# Gone Astray

BY

## SUSAN ERLANDSON WASHBURN

ISBN: 978-81-19654-45-1 Cyberwit.net
*Gone Astray*

"To reach something good it is very useful to have gone astray, and thus acquire experience."

—St. Teresa de Avila (1515-1582

One

Dorie Winslow realized too late that she had completely missed the signs that something was seriously wrong with her daughter. A good mother, she chided herself, would have noticed. Even if that good mother were overworked, underpaid and frustrated by her overprivileged and undermotivated students at West Fork State, an institution better known for proximity to three Colorado ski resorts than rigorous academics.

But what had she, an obviously lax mother, done? She'd been so preoccupied with her personal problems that she'd passed off the dramatic transformation in Phoebe's wardrobe and CD collection as just another adolescent phase-change, the newest experimental persona in the "who-am-I-this-year" game. After all, pastel baby tees, pink lip gloss, and the surprisingly harmonic music issuing from Phoebe's room were a welcome change from last year's torn black t-shirts, venous- blood- red lipstick and the heavy metal dissonance of Marilyn Manson. Dorie was so relieved that her daughter now looked like a throwback to the Eisenhower years rather than a contestant in a Little Miss Goth pageant that she didn't think to ask why.

Then, on a disarmingly sunny mornng in June 2004, a few days before Phoebe's sixteenth birthday, the caca hit the fan. Dorie, hoping to make up for her maternal benign neglect, had made all the arrangements for a blow-out celebration. First, Phoebe and three friends would be treated to a non-extreme makeover, courtesy of Dorie's next door neighbor, Sharon Folsom, who sold skin care products whenever she wasn't trying to keep her twin boy toddlers from murdering each other. Then there would be dinner out at the Grubstake Hotel, West Fork's premiere historically preserved Victorian hostelry, followed by a movie and a sleepover. Dorie felt she had done herself proud, at least by West Fork standards, which were admittedly low compared to those of her yuppie friends back east who had to shell out major bucks for orchestra seats at Broadway shows. However, B-day was rapidly approaching and she still hadn't bought Phoebe a present.

Overwhelmed by sentimentality and memories of her own sixteenth birthday, when her father had presented her with a gold charm bracelet ordered from a discount catalogue, Dorie had been considering jewelry, maybe a ring set with a pearl, Phoebe's birthstone, but her daughter had such definite tastes that she had hesitated to pick out anything without a consultation.

So, when Phoebe skipped down the stairs to breakfast that Saturday morning wearing cute little cutoff jean shorts that complemented her tan legs and an aqua tee with a rhinestone heart placed fetchingly over her left breast, Dorie proposed a trip to Weiss's Jewelry for the bauble of her choice.

"Anything you like, muffin," she offered magnanimously. When Phoebe beamed, she added, "So long as it doesn't involve piercing your nostrils, nipples or any unmentionable mucous membranes."

Phoebe frowned and tucked an errant strand of hair neatly behind her ear. The black dye from her punk rocker incarnation had been mercifully semi-permanent and, to Dorie's great relief, her daughter's straight, dark brown locks, a long version of Dorie's own short bob, had survived their chemical bath unscathed.

"Mother," she said, "that is not my style anymore. That sort of self- mutilation disrespects the body."

"That's more or less what I told you when you wanted a barbed wire tattoo on your ankle," Dorie reminded her.

Phoebe, to her credit, ignored the remark. She opened a cupboard, extracted a bag of granola and studied the list of ingredients.

"Actually," she said, gathering her hair into a low ponytail and securing it with a scrunchie she slipped off her wrist, "there is something I've been wanting." She replaced the granola and fingered a box of corn flakes.

"Then you shall have it," Dorie said, trying to make amends for her verbal jab.

"What I'd really like," Phoebe said gravely, still addressing the open cupboard, " is a little gold cross on an eighteen inch box chain."

Dorie was confused. She thought crosses had gone out of style six years ago when Madonna took up the Kabbalah, but then she wasn't really au courant with accessories favored by the young and hip.

"I think, " Phoebe continued in the same even tone," that it's important to show where you stand." She turned around to face Dorie, blinked several times, and said, in a vaguely defiant, run-on mumble, "And now that I've been born again I need to wear a cross as a symbol of my new life in Christ."

"Now that you've been what?" Dorie said, sloshing tea all over a new handwoven placemat.

"Born again. You know, accepted Jesus as my personal savior."

Dorie coughed to clear her windpipe of the tea that had gone down the wrong way. I cannot believe this, she thought. Phoebe must be putting me on. She scanned her daughter's face for signs of suppressed amusement but found none. She decided to proceed with caution; if Phoebe were indeed serious there was nothing to be gained by offending her.

"When exactly did this happen?" Dorie asked, "and why have you not told me about it?"

Phoebe heaved a long sigh of terminal exasperation, leaned back against the counter, and folded her arms across her chest.

"I did tell you. Sort of anyway. You know I've been going to the rec center every Friday night with Kimberly."

Dorie recalled that Phoebe and her new best friend, a chatty blonde cheerleader type who insisted on addressing Dorie as "Ms. Winslow" despite an invitation to use her first name, went down to the municipal recreation center on Friday nights. However, she hadn't given much thought to what they actually did there. Kimberly and her friends were such an improvement over the spike-haired, ghoulishly eye-shadowed girls that Phoebe hung out with when they first arrived in West Fork a year ago that she was too relieved to ask questions.

"Well, of course I knew you went to the rec center , " Dorie replied. Then, forgetting her intention to proceed with caution, added, "but I figured you were playing ping pong, not being dipped in the blood of the lamb."

Phoebe gave her a black look.

"That's because you weren't listening. As usual. I told you I was going to the TFC meetings there."

"TFC?" Dorie said blankly. "What's that?"

"Teens for Christ. Kimberly's the president."

Dorie took the tea-soaked placemat to the sink and rinsed it while she attempted to process Phoebe's revelation. She'd raised her daughter on the same masala of Eastern religions peppered with a dash of quantum mechanics that she had embraced during the seventies and still invoked during moments of ecstasy and/

or despair. Both she and Phoebe's father had been outspoken advocates of scientific method and rational thought—- leavened with the occasional use of mind-altering substances. The G-word, much less references to the purported son thereof, was rarely uttered in their household save in conjunction with "damn it." No daughter of theirs could possibly fall for the pie-in-the-sky promises of evangelical Christianity.

"And what exactly goes on at these Teens for Christ meetings?" Dorie asked, realizing too late that her sardonic tone of voice was unlikely to encourage true confessions.

Fortunately, Phoebe seemed to overlook it.

"First we have Musical Praise Circle, "she explained. "Then Pastor Charlie plays the harmonica and Jared, this boy I know, he plays guitar. Then we discuss the Scripture of the Week, and then we Witness and then we sing some more and at the end we have refreshments and social hour."

Her entire recitation was delivered with bubbling enthusiasm. Dorie felt the tiny fingers of incipient panic tickling her chest. Phoebe was completely serious. A discomfiting vision of her daughter clutching a Bible as she boarded a bus bound for Jesus Camp flashed across Dorie's mental screen. She had to do something, fast. She could barely manage to relate to Phoebe as it was. Whatever minimal family values they shared would never survive Musical Praise Circles and Witnessing. Not to mention this Pastor Charlie, who could very well be one of those hypocritical Christian leaders who were constantly being revealed as philandering perverts.

"And just who is Pastor Charlie?" Dorie asked. She managed a tone of studied neutrality this time but it was a major effort.

A beatific smile crossed Phoebe's face.

"He is just the most cool minister on the planet. I mean, he really knows what's happening. You can tell him anything. Because he listens."

This last was accompanied by a pointed stare at her mother.

By now Dorie was in such a state of shock that she wasn't even tempted to defend herself against the implicit accusation of parental inadequacy.

"Phoebe," she asked, "you don't really believe that fundamentalist crapola about heaven and angels and hellfire and brimstone? "

Phoebe turned away and crossed the room to the refrigerator.

"I knew you'd be like this, " she said. "You're always so ...so...." She searched for a suitably damning adjective as she extracted a carton of peach yogurt. "...cynical." She grabbed a spoon from the table and clomped upstairs.

Dorie poured herself another cup of tea and sat down to reflect on the state of the mother-daughter union. She'd given up coffee as part of a campaign to combat perimenopausal irritability so that she could better cope with Phoebe's mood swings but now she was addicted to an expensive Irish breakfast tea ordered from an intimidatingly refined tea company in Massachusetts and her nerves were as frazzled as ever.

She looked around the sunny yellow kitchen that had inspired her, always a reluctant cook, to take up brownie baking and crockpot cookery in a belated attempt at traditional nurturing. The sliding glass door opened onto a deck with a Weber grill, a hummingbird feeder and a view of a rock escarpment that turned gold in the reflected light of sunset. There was an explosion of multi-colored sweet peas on the trellis attached to the weathered cedar siding and a blue spruce in the fenced yard, a yard just right for the kind of big, smelly dog that would never have been allowed in the Newton, Massachusetts townhouse where she and Phoebe used to live. What was wrong with this picture? Rabbit Valley was exactly the kind of unpretentious semi-rural neighborhood she'd always been drawn to and their house, while something of a relic from the early seventies, was roomy and comfortable. Why didn't she and Phoebe have the happy, relaxed domestic life she had envisioned when she traded a pprestigiousassistant professorship in Boston for a low-stress job at West Fork State College?

Part of what was wrong was the same thing that had been wrong back East. No man. No hubby, daddy, partner, or significant other. No co-parent to pour her a drink and assure her that, despite Phoebe's increasing truculence, they would not end up on Dr. Phil hurling accusations at one another.

Of course, Dorie had to admit, she hadn't put much effort into acquiring a significant other during her eight years of widowhood. She had been so devastated by her husband's sudden death she could barely manage to drag herself to the requisite, and useless, grief counseling at the Newton Mental Health Center and take Phoebe to an expensive pediatric therapist who encouraged pillow-punching and the liberal use of finger paints to sort out her daughter's tumultuous feelings. And the physical aftermath of his death had been overwhelming: the endless legal papers and financial documents, the closet full of male clothing that disconcerted her with his scent; the scuba gear and skis in the garage that reminded her of happier times, his technical books and journals stacked knee high on the study floor. She had finally cleared the house of all his possessions in an attempt to pull herself out of her lingering depression and make a fresh start, but then Phoebe, always a temperamental child, hit thirteen and morphed into a secretive, rebellious adolescent. After full days at work and evenings rife with slammed doors and evasive silences, all Dorie wanted to do was go to bed with a Stephen King novel.

Dorie dumped the remainder of her tea into the sink. Given Phoebe's heavy-footed departure, it looked as if the Saturday morning shopping expedition was a no-go. This meant that she could either do something useful around the house, like finishing unpacking the boxes of books in her home office, which she'd ignored for nine months while she attended to more pressing concerns like stripping the dizzyingly floral wallpaper off her bedroom walls. Or she could go for yet another solitary hike in the hills. Phoebe was probably already on the phone with Kimberly or another new best female friend, arranging some activity that didn't involve her mother. Not that it should have. In all honesty, Dorie had to admit that her daughter had made more friends in West Fork than she had.

She rinsed her tea mug and put it on the drainboard to dry, gave the fake butcher-block laminate countertop a swipe with a sponge, wishing as usual that she could afford to replace it with granite tiles, and grabbed an orange and some cheese and crackers to stuff in her backpack. Faint bass booms from Phoebe's stereo seeped through the ceiling. At least she wasn't listening to one of those saccharine pseudo-pop ballads about God's boundless love that dominated Colorado's Christian bandwidth. But what on earth was she listening to? Soprano voices that sounded like the Hallelujah Chorus as rendered by the Supremes rose above the bass line.

Dorie shouted upstairs loudly enough to penetrate the booms.

"Phoeb, I'm going for a hike. Wanna come with?"

A muffled "Whatever" came back.

"Right," Dorie felt a pang of disappointment, but then why on earth would Phoebe want to come with her? It was normal for teenagers to prefer the company of their peers to that of their boring parents. Besides, she 'd just managed to further alienate her daughter by dissing something that was obviously dear to her heart.

Dumb, dumb, dumb, Dorie admonished herself. Why can't I keep my big smartass mouth shut? Phoebe's right. I don't listen. I can't wait to interject my own opinion and set everybody right. My damn ego is still running the show.

This line of thought was so discouraging that she turned to more practical matters. She filled her Camelback with bottled water—the stuff from the tap stank of sulfur—and went out to the deck to lace her hiking boots and consider her options. Those involving her hiking route were easy; she'd do the four-mile loop trail that led up the mesa that rose above the north edge of Rabbit Valley.

Those involving her daughter's newfound religious fervor were trickier. If she didn't nip this religious obsession in the bud, Phoebe could turn into a full-fledged evangelical, marrying young and spawning a brood of home-schooled kids, all of them estranged from their heathen grandmother. Dorie felt vaguely nauseated. Phoebe was her only living kin, the one person on earth to whom she felt really connected. Losing her was unthinkable.

She took a deep breath, exhaled slowly, and told herself to get a grip. She had to remain calm and rational. She had to explain to Phoebe that the Bible was more or less what was currently referred to as Creative Nonfiction and not to be taken literally.

Or maybe she should just step back and wait for Phoebe's religious mania to fade away like her dreadful black goth hair. The latter plan was probably best, but Dorie suspected that, given her intolerance for warm panaceas and fuzzy thinking—a quality that had already spread fear and awe among her students at West Fork State College—she might not be capable of carrying it out.

The mesa trail began with a series of steep switchbacks dotted with increasingly taller Ponderosa pines and Dorie was winded by the time she reached the top. She sat down on a rock, swigged lukewarm water from her Camelback, and watched a crow circling overhead trying to decide if she were a potential source of lunch.

The strenuous trek had, as usual, improved her mood. Returning to Colorado had been a good idea. West Fork reminded her of the Boulder she had known as a graduate student at the University of Colorado, before condos and McMansions had metastasized throughout the open spaces that kept Denver at bay. Maybe, she mused, I am trying to go home again. But why not? She opened her arms wide, belted out a few off-key bars of "Country Roads," and asked the crow, who was watching her from the top of a Ponderosa, "So who's right, anyway? John Denver or Thomas Wolfe?"

The crow didn't answer.

"I don't even rate a 'nevermore?'" Dorie shifted into a cross-legged position to stretch her inner thighs and extracted the orange from her backpack. As she dug her fingernails into its oily skin, releasing a nose-stinging pungency, she pondered Phoebe's new incarnation as a Jesus freak. In the context of West Fork, which had some brand of Christian church on every corner, it looked downright mainstream. If Phoebe goes mainstream, Dorie thought, as panic once again gripped her throat, where will that leave me?

Two

Dorie took a shortcut down an arroyo on her way home so barely three hours had elapsed by the time she was on her back porch again. She opened the slider to the kitchen and announced her return.

"Phoebe? I'm home! I can shower in a few minutes and then if you want we can go to Weiss's to shop for your birthday present."

No answer. Maybe Phoebe was in her room. She went to the foot of the stairs and called upwards.

"You can have the cross of your choice."

Silence.

"So long as it doesn't have a dead Jesus hanging from it," she added to herself.

Still no answer. She returned to the kitchen and checked the whiteboard on the side of the fridge for messages.

"Gone to Kimmi's. Back later.—P."

Well, Dorie thought, at least we're still communicating. Sort of.

Dorie spent the rest of the afternoon in her home office, a converted screened porch off the living room that the real estate agent had declared "just perfect for a media room." When Dorie said that her preferred medium was the written word, the agent had promptly pointed out two walls suitable for built-in bookcases and recommended a carpenter who could do the job.

Dorie unpacked and shelved two boxes of books, filed a stack of lecture notes for classes she hoped never to teach again, and shifted a box of ancient financial records she kept in case the IRS ever decided to audit her. Behind it sat a dusty carton labeled "Memorabilia—To Storage" that the movers must have dredged up out of the townhouse cellar when they left Massachusetts. She couldn't remember it or its memorable contents at all.

The accumulation of paper representing the past was so disheartening that she fled to the kitchen and made a large salade nicoise for dinner. Phoebe was partial to salads these days; Dorie hoped it was just a reflection of her own love of raw vegetables and not a symptom of an eating disorder. Just to make sure they didn't become too disgustingly wholesome, she made a quick fruit crumble with frozen mixed berries and an oatmeal and walnut topping. Then she opened a Corona, jammed a slice of lime into the bottle,-and sat down in the living room to catch the news and await the prodigal daughter.

Said daughter walked in the front door at 6:10, well in advance of their more-or-less standard dinner hour of 6:30. Whatever she'd been up to all afternoon had evidently improved her mood as she actually smiled and asked if Dorie had a good hike.

"Sure did," Dorie said. "I wish you'd come with me sometime. The view from the top makes West Fork look like Whoville." Phoebe, Dorie remembered, had loved the movie version of "How the Grinch Stole Christmas" when she was a kid.

"No way. " Phoebe shot back. "I've got better things to do. Hiking's dorky."

Well, Dorie thought, so much for passing on my love of the Great Outdoors.

They ate in the kitchen, at the round pine table in the windowed northeast corner. Phoebe approved of the menu, complimented the vinaigrette salad dressing, and ate heartily. She was so agreeable that Dorie took a stab at initiating a little heart-to-heart talk.

"Were you over at Kimberly's this afternoon?" she asked, in what she hoped was a pleasantly neutral tone.

"Yup," Phoebe replied and carefully dipped a chunk of sourdough bread into a saucer of seasoned olive oil.

"What do you guys do together?"

Phoebe raised an eyebrow as if she found her mother's display of casual interest suspect.

"We just, you know, hang, " she replied. She picked up a knife, painstakingly cut an anchovy fillet into minute pieces, then mixed them into the remains of her salad.

"Cool," Dorie said, adopting the vernacular to encourage rapport. "But what exactly do you do while hanging?"

"Oh, listen to music, talk. That kind of stuff." Phoebe continued to rearrange the components of her salad..

"Yeah?" Dorie said encouragingly, leaning forward to indicate interest. "And? What else?"

"Sometimes we, like, do each other's nails."

At this rate, Dorie realized, they were never going to make it to heart-to-heart land. She decided on a full-frontal approach. She placed her knife and salad fork on the edge of her plate, straightened up, and looked directly at Phoebe until her daughter gave in to the force of her stare and met her eyes.

"Phoeb, I just don't get this Christian thing you're into. I didn't mean to hurt your feelings or anything this morning. But Teens for Christ? I mean, given your level of..." she started to say "intelligence" but realized that was the wrong tack. "Given your background, I just would never have expected..."

"You mean given the way you brought me up," Phoebe broke in. "All those little Buddha statues and incense and that dopey meditation alcove in your bedroom?"

"I haven't done that for years," Dorie said indignantly. "Not since you started grade school and I used my few precious minutes of spare time to go to parent-teacher conferences. Where we dealt with your negative attitude toward group activities, you might recall."

"Well maybe you should have spent more time meditating," Phoebe shot back. "Then you wouldn't have been so cranky." She speared a piece of tomato with her fork, bit off half of it, frowned, and replaced the other half on her plate.

Dorie resisted the impulse to remind her daughter how hard it had been to maintain a nominally middle-class lifestyle in Newton as a single parent, how exhausting it was to teach a double course load to pay the bills while trying to research a post-feminist study of Nathaniel Hawthorne's heroines in order to stay on a tenure track. She reminded herself to listen actively and express understanding.

"You're probably right," she admitted. "I was cranky. Too much work and not enough sunshine. The New England syndrome. Things are better now, aren't they? I know I'm happier out here and it seems like you are too..." She refrained from adding "Now that you've found Jesus." She wanted to steer the conversation back to Teens for Christ but sarcasm wasn't going to help. She continued, "...now that you're friends with Kimberly and those other two girls, I forget their names."

Phoebe sighed resignedly.

"Nicole and Amber," she said. "I've told you a hundred times."

I'm getting nowhere, Dorie thought. She's not going to talk about Teens for Christ unless I approach the topic obliquely.

"So how come you dropped your old crowd and took up with these new kids?"

"Well isn't it obvious?" Phoebe said with a withering stare. "They're way cooler. Those goths were losers. I just went with them because it was easy. Kimmi and the others were sort of above me when I first came. Like, Kimmi's probably the most popular girl in her class and Nicole's a cheerleader and Amber's on Student Council. But after Christmas break they started being really nice to me, you know? Kimmi invited me to sit with them at lunch and we, like, started going around together."

Dorie wondered if Kimberly and her little salvation army were being friendly or just trying to win another convert but she thought better of bringing up this devastating possibility. There was no point in undermining Phoebe's emerging self-esteem.

"But what about Teens for Christ?" she continued. "Did you feel like you had to join to be friends with these girls?"

Phoebe frowned. "No," she said. "It wasn't like that at all." She paused and twirled a piece of her hair into a ringlet. "Well, maybe a little, at first. I kind of wondered about it but the way they talked about the things they did made it sound really fun." She smiled as she uncoiled the ringlet. "And I kind of thought it would be a good way to meet Jared."

"Jared? The guy who plays the guitar?" Dorie's anxiety about Phoebe's new-found religion was momentarily assuaged by the possibility of a boyfriend, which would be a first for her petite and pretty but socially awkward daughter. Possibly Jared, not Jesus, was the real draw to TFC.

"Yes," Phoebe said. "He is majorly cute. He's on the soccer team. And he's taking four A.P. classes."

Dorie knew this last was a sop to her intellectual snobbery but she didn't mind. She was just relieved that Phoebe was showing signs of a normal, teenage crush. This she could deal with. Getting born again was another matter.

"Jared's applying for early admission to Stanford…"

Dorie smiled approvingly.

"…and he's applying to Biola too."

Dorie's smile faded.

"Isn't Biola some evangelical school in L.A.?" she asked.

Phoebe stared at her unblinkingly.

"Of course it is," she replied coolly. "Jared may have a calling. So Biola's his first choice. If it's the Lord's will."

Dorie couldn't hold back any longer.

"Phoebe, tell me straight out right now. Do you really, truly believe you have been born again? Whatever that means?"

Phoebe stood up and carefully took her dishes over to the sink and dumped them in noisily. Dorie saw her shoulders rise as she inhaled deeply, then fall as she slowly exhaled. She turned around and smiled sweetly.

"Yes, mother," she said. "And I pray every night that you'll find your way to Christ too."

The next morning Phoebe came into Dorie's study and announced that she was going to church. Pastor Charlie's church, of course. The Circle of Friends in Christ. And no, she didn't need a ride because Kimberly would be picking her up at 9:30 and bringing her home again.

Dorie looked up from the file drawer where she was sorting home repair invoices, of which there were an alarming number, into color-coded folders. She made a valiant effort to be both non-commital and agreeable. She didn't want to squelch her daughter's enthusiasm, no matter how ill-founded, or turn what could be a passing fad into a major doctrinal issue. Not that she hadn't been brooding half the night about some subtle way to bring Phoebe to her senses. So she merely told Phoebe that her outfit, a knee-length black cotton skirt and a white blouse, was dynamite and asked her if she needed money for the collection plate.

Phoebe looked blank, which was understandable since, to Dorie's knowledge she had never attended a conventional church service in her life. Dorie felt a pang of guilt; perhaps her laissez-faire approach to her daughter's religious education had created a spiritual vacuum that Pastor Charlie was only too willing to fill.

"How much do I put in?" Phoebe asked. "I don't want to look stupid."

It was Dorie's turn to be stumped. All she could remember about collection plate etiquette was based on childhood visits to her granny, who took her to the First Presbyterian Church of Moline, Illinois with a fifty-cent piece tied in the corner of her hanky. Given the rate of inflation since the 1960's it was likely that folding money might now be required. She picked up her purse from beside her desk and rummaged for her wallet. An indirect donation to Pastor Charlie's coffers might buy her some filial goodwill. She handed Phoebe a wad of ones and told her to give whatever Kimberly did.

Just then a car pulled into the driveway.

"Kimmi's here. I've gotta go," Phoebe said. "Thanks for the money." She was half out the front door when she stopped and turned around.

"Have a good day, Mom," she called and pulled the door shut.

How can Mom possibly have a good day? Dorie thought. Sundays had always made her uneasy. Saturdays were for catching up on the trivia of life, shopping, yard work, cleaning out closets. But Sundays called for contemplation or socializing, both of which she generally avoided by plowing through the New York Times and then torturing herself with the crossword puzzle.

Since she didn't feel like driving downtown to pick up a paper, she'd have to fill the Sunday void some other way. She'd explored various hiking trails on previous Sundays, but after climbing the mesa yesterday she wasn't up for more outdoor exertion. That left her default recreational mode: home improvement. Which meant, at the moment, tackling more of the dreaded boxes in her home office.

She poured another cup of tea, put "The Best of Elvis" in her office CD player, located the utility knife underneath a pile of mail-order catalogs and set to work. But after three boxes of books had been dispersed to appropriate categories on the rapidly filling new shelves, her enthusiasm for establishing order waned. The mystery carton labeled "Memorabilia—To Storage" was bound to be more interesting.

The carton had a musty, moldy smell that suggested a lengthy subterranean sojourn. Dorie recognized the handwriting on the outside as her own but the carton must have been relegated to the cellar so long ago that she had forgotten about it. She ripped off the brittle strapping tape that was holding the battered cardboard together and opened the flaps.

A See's candy box labeled "Family Snapshots" in her mother's neat cursive backhand was on top. Dorie examined a few: her parents, young and smiling beside a 1930s Dodge on a two-lane road in an unidentifiable desert. Her mother, wearing a seersucker summer dress, shucking corn on the porch of their Iowa farmhouse. Her father with one of their succession of collies at his feet, his left hand on the front wheel of his new John Deere tractor. That tractor had been his pride and joy, but the color print had faded so much that its kelly green and bright yellow paint now appeared khaki and beige and the cloudless midsummer sky had washed out to a dull grey-blue.

Dorie sighed. The impermanence of Kodachrome struck her as a fitting metaphor for the ephemerality of life. She felt a sudden stab of longing for her parents, both gone abruptly and too soon. Her mother eaten from within by ovarian cancer; her father, dead a year later of a heart damaged as much by grief as artheriosclerosis. She grimaced as she recalled the terrifying desolation that had haunted her after their deaths; she'd been so depressed that she dropped out of college for a semester.

Would have been easier if I'd had a brother or sister, Dorie thought. Only children aren't equipped to be orphans. She put the candy box aside. She was not in the mood for family snapshots.

The rest of the carton contained verbiage of one sort or another. Old birthday cards, diplomas and certificates chronicling her progress from high school to a Ph.D., yellowed clippings of the humor column she wrote for her college newspaper, an engraved invitation to her wedding to Phoebe's father. She fingered the heavy ivory paper, now frayed at the edges. They'd been so optimistic and full of hope, a perfect match, according to their friends. How could something that had begun so brightly have ended so darkly?

Dorie sandwiched the invitation between a hand-lettered natal astrology chart and a poster for her high school prom. She should preserve it for Phoebe if nothing else.

At the bottom of the carton she came across a manila envelope with "Summer of 1978—Journal" written in fat black marker pen on the outside.

"Jackpot!" Dorie cried. Here was a worthy bit of memorabilia. She had looked for this journal several years ago but its whereabouts had eluded her and she'd given it up for lost. Its rediscovery now was serendipitous, given what was happening with Phoebe.

She opened the envelope, pulled out a tan spiral notebook, and sneezed. The cover was spotted with mildew, the scourge of New England basements, but the pages seemed to be intact. She made herself comfy in her upholstered desk chair, which, despite its ergonomic design, required placing one's feet on the desk in order to avoid back strain. She opened the cover, looked at the first page, and reached for her reading glasses; she had written the journal in the minuscule hand of her youth, which was now indecipherable without magnification.

Then first sentences came into focus and Dorie plunged down a rabbit hole into the wonderland of her past.

$$\mathcal{T}hree$$

## Monday, June 5, 1978, Boulder, CO

I made a big mistake coming here for the summer. I don't know anyone in this town except my graduate advisor and she's in Italy. My apartment is hot and stuffy and the toilet runs and the kitchen faucet drips all night so I can't sleep and I lie awake thinking about Roger, the bastard. I don't care that he dumped me but I hate that I was the last person to know he was cheating.

So now what? I can: 1. Stick it out here and go to grad school in the fall like a good girl. 2. Break my lease and go back to Ames where I'll run into Roger and his airhead girlfriend every time I walk across the campus 3. Join the Peace Corps so I can do something useful with my miserable life.

I wish I could talk to Mom. Or even Dad. I want to go HOME. If the farm weren't sold I could hole up there and become a recluse. Like in "A Rose for Emily." But I guess that would mean I have to murder Roger so I can keep his dried up body in my bed.

Never mind. Tomorrow I will get dressed and go out and meet people. Starting with whoever lives downstairs in this old house and leaves that damn bike in the hall so I keep tripping over it in the dark.

## Tuesday, June 6

The bike guy is named Bruce and he's a free-lance handyman. He fixed my leaky sink tap with a new washer, which was great, but then he subjected me to a half-hour discourse on his guru. Like so:

He pulls two teabags out of his pocket and asks, very innocently, if I've got a minute for a cup of chai and a chat. Being desperate for company, I leap at the chance. So he sits himself down at my kitchen table like he owns it and says, "Do you ever wonder about the purpose of human life on earth?" I say "Well, of course I do, particularly my own because it's a total mess right now." And he practically yells, "Aha! I knew you were a black sheep!" and pulls a dog-eared paperback book from the pocket of his filthy jeans and thrusts it at me.

"You might be interested in this," he says. I thumb through the book, which is written by someone called I.M. Budd, who has only a rudimentary grasp of the English language as he omits articles and sprinkles his aphorisms with random capital letters, i.e. "You all Dumbkopfs. You think Work on Self Big Chance for glory when it really just Taking Out garbage."

Turns out this Mr. Budd is a big-league spiritual teacher. "A thinking man's guru," Bruce tells me solemnly, "not for the masses but for the critical few." Of whom, he suggests, I may be one.

## Friday, June 16

I actually read The Watercloset Tapes and it was weirdly interesting. It's supposed to be transcripts of this Mr. Budd's talks to his students during his morning toilet routine. Gross! But the message is that the world is seriously screwed up and much "voluntary suffering" and great quantities of Work with a capital W, which is different from ordinary work like digging ditches or selling used cars, is required to set the collective human psyche in order. I don't get that, but I do get the part about wandering through life in a fog of preconditioned concepts and associative dreams that keep us from experiencing our experiences. Especially since I'm still obsessing about Roger's betrayal and crying myself to sleep. And obsessing about whether I really want an academic career or am just doing it because I can't think of anything better. It's like my mind has a mind of its own and my thoughts aren't ones I want to be thinking.

Maybe I should see a shrink. Or maybe I should check out Bruce's guru. He's bound to be cheaper and he probably won't try to put me on anti-depressants. Bruce has invited me to accompany him to the guru's lair, up in the mountains. He says I would benefit greatly from meeting Bud, as he's known among his intimates. "He'll scare the pants off you but he'll also give you a kind of perspective you can't get any place else," Bruce says. I could use a new perspective because right now I have no idea where I'm going or why.

Rhea, my other downstairs neighbor, a large lady with shoulder-length frizzy grey hair, has a different opinion of Mr. Budd. Being obsessed herself, with the Sexploitation of Womin, she is of the opinion that my pants may very well be removed, but not through fright. "Those gurus, they're all alike. They got strings of women as long as their prayer beads," she tells me darkly. "You go nosing around them looking for truth and enlightenment, well, you better watch your backside, hon."

## Friday, June 30, Marmot Rock, CO

I'm in the soup now. I committed myself to two months of spiritual boot camp. Drove up to this funky mountain village in an old VW van with Bruce and the other members of Bud's Boulder study group. They are: Omar, the control freak leader of the group; Ianna a skinny woman who seems to be Omar's girlfriend, Annie, who just graduated high school, and Alfredo. Alfredo's a sheet metal fabricator and very practical. He's the only person who thought to check the van's coolant level when it kept overheating.

The Community—that's what Bud's long-term students call themselves—hangs out in a kind of permanent camp in the woods outside Marmot Rock. The people look like ex-hippies and artists and college dropouts, mostly in their twenties and thirties. Some scruffy little kids running around too. But there's a good vibe going. Everybody's friendly and glad to see us.

The place is actually quite beautiful, tall pine trees and meadows full of yellow wildflowers, but the buildings are tacky. Old log cabins and doublewides stuck in the trees around a long green shed that contains the communal kitchen and a big dining hall with long tables and benches. Looks like a second-rate summer camp for underprivileged city kids.

But then I go inside to register (giving name, address, next of kin and astrological sign) and I see this huge photograph of Bud-the-guru on the wall. He's wearing a gold turban and smiling with his eyes half-closed. This freaks me out. What if this is some kind of cult? I'd better work out an escape route to the nearest paved road, just in case.

There are little prints of that Bud photo everywhere, in the women's bunkhouse where I stow my backpack, and even in the unisex portable johns. It's hard to pee with a photo of the guru staring at you but I guess it's supposed to encourage self-awareness.

But where's the guru himself? During dinner, which is the usual New Age brown rice and steamed veggies, I'm seated next to a thin dark-haired older guy named Leonard. He used to be a public defender but he now takes care of the Community's legal affairs. (He says he keeps the Health Department out of the kitchen and the IRS out of the books.) I point at the throne-like carved chair at the head table and ask him why it's empty and he tells me Bud often disappears for days at a time without explanation only to reappear as if out of thin air. "Does he go sit on a mountaintop and meditate?" I ask. "No way," Leonard says. "He goes to Las Vegas. Bud's a world-class gambler."

I can just see the Great Man in his gold turban sitting in the lotus position on a stool at a poker table raking in the chips.

## Monday, July 3

I've mislaid my watch somewhere, which is a royal pain. At least I think I mislaid it. I don't think anyone here would nick it. On the other hand, judging from the beat-up vehicles in the parking lot, they're living on the edge of poverty, so who knows?

Big Daddy still hasn't put in an appearance and I'm wondering if this summer workshop is a con. Maybe I should have paid more attention to one of Bud's aphorisms in "The Watercloset Tapes," the one that says "There's always free cheese in the mousetrap."

Oh well, tradition has it that when the student is ready, the teacher will come. Guess not a single one of the twenty-eight spiritual seekers here, myself included, is ready because the Living Master seems to have vanished into the thin mountain air.

$$Four$$

The phone rang, catapulting Dorie back into the present. She closed the notebook and reached for the handset. The sudden move elicited a twinge of protest from her lower back. Where had all the flowers gone? And what was she doing inhabiting a middle-aged body with creaky joints, sun-damaged skin, and a haywire thermostat? That strange, unpredictable summer of 1978 had been, in an unsettling way, one of the most exhilarating periods of her life. Yet its memories seemed to have been buried as deeply in her subconscious as the journal had been in her basement.

Remembrance of things past would have to wait. Phoebe's cell phone number was on the caller ID screen.

"Mom?"

"Hey, baby, what's up?"

"Have we got any food?"

"Of course we have food," Dorie said. "Since when do we not have food?"

"Whenever you get too busy to be bothered to shop," Phoebe replied. "Which always happens when you're working on your book."

"Ummm," Dorie said, for lack of a good defense.

"Anyway," Phoebe went on, "Kimberly and Jared and I need to work on a project together and I thought maybe we could do it at our house but we're starving and if you don't have anything for lunch we'll stop at McDonald's and eat junk food."

Dorie informed her that threats weren't necessary; she would gladly provide something nutritious. Very gladly indeed, since this would give her a chance to meet the object of Phoebe's affections, Jared of the divine calling.

She put her musty notebook in a bottom desk drawer. She felt a wash of sweet nostalgia for the oddballs and misfits, including her own younger, more exuberant self, who lived in those pages. She looked forward to another session of recherché du temps perdu as soon as possible.

The refrigerator was a little low on raw materials, but Dorie scrounged the makings of grilled cheese sandwiches and coleslaw and excavated some frozen homemade tomato soup from the freezer. She didn't want Jared, whom she assumed would have the typical adolescent male bottomless stomach, to go hungry.

She had the kitchen table set, complete with centerpiece, a bunch of early-blooming pansies from the backyard, by the time she heard Kimberly's car crunching onto the gravel driveway. By virtue of her father's ownership of the local GM dealership, Kimberly had her very own gas-guzzling SUV, a shiny cobalt blue Envoy that loomed over Dorie's five-year-old Subaru Forester.

Such are the rewards of being born to parents with a commercial bent, Dorie mused. Phoebe had been lucky to get a new mountain bike last year. A car, not to mention the huge insurance premiums for a teenage driver, was out of the question even though Phoebe expected to get her license next week and had left the used car section of the classifieds on Dorie's desk with an ad for a 1989 Jeep circled in red.

The aroma of scorching cheddar wafted up from the broiler. Dorie snatched the sandwiches from incendiary disaster just as Phoebe and her friends opened the front door.

"Eeew, what's that smell?" Phoebe called out.

"That's your lunch, sweetie," Dorie called back. "I hope you all like your grilled cheese well done."

Phoebe came into the kitchen, followed by Kimberly. The girls were a study in contrasts. Kimberly was model thin and tall, with long straight baby blonde hair. Phoebe, petite and olive-skinned, her dark hair a tangle of unruly curls, looked like a little gypsy tagalong.

"Hello, Ms. Winslow, it's so nice of you to have us for lunch at the last minute," Kimberly said, her wide smile revealing beautifully aligned and probably professionally whitened teeth.

Score two for parents in business, Dorie thought sourly.

"My pleasure," Dorie said automatically, peering over Kimberly's shoulder in search of the object of her daughter's nascent affection.

"Jared's getting some stuff from the car," Phoebe said, scowling at her.

"Okay," Dorie said, "I'll just finish salvaging the sandwiches." She turned away and busied herself at the kitchen counter to reassure Phoebe that she could control her curiosity. Just then the front screen door banged shut, something clattered on the hardwood floor, and someone exclaimed, "Oh, shit!"

Phoebe and Kimberly exchanged meaningful glances. Kimberly smiled apologetically.

"Jared has a little problem with his language," she murmured, "but we're working on it."

A lanky youth with floppy light brown hair shuffled into the kitchen, clutching an untidy stack of poster boards and a backpack.

"I dropped the markers," he said sheepishly.

"Oh Jared," Kimberly said. "You are such a klutz."

She grabbed the poster boards, which were about to slide to the floor, and looked at Phoebe, hissing "Introductions...?"

Phoebe followed Miss Manners' cue and waved an arm in Jared's direction.

"Mom, this is Jared Lepawski, Jared this is my mother Dorie Winslow," she mumbled, then added, "You can call her Dorie."

"Pleased to meet you, Missus Winslow," Jared said, opting for an old-fashioned formality that topped Kimberly's "Ms." He stepped forward and extended his hand; his firm capable grip belied his gawky movements. Dorie could see why Phoebe found him appealing; he had a sweet shy smile, gentle blue eyes and a lovely voice, a man's baritone that his body had yet to grow into. Dorie imagined teenaged girls swooning when he did a riff on "Jesus Loves Me," or whatever it was that Pastor Charlie's angels sang at their little get -togethers.

Kimberly collected the scattered markers from the living room and stacked the poster boards in a corner while Dorie ladled soup and scraped the burnt bits off the grilled cheese sandwiches. She found some cans of soda in the pantry and instructed Jared, who had politely asked if he could help, to fill glasses with ice. Nice manners, Dorie thought, and nodded approvingly at Phoebe, who shook her head violently and mouthed "Mu-ther."

Kimberly, polite as always, asked Dorie if she were joining them for lunch, but Dorie had already decided Phoebe and her buddies would have more fun without Missus Winslow at table. She declined and started cleaning up the mess she'd created with her hasty lunch preparations. That, of course, allowed her to eavesdrop openly while pretending to be otherwise occupied.

However, her expectations of overhearing tidbits of gossip about high school romances and impossible teachers went unfulfilled as the three teenagers joined hands and Jared, their de facto spiritual leader, intoned a resonant blessing.

"Dearest Lord," he said," we want to thank you for the bounteous repast you and Missus Winslow have laid before us today, and we want to thank you also for the blessing of good fellowship we enjoy under the guidance of Pastor Charlie, and we pray that you will help us spread the Good News to those lost souls who have not yet opened their hearts to your Son and our Savior. In Jesus' name, Amen."

"Amen," Phoebe and Kimberly chorused, rather more enthusiastically than necessary Dorie thought. But then she was a mere lost soul who hadn't yet opened her heart to the Son and Savior so what did she know?

As lunch progressed, Kimberly kept the conversation focused on the project Phoebe had alluded to on the phone, a TFC carwash. Her verbal style resembled a PowerPoint presentation.

"A," she announced. "Delegation of Responsibilities. One. Phone roster. Phoebe, that's you. You call all the members of TFC and make them promise to show up at 8 a.m. on the morning of the car wash. Write down everyone who's coming and if anyone isn't, write down why they aren't."

She turned to Jared. "Two. Equipment. Jared, I want you to make a list of everything we need. You know, buckets, sponges, rags, car shampoo or whatever it's called, wax. All that stuff. We can borrow lots of it from my folks and the rest we'll get at Wal-Mart. But be sure you think it all the way through so you don't leave anything out, okay?"

Jared nodded meekly. Dorie speculated that he was the baby in a family of bossy older sisters.

Kimberly, naturally enough, was to be the liaison with the managers of the venue, her parents, who had offered the front parking lot of the GM dealership for the event.

"And I'll handle the media, too," she said airily. "I'll put an ad in the Shoppers Guide and I think I can get us a radio spot on the Village Corral. The guy who does the current event announcements owes us a favor because my dad let him keep a loaner car way longer than he should have."

This girl, Dorie thought, has a brilliant future, probably as some senator's press secretary.

After lunch, Phoebe took her friends upstairs to her room to make posters for the carwash. Dorie retreated to her office, intending to go online and search out a few more boring articles for her increasingly boring magnum opus on the contemporary relevance of Nathaniel Hawthorne's exploited heroines. She had begun the project years ago in hopes of getting a position at Harvard, but she had gotten bogged down in the middle, probably, she had to admit, because she didn't really want to dwell in those highly competitive halls of Ivy. Now she simply wanted to finish the manuscript just to prove she could write an entire book.

Fortunately, the moldy journal in her bottom desk drawer provided an excuse for procrastination. She pulled it out and flipped to the page where Phoebe's call had interrupted her reading.

# Five

## Sunday, July 9

The dreaded stomach flu has laid me flat. I haven't left my bunk all day, except for mad dashes to the nearest john. Annie brought me acidophilus tablets and a hot water bottle. Ianna dispensed peppermint tea but no sympathy. "Physical illness is a manifestation of blockage on the spiritual plane," she told me loftily. "Probably the same blockage that's responsible for your attitude of superiority."

I should spit on her toothbrush and see what she says about the spiritual plane when she's lying in bed with stomach cramps.

## Monday, July 10

Today things started to get really interesting. In a kind of scary way.

This morning I'm feeling almost human so I wander up to the kitchen to look for something to eat that isn't granola. Everyone's gone except for a few staff members because Omar has organized an expedition to a nearby mountain that's supposed to be some kind of Apache sacred site. Ianna told me yesterday that he's going to conduct a ritual designed to "tune in" to the "entity" that inhabits the peak.

So I'm just outside the dining hall when a big flashy pickup truck with a CB antenna skids to a stop in the driveway. A short, muscular guy wearing a cowboy hat and boots jumps out. "Howdy," he says and sticks out his hand. I howdy him right back while I wonder what the heck this ranch hand is doing on Community property. Then he just about crushes my fingers with his handshake.

"You don't look too well," the cowboy says. "Had the stomach flu?" "How did you guess?" I say. He shrugs. "Everybody here gets it sooner or later. The sanitation is awful. So's the food. Let's go find some coffee. There's a stash behind that godawful herb tea."

The thought of having a cup of real coffee instead of Dharma Tea Company Hokey Moka Dandelion and Chicory Blend, and a bit of small talk with an ordinary, unspiritual person, even if he does appear to be a redneck, turns me on. I follow him into the cookhouse, where he heads for a corner cupboard and rummages around on the top shelf.

"Got it," he exclaims. "My special blend. I get it from a boutique roaster in Berkeley." He turns around and brandishes a coffee can at me. I get a good look at his face. Despite the luxuriant Wyatt Earp moustache and the slightly receding, wavy dark brown hair, there's an unmistakable resemblance to the saintly, turbaned countenance in the flower-garlanded portrait above the refrigerator. The same twinkly brown eyes, with slightly hooded, Asiatic lids, the same cleft chin. It is Bud himself.

I blurt, "You're the guru!" I'm not so much awe-struck as surprised, both at his unexpected appearance and the fact that I like him. "One and the same," Bud replies, with a big grin. "And who are you? And why the hell are you here? I hope you're not looking to be enlightened." I introduce myself but it's hard to tell him why I'm here since I've been wondering myself the past few wretched days. "I guess I just wanted to find out what was going on," I mumble stupidly.

He nods, and scoops coffee into a French press he takes out of a box marked "Keepa Da Hands Off Or I Breaka Da Head." "That's as good a reason as any," he says, "although that kind of curiosity can get you into trouble." I'm practically hypnotized by the way he's making coffee. He's like a Zen master performing the tea ceremony.

I ask him what's wrong with curiosity. He says, "What I mean is, the cat got killed that way." He pushes the plunger down with exactly the right amount of force. "On the other hand," he continues, "nothing ventured, nothing gained, and the Lord helps those who help themselves, etc., ad infinitum. There is deep truth in trite proverbs. The trick is recognizing the situations to which they apply."

He pours coffee into two gilt-edged porcelain mugs and hands me one. It's black as swamp water but it smells great. "Drink up, Cookie," he says. "It'll put hairs on your chest." He grins at me again. "You do want hairs on your chest, don't you?"

"Not really," I reply, wondering what he's on about. "Aren't you into women's lib and all that?" he says. "Well, I'm for equal opportunity and careers for women, if that's what you mean," I say. "But that's only common sense. Women should use their talents just like men do."

"Should they now," he says, with a wicked gleam in his eye. I'm getting a little pissed off. I'm trying to think up a good retort when I hear scuffling and thumping noises in the entryway. "In here, **girls,"** Bud sings out, looking teasingly at me.

Two women about my age stagger into the kitchen carrying an enormous cardboard box between them. "Where do you want it, Bud?" the taller one asks. Bud turns to me. "See? I too am for equal equal opportunity. I always give the girls an equal opportunity to carry the groceries." He tells "the girls" to put the box down and come meet me.

"This is Cookie," he informs them, waving a hand to shush me when I try to introduce myself. "Bruce enticed her into Omar's study group by fixing her leaky faucet." I have no idea where he got that bit of information, but it doesn't prove he has paranormal abilities. He may just have a good intelligence network.

The taller woman says "Hi, I'm Corinne," without a trace of a welcoming smile. She has big brunette hair and she's wearing designer jeans and an ornate, embroidered western shirt. She reminds me of those Dallas oil wives you see buying up entire floors of Neiman-Marcus and she makes me nervous.

Polly, the shorter and younger of the two, is as friendly as Corinne is aloof. She's wearing non-designer jeans and a blue chambray work shirt and her sandy hair looks like she cuts it herself. I like her right away.

Corinne says something about how it's nice that I've found time to pay Bud a brief visit. I get the distinct impression that she means the briefer the better.

While the Dragon Lady and Polly bustle about in the kitchen, Bud settles himself at a round table in the breakfast nook and props his feet up on a chair in flagrant defiance of rule five in the Contamination Proclamation posted on the refrigerator door. I'm feeling very out of place. I try to be useful by taking the empty coffee mugs to the sink. Corinne gives me a dirty look but I go ahead and wash and dry them anyway.

"Glad to see someone doing something productive around here without being told," Bud observes. I say I don't think dishwashing's productive, it's just boring maintenance work that nobody notices unless it doesn't get done.

"Hah!" Bud retorts, "then you know how God feels." I ask him what he means. He goes to the refrigerator and gets a Perrier off a shelf labeled "Bud's Stuff—Not For You," then turns and leans against the door.

"Old Mr. God doesn't hear a lot of thanks for keeping the creation going. A few perfunctory hymns of praise and the occasional prayer or candle when someone thinks he's granted them a special favor, but generally the effort he puts into keeping the whole ball of wax together is taken for granted. Nope, no one bothers to tip the cosmic maintenance man, not even at Christmas. Well, he might get a few cheap Hallmark cards with sentimental messages. But no one offers to lend him a hand."

Bud twists the cap off the Perrier, takes a swig, belches loudly, and looks at me to see my reaction. I must look bewildered because he abandons his metaphor.

"Don't you see," he says, advancing on me until I'm backed up against the table, "every single moment of existence is a miracle. Yet you pass through your days oblivious to the continual renewal of the creation in which you are an unwitting participant. If you realized what you've been given, what a wonder it is to exist, regardless of the form of that existence, your every breath would be filled with gratitude."

He looks at me with an intensity that would be unbearable except for the strange, almost palpable calm that suddenly surrounds us. I'm standing stock-still, vaguely aware that I'm holding a dripping dish sponge in my hand, while I try to understand what he means. His words don't really make sense—they're just sounds that occupy my mind while some other part of me is absorbing the actual message.

We stay like that for a while, just standing and looking at each other. Except I'm not exactly looking at Bud. I'm looking through his eyes into an endless void that is both black and brilliantly lit at the same time, and while I'm looking into it, I'm also in it. Or maybe it's in me. Whatever it is, it's like nothing I've ever experienced before and it blows me away.

After a while, Bud breaks the spell by slurping some more of his fizzy water. He smiles at me. "You don't know what I'm talking about, do you, Cookie? You're close, but no cigar. Well, you might just get it someday." He whirls around and leaves the kitchen, letting the screen door slam behind him, while I stand there clutching a wet sponge and trying to figure out what just happened.

On a more profane note, now I can't find the packet of travelers' checks that I stuck in my backpack as emergency mad money. Either I'm going completely bonkers or someone's pinching my stuff.

• • • • • • •●● ● ●●● • • • • •

Dorie smiled to herself as she closed the journal and leaned back in her chair. Bud had been something else. Unpredictable, outrageous, and magnetic. The very air around him had been supercharged, like the atmosphere preceding an electrical storm. She had never, before or since, felt so alert, so open to indefinable possibilities, as she had that summer. Back then she'd been willing, even eager, to leap before she looked—and assessed—where she might land.

Miniscule dust motes floated aimlessly in the afternoon light that leaked in between the slats of the wooden blinds. The house was quiet. She dimly remembered having heard voices and a door closing at some point while she was reading. Evidently, Kimberly and Jared had left and Phoebe had gone upstairs to her room.

She stood up and rolled her neck in a semicircle to release the tension that had crept into her shoulders. Her cervical vertebrae crackled in protest. She pictured Bruce, disheveled and earnest; she wondered if he had ever found what he was looking for, whatever it was. And the rest of the motley crew that made up the Community, whatever had become of them? Funny how she had completely forgotten them even though they had come to share an intense, if temporary, intimacy.

Bud, however, was another story. His face had popped up in her dreams over the years, but she had promptly banished it behind the practical concerns of waking life. She hadn't thought seriously about him since Phoebe was born.

"I wonder," she said aloud, "what he's up to now?" On the other hand, she reflected, maybe I don't want to know.

*Six*

D orie was one of the few people she knew who actually liked Mondays. Monday meant the return of structure: office hours, appointments, classes, a general busyness that filled the day and brought a satisfying, if illusory, sense of accomplishment.

So even though she wouldn't be teaching until the third summer session began in July she intended to be in her office by early morning. She had been assigned a new course on Southwestern literature and, given her geographically inappropriate expertise on New England writers, she needed to do some fast pedaling. She had composed a tentative reading list that included "Death Comes for the Archbishop" and books by Frank Waters and John Nichols but she needed more and she didn't think Tony Hillerman's mysteries would be deemed sufficiently literary. She briefly considered inserting "The Last of the Mohicans" on thematic grounds, but since the Adirondacks were a couple of thousand miles too far northeast she nixed that idea.

She drank a hearty mug of "River Shannon" Irish breakfast tea while she watered the little cutting garden in the backyard and contemplated the peaks east of Rabbit Valley. The rising sun backlit them with a rosy glow and she couldn't resist declaiming a bit of Shakespeare to the baby snapdragons and cornflowers.

"Full many a glorious morning have I seen flatter the mountaintops with sovereign eye," she intoned. She could never remember the rest of the sonnet, but those two lines seemed an appropriate paean to a glorious Colorado summer morning

Before leaving the house, she made a huge protein shake with whey powder and frozen raspberries, drank half, and put the rest in the fridge for Phoebe. Dorie knew her daughter would be oblivious for another hour, deep in the heavy morning sleep of adolescence, but she trusted Phoebe to wake up in time to bike to her summer job as a junior barista at The Coffee Connection. It was a four-mile ride, but mostly flat or downhill, and Phoebe had done it twice before without difficulty. Dorie left her a note on the kitchen whiteboard saying that she would pick her up when her shift ended at four p.m., shouted a goodbye in the general direction of the stairs just in case her daughter was conscious, grabbed her briefcase, and set off for work.

West Fork State College was perched on a mesa to the east of town. The drive took fifteen minutes, long enough for a bit of brooding. She decided that coming across her old journal had been a mixed blessing. It did remind her of the exhilarating hopefulness of her youthful spiritual search, but the contrast between her naive flirtation with Eastern mysticism and her daughter's fervid infatuation with a simplistic version of Christianity was depressing.

It's all my fault, Dorie thought glumly. Phoebe's taken up with a bunch of preppy Jesus Freaks just to piss me off. Why didn't she just join the Hare Krishnas? That I could handle.

Dorie parked the Forester in the lot near Burgwin Hall. Like the rest of the college buildings, it was a low, contemporary structure clad in buff-colored sandstone and capped with a practical metal roof. The entire campus was as unlike the turreted and pedimented colleges of New England as West Fork itself was to Newton, Massachusetts.

I wanted a change, Dorie thought. And here I am. A stranger in a strange land. Like Bud used to say, be careful what you wish for because you may get it.

When she got to her office, she saw a Post-it note stuck to the door. This one was yellow; last week's had been pink and the one before that blue. She read the loopily scrawled message.

"Venus fly traps are purple

ragweed is yellow

when will you see

I'm a truly nice fellow?

How about dinner this Friday? My treat as long as the entree isn't over $9.99 and you don't order a French wine--Doug"


Dorie smiled and rapped on the door next to hers.

"You may approach," a pleasant bass voice called.

She pushed the door open. Doug Brenner, ex-ski bum turned poet and creative writing teacher, leaned back in his chair and grinned at her, then turned to his teaching assistant, who sitting on the edge of his desk.

"Is she going to say yes this time, Tony? Or is she going to spurn my advances yet again and miss out on what could be a mad, passionate affair, possibly leading to an LTR? Which, in case you don't know, stands for" long term relationship" in personal ad talk."

Tony Begay, a stocky Native American wearing a sweatshirt depicting the Mt. Rushmore Monument presidential heads with Indian features, shook his head vigorously.

"Sheesh, Doug," he said "I don't think your doggerel cuts it. You should try chocolate."

"Okay, okay," Dorie laughed. "I'll think about dinner but it's not likely. I've got too much work to do and besides I'm too old for Doogie Hauser boy-wonder-poet."

"I dunno," Tony said. "You guys look the same age to me."

"Looks are deceptive," Dorie replied. "Doug didn't use sunscreen in his misspent youth so he's got wrinkles. And many, many silver threads among the gold. I, on the other hand, believe in zinc oxide and Miss Clairol. And I'm a compulsive hiker and eat vitamins like candy while Doug is a junk food addict."

"Well, we think you're a still a fox, don't we Tony?" Doug said encouragingly. "And seven years age difference is nothing. Of course, if we get married I'm counting on you to die first and leave me that sweet little house of yours out in Rabbit Valley."

"Not on my prenup," Dorie shot back. "That's for Phoebe and my unborn grandbabies. But enough of this. I've got a problem."

She sat down in the visitor's chair that Tony had spurned. She admired Doug for mentoring him academically and for playing a fatherly role in his life. In her weaker moments, she could see Doug playing a fatherly role in Phoebe's life, but that was a place she really didn't want to go. Not yet, anyway, and maybe never. Better to get a large hairy dog, she had decided, preferably a neutered male.

"A problem," Doug mused. "Let me guess. Your car is going wonka wonka wonka and black stuff is dripping out of the tailpipe?"

Dorie shook my head. "Worse than that."

"You just found out your house was built on a bentonite deposit and may be swallowed up in a sinkhole?"

"Worse yet." She feigned a tragic sigh. "My daughter has become a born-again Christian."

Doug looked at her quizzically. He ran his hand through his overgrown salt and pepper curls and shrugged.

"Could be worse," he said. "She could be pregnant. Or anorexic. Or snorting the evil white powder."

"But it doesn't make any sense," Dorie complained. "She's smart and she's not naïve. I deliberately exposed her to Buddhism and Sufism and all that good stuff. And she's always liked science and computers. I just don't see how she can believe in a literal interpretation of the Bible. She talks about this Pastor Charlie who leads her Christian youth group like he's some kind of oracle. She's completely hooked."

"Is that Charlie Pritchett?" Tony asked. "The guy that pastors the Circle of Friends in Christ church over on Wyoming Avenue?"

"I think so," Dorie said.

"Oh, he's not so bad," Tony said. "He's great at motivational talks and I think he really cares about kids."

Dorie looked at Tony carefully. Maybe he was a born-again, in which case she'd really put her foot in it. She tried to think of some way to cover her tracks but Tony rescued her.

"Don't worry, Dr. Winslow," he said. "I'm not a Christian. I'm more into my own people's religion. I only met Pastor Pritchett at an ecumenical counsel on substance abuse."

Doug had told her that Tony's parents, Dine from Shiprock were both alcoholics but that Tony had been raised by an auntie who had made sure he attended school and was adequately nourished. In gratitude, he counseled his peers on the dangers of addiction.

"But I kind of think you're overreacting," Tony continued. "Kids have to try on a lot of philosophies before they find one that fits. Besides, it's your daughter's life, not yours. You can't choose a religion for her."

"But I can guide her, can't I?" Dorie asked indignantly. "I mean, isn't that what parents are supposed to do?" She looked at Doug for affirmation. Not that he'd ever had any children, she thought, given his protracted adolescent obsession with skiing and mountain biking.

"All you can do is present a range of possibilities and state your own position," Doug said. "Then you have to let the kid make her own choices, Dorie. Especially when it comes to religion, which is even more personal than sex. Maybe you'll agree with the choices and maybe you won't. But unless you can see a clear and present danger you need to back off and let Phoebe find her own way."

This wasn't exactly what she wanted to hear but she couldn't argue with it. She thanked Doug and Tony for listening to her rant and turned to go.

"Hey," Doug called after her. "What about that dinner invite?"

"Not this time," she said. "I've got to get my Southwestern lit course together and I've got Phoebe's birthday party on Saturday. And I need to clean the house and I still haven't unpacked the boxes in my office..."

"Lame excuses, Dorie," Doug responded. "Truth is you've got this strange immunity to my charm. Although I can't imagine how. All the other ladies succumb. But you," he thumped the desk in a doo-wop beat and sang, "you're the one, you're the one that I want."

Dorie slipped out the door as Tony joined the chorus by slapping his knees to the beat and adding a falsetto descant, "Öooo...ooo honey..."

Dorie made some progress on her course outline, adding a couple of books by Denise Chavez and Sandra Cisneros to her reading list. By the time she finished a little online research for her Hawthorne manuscript, she was ravenous. She decided to drive into town for a sandwich and a visit to Weiss's Jewelry, where she intended to buy Phoebe the prettiest little gold cross she could find. Doug and Tony were probably right about backing off to a neutral, albeit uncomfortable, corner. Giving Phoebe the symbolic trinket she wanted would be a meaningful concession.

Weiss's Jewelry was on the ground floor of a late nineteenth century red brick building at the less fashionable north end of Main Street, next to a small hardware store that was struggling to survive the arrival of a Home Depot on the outskirts of town. The south end of Main Street, which had once held a drug store with a genuine marble-countered soda fountain, a J.C. Penney's retail outlet, and a shoe repair shop, was now all trendy eateries, real estate agencies, and shops selling overpriced Western-themed decorative items made from castoff antlers and used horseshoes. Dorie avoided it whenever possible save for an occasional guilt-ridden purchase of pecan cinnamon buns at The Rocky Mountain Bakery.

Avram Weiss looked up from the workbench at the rear of his store. He appeared to date from the late nineteenth century himself, with his hunched back, bald pate, and abundant liver spots. However, he still had the visual acuity and manual dexterity needed to replace watch batteries and repair broken jewelry clasps, which is how Dorie had met him.

"Hi, remember me?" she said. "I came in to get my bracelet fixed after it fell off into a grate?"

Mr. Weiss's wrinkles rearranged themselves into a deeply creased smile.

"Yes, yes," he said. "The lady professor from Boston, come to Colorado to escape the big city. You settled into West Fork now? You got a nice boyfriend yet?"

Dorie replied that yes, she was settled, and no, she didn't have a boyfriend, she needed a birthday present for her daughter.

Mr. Weiss suggested something involving pearls, June's jewel of the month.

"Good idea, "Dorie said, "but she has a specific request."

"If she wants a ring for the belly button I don't have," Mr. Weiss announced.

"Don't I wish," Dorie replied. "Unfortunately, she wants a gold cross on a chain."

Mr. Weiss raised his eyebrows.

"Funny," he said. "I thought you were Jewish."

Dorie smiled. It wasn't the first time she had been thought to be Jewish; she liked to believe it was because of the unbeatable combination of her olive complexion, dark hair and rapier wit.

"Nope," she said, "I'm just a plain old lapsed Presbyterian from Iowa."

Mr. Weiss nodded slowly and walked over to a display case on the left side of the store. He pulled out a black velvet tray with an assortment of crosses, miniature praying hands, hearts, tiny bear fetishes, aspen leaves, and a lone Star of David.

"Something for everyone," he said. "Even the hippies." He pointed to a tarnished silver peace symbol that looked as if it were left over from the sixties.

Dorie examined the crosses. She settled on a sleek contemporary design, narrow and tubular with a tiny diamond at the intersection of the arms. As a piece of jewelry, it was quite elegant. She hoped Phoebe wouldn't consider the diamond sacrilegious.

Mr. Weiss helped her select a complementary chain with a close-woven snaky construction. He placed the chain and cross in a blue velvet box, put that in a white cardboard gift box, wrapped it in glossy dark blue paper and tied the package up with gold cord.

"There now," he said, handing Dorie the package. "The little miss should be pleased."

"I guess so," she said. "But I hope she comes to her senses before someone entices her to go out and bomb an abortion clinic or something. What these people do in the name of religion is beyond me."

Mr. Weiss raised an eyebrow as he ran Dorie's Amex card through the machine.

"Oy," he said. "Religion. A blessing and a curse."

He gave her the card and her sales receipt, then looked into her eyes and shook his head slowly.

"To bomb an abortion clinic is not good. But worse has been done in the name of God. Much worse."

Dorie nodded in agreement. Mr. Weiss was right. And so was Doug. She needed to back off, give Phoebe some space and pray, pardon the expression, that her daughter came to her senses.

# Seven

The Coffee Connection occupied a refurbished gray and white Victorian house on the edge of West Fork's historic district. As Dorie pulled into the parking lot, she spotted Phoebe's silver mountain bike chained to a rack. That bike had cost a bundle. It was gratifying to see Phoebe was being more careful with it than with the rest of her regularly lost or misplaced possessions.

Dorie opened the front door and stopped in her tracks. Phoebe was behind the pickup counter, leaning forward, winding a tendril of hair around her finger as she listened to a pair of teenage boys recount something involving abundant gesticulations and exclamations.

Dorie recognized the taller of the boys as Jared; his height and disheveled hair were unmistakable. As were Phoebe's rapt facial expression and body language. Boy number two, and any customer in need of a latte, might as well abandon all hope of being served.

"Hellloooo," Dorie called, resisting the temptation to lurk behind a coat rack and watch her daughter's budding romance unfurl.

Jared turned around and smiled. "Missus Winslow!" he called enthusiastically. "How you doing?"

Phoebe was less effusive. "You're early," she accused.

"It's only ten 'til four," Dorie said, "and I really needed a hot chocolate pick-me-up." Why, she chided herself, do I sound so apologetic?

Jared introduced his companion, a burly kid in baggy shorts and baggier shirt, as Chris French. "Chris is helping us with the car wash," Jared said cheerily. "He's kind of an adjunct member of TFC. He's holding out, but the Lord's got him in his gunsights and he's gonna bring him down pretty soon."

"Uh, that's good, I guess," Dorie said, resisting the urge to comment on Jared's choice of metaphor.

Phoebe thrust a hot chocolate at her. "It's on the house. Employee perks."

Dorie interpreted this as a gesture of appeasement; Phoebe's irritation at the unexpected maternal intrusion into Teen World appeared to have dissipated.

Jared and Chris excused themselves—-something about needing to get over to the church to pick up some sheet music—-and left in Jared's old Toyota Tacoma. Dorie noticed that he used his turn signal when turning into the street even though he was only exiting a parking lot. A careful driver, she mused. And he does have impeccable manners. If courtesy to one's elders is a corollary of Christianity, perhaps TFC has some redeeming features.

Dorie drank her hot chocolate while Phoebe signed over the cash register key to the next barista, a young woman with pale skunk stripes in her dirty blonde hair. No class there, Dorie thought, and immediately felt guilty for being a snob. Nevertheless, she glanced at Phoebe's luxuriant brown mane and felt a warm wash of maternal pride. Phoebe, despite her sporadic fits of bad temper, definitely had class; it was inherent in her delicate features, graceful movements, and cool, assessing gaze. Moreover, she appeared to be a conscientious employee. Dorie watched with amazement as she aligned clean cups according to size, scrubbed all the sticky spots off the counter, and made sure the self-serve water dispenser was filled. Surely this was not the same girl who left shoes, books, and CDs scattered at random on the living room floor.

On the way home to Rabbit Valley Dorie decided to take advantage of Phoebe's vehicular captivity and extract some information about Jared.

"You know, Phoeb," she began, "I really like Jared. He seems like a genuinely sweet guy."

"Uh huh, Phoebe said and turned to look out the passenger window.

Dorie tried again. "Did he grow up in West Fork?"

"Uh uh. He moved here from Chicago."

Dorie persisted.

"What about his family? What brought his mom and dad to West Fork?"

"He doesn't have a mom. Not here anyway. His mom and dad got divorced and his dad got custody and they moved here."

"But why West Fork? That's a big change from Chicago."

"His dad's brother lives here. They wanted to be close to him."

Dorie wasn't giving up. "Does Jared have brothers and sisters?"

"Nope. He's a lonely only, like me," Phoebe said," except he has two live parents, which I don't."

Dorie's jaw tightened. She wasn't going to let Phoebe start another one of those pointless, recriminatory conversations about how much she missed her father. They'd had enough of those back in Newton. It was time to move on.

"Well, it's nice that you're both only children," she said brightly. "It gives you something in common."

"Mother, that's not exactly a big deal. We have something much more important in common."

Dorie could guess what was coming but she asked anyway. "And what's that?"

"Our life in Christ," Phoebe replied with a sly smile. "What did you think I was going to say? Snowboarding?"

When they got home Dorie sorted through the usual assortment of unwanted catalogs in her mailbox—an impulsive late-night online purchase of bed linens and fireplace tools had gotten her on every junk mailing list in the country. Then she checked her email in case any of her Boston friends still remembered her. They'd kept in touch for the first six months she was in West Fork, largely, she suspected, out of morbid curiosity about the consequences of what they considered her suicidal career move. But as time went by, she had found it increasingly difficult to share the details of her quiet, small-town life with people who accepted traffic jams spanning five lanes of the Massachusetts Turnpike as an inconvenient but unavoidable part of their daily routine.

There were no emails demanding prompt replies so Dorie poured herself a Jack Daniels and water and plopped onto the sofa with a fresh issue of The New Yorker. She was savoring a particularly vicious movie review when Phoebe came into the living room.

"What's for dinner?" she asked.

"How about pizza?" Dorie said. "I don't feel like cooking tonight."

"Okay," Phoebe agreed as she picked up Dorie's drink from the end table and sniffed it

"What on earth are you doing?" Dorie asked.

"This stuff in your glass. What is it?"

"Bourbon and branch. Why do you ask?"

Phoebe twisted her ponytail into a spiral and looked down at the floor. "You have beer or whiskey or something every night. You could have an alcohol problem and not know it."

Dorie took a slow, deliberate sip of bourbon and rolled it around on her tongue before replying. "Phoebe, have you ever seen me drunk? Or even tipsy? You know, talking too loud and acting weird?"

Phoebe admitted that she hadn't.

Fortunately, Dorie thought, she's never been to a faculty cocktail party.

"Right. So what's the problem?"

"Well," Phoebe said. "Well..." She sat down in the armchair next to the sofa and tucked her bare feet under her. "Well, Pastor Charlie says substance abuse is like a slippery slope. You take one step on it with your first drink and then all of a sudden you're at the bottom. Like, in the gutter."

Dorie suppressed a smile. Phoebe's concern seemed sincere but this parent-child role reversal was too much to take.

"I don't disagree with your Pastor Charlie," she answered, "but one drink a day isn't going to put me on skid row. All it's going to do is raise my good cholesterol and calm me down so I don't get upset by the atrocities on CNN."

"But that's just it," Phoebe wailed. "You're always getting upset. You get upset about the news, you get upset about the papers you have to grade, you get upset when you pay the bills, you...you..." She examined the pink polish on her toenails, then looked up at her mother and said softly, "You don't have peace in your heart."

Dorie didn't know what to say. Phoebe was right. She didn't have peace in her heart. An armed truce, maybe, but not peace. She wasn't unhappy, but aside from her Rocky Mountain highs in the great outdoors, she was continually fending off a cloud of small buzzing anxieties, worries about her finances, her unfinished book, her health, her age, and, of course, Phoebe's state of mind. Which at present was even more anxiety-provoking than usual.

"So," she asked her daughter, "just what do you who suddenly seem to have all the answers suggest I do about it?'

"If you were saved," Phoebe said, "you wouldn't worry so much. You'd know that Jesus would take care of all the stuff you can't handle and that whatever was happening was part of God's plan for you. If you were saved you could relax. You wouldn't have to drink."

"Phoebe, I am not an alcoholic nor do I have to drink. I drink because it relaxes me and I enjoy it and that's all," Dorie burst out, realizing too late how non-relaxed she sounded. She took a deep yoga cleansing breath and began again. "But now that you've brought it up, how about telling me about this being saved business. What does that really mean to you?"

Phoebe looked surprised. "Everything. It means just everything."

"I need more than that," Dorie said. "I want details. How did you get saved? What happened? "

Phoebe unfolded herself from the armchair and started towards the front hall. Dorie wondered if she were going to do one of her disappearing acts, but Phoebe turned around and smiled radiantly.

"Just a sec," she said. "I'll be right back." She bounded upstairs and returned in less than a minute carrying a large paperback book. She sat down on the sofa and passed it to Dorie.

Dorie examined it. The glossy cover featured an expanse of blue sky with a mischievous cherub in a baseball cap reclining on a fluffy white cloud. He, or it, was giving a thumbs-up. A tiny red biplane in one corner spewed wispy skywriting above the cherub and his cloud. It read: "The Radical Teen Bible: The Best Book You'll Ever Read, The Only Book You'll Ever Need."

A four-letter Anglo-Saxon expletive nearly escaped Dorie's open mouth.

"This is what we use in our study groups," Phoebe said. "It's a regular Bible but it's got these special parts that explain how the stories and the Proverbs and everything relate to kids like us. So it's actually fun to read. Except for the begats. I always skip them."

Dorie thumbed through the book. It appeared to be a normal New King James translation interspersed with sidebars outlined in turquoise and fuchsia. They bore titles like "Dating: What Would Jesus Do?" and "Vanity: The Devil in the Mirror." There were also full-page sections on marriage, family, sex, and abortion, accompanied by line drawings of teenagers and parental figures in dowdy sixties-era clothing.

"Here's the part I want you to read, Mom," Phoebe said. She leaned over and opened the book to an earmarked page.

Dorie looked at the chapter heading. It said: "Salvation: You've Got a Ticket to Ride."

"Read it, Mom. It explains everything better than I can."

Dorie swallowed hard and began reading.

*"Do you want to get to Heaven? Do you want eternal blissful life? The bad news is, no matter how hard you try to be good and do God's will you're going to fail. That's right. We're none of us perfect enough to get into Heaven under our own steam. As it says in Romans 3:10 and 3:23 'There is no one righteous, not even one, for all have sinned and fallen short of the glory of God.'*

*"The good news is that there's a free ticket waiting just for you. God truly wants you to be Saved. Nothing makes God happier than having another one of His children come home to him. So God sent his Son to pay for your sins. All you have to do is to admit that you are lost, separated from God by your human weakness, as it is written in Isaiah*

*53:6, 'We all, like sheep, have gone astray, each of us has turned to his own way.' All you have to do is accept Jesus as your personal Savior and you will be assured of a blessed life on this earth and eternal life after that. Remember John 3:16: 'For God so loved the world that he gave his one and only Son that whoever believes in him shall not perish but have eternal life.' Now is that a deal, or what?"*

Dorie closed the Bible. She didn't want to rain on Phoebe's parade, but these bromides about salvation were infuriating.

"Phoebe, do you think this is literally true? About Jesus being the Son of God, and about Heaven and damnation and all? Don't you think these are just ways of describing certain states of consciousness? You know, metaphors?"

Phoebe grabbed the Bible and clasped it to her chest. She drew her breath in sharply.

"I should have known you'd say that," she said, her voice trembling. "I should have known you wouldn't get it."

"I'm trying to," Dorie said, "I really am. But I just don't see how you can believe this nonsense."

Phoebe stood up, holding the Bible in front of her like a shield. "Because I feel it," she said defiantly. "When Pastor Charlie talks about the Lord, and sometimes when we're praying, I feel something huge. Something awesome. Like my heart's going to explode with happiness." She pressed her hand to her heart. "I know it's true because I feel it. Here."

And with that, she retreated upstairs to her room.

"I'm sorry, "Dorie called after her. "I didn't mean what I said. I didn't mean to…" She stopped. Phoebe was too far away to hear and besides, while she hadn't intended to hurt Phoebe's feelings, she had indeed meant exactly what she said.

Eight

There were no more references to salvation the rest of the evening. Phoebe reappeared for dinner, distant but cordial, and a TV documentary on the Great Barrier Reef provided a shared diversion along with a large pizza margherita. Just to be on the safe side, Dorie had a diet Pepsi with her pizza instead of the beer she really wanted. She wasn't sure whether she was being diplomatic or cowardly but she felt it best to avoid any possibility of further offending her daughter. Nevertheless, she was relieved when Phoebe said goodnight and went upstairs to bed.

Dorie too went upstairs, but not to bed. She ran a steamy lavender-scented bubble bath in the master bathtub, pulled a stool over by the tub and set her journal, which she'd fetched from her study, on it. She slid into the hot water and felt the tension in her shoulders and lower back melt away

She pondered the Phoebe situation. Was it really so dire? Phoebe was happier than she had been in years. That was good. But this happiness was based on dogma. That was bad. But then who was she to judge? Hadn't her own spiritual search been permeated with patchouli, pot, and a hodgepodge of Eastern mystical beliefs? Was the evangelicals' fervent obsession with Biblical inerrancy really any worse than the fantasies about Enlightenment that ran rampant through the Community?

"We all like sheep have gone astray, each of us has turned to his own way," she murmured. With that marginally comforting thought in mind, Dorie wiped her hands on a towel and opened her journal.

## Sunday, July 16

I made it into the Inner Circle today. Bud invited me to have breakfast with him and his groupies, i.e., Corinne, Polly, and Rosa, a matronly thirtyish woman who keeps the Community's books and pretty much runs the practical side of things, like ordering brown rice and toilet paper.

So we all go rolling off to the pine-paneled Kozy Kafay in Marmot Rock, squeezed into Bud's truck, with me next to Bud, which Corinne does not like, and Polly perched on Rosa's lap. Corinne also doesn't like it when Bud makes me sit by him in the booth in the restaurant.

But here's the fun part. We're all sitting at this booth with menus in front of us. Bud picks one up and looks at it and so do I but the other three women don't touch them. Polly whispers to me, "Bud always orders for everyone." And so he does. He selects completely different dishes for P., C., and R. based on mysterious dietary or esoteric requirements known to him alone. Then he tells the waitress that "Cookie here will have the mushroom and cheese crepes." I say "Oh no she won't." P. C. and R. look shocked. Bud smiles. I realize too late that he knew exactly how I would react.

Then he arranges his face to express profound disappointment and says, "But mushrooms would be good for you, Cookie. You need some yin foods to provide balance. But who am I to say what you need..." His voice trails off sadly and his shoulders slump.

I almost fall for his Jewish mother food-as-love guilt trip combined with an appeal to my egotistical curiosity, i.e., what does he know about me that I don't? But I catch myself and explain in a calm, mature manner, that heavy food in the morning gives me heartburn. Then I order toast and grapefruit juice, feeling smug about my non-reactive performance.

"Give her what she wants," Bud smiles at the waitress. The ladies heave a collective sigh of relief—he isn't staging one of his famous rages over my rebellion—and start gossiping about some Community incident. Bud leans toward me and whispers, "Nice try, Cookie, but you blew it." "What do you mean?" I ask. "You had to justify insisting on your own choice," he says. "You apologized for asserting yourself. That's just another knee- jerk reaction no better than your first defiant one. You're not home free yet, kiddo." Chalk up another "gotcha" moment for the guru.

### Wednesday, July 18

About 4 p.m. this afternoon Corinne rushes into the shed that serves as a sweatshop for the Community's Authentic Native American Beaded Moccasins business. (Rosa orders case lots of cheap leather moccasins from a factory in Chicago and the women sew glass beads onto them in geometric patterns and retail them through local souvenir shops.) She tells us to drop everything and come to the dining hall because there's a Work Emergency.

Carole, the California woman who is supposed to be spiritually contaminated because of an affair she had with a Rajneesh follower last year, is so terrified of Corinne that she leaps to attention, knocking over a bottle of itty bitty fake turquoise beads that scatter to the four corners of the room. Corinne averts her eyes and remarks to no one in particular that Bud always said that contact with poison lineages causes long-term damage to the moving center.

I deliberately hang back as Corinne races around the compound hustling people into the dining hall as if we've just had a five-minute warning of nuclear attack. By the time I sneak in through the closed doors, the entire Community is assembled. Bud is at the far end of the room with his consigliere, Leonard, and Ned, a shy, balding man who works as a sous chef in a New York restaurant. Bud has his arm around Ned's shoulders and is talking to him quietly. I catch Leonard's eye and mouth "What's happening?" He shakes his head and puts his finger to his lips. Bud hugs Ned, pats him on the back, and then steers him towards Leonard, who takes his arm and leads him, head down and stumbling, out of the room.

I sit down next to Rosa. She has her face in her hands and doesn't look up. Bud goes to his chair at the head table and pulls it out like he's going to sit down, then pushes it back and walks around in front of the table. He stands there without saying anything and seems to look directly at every single person in the room in a matter of seconds. Everyone stops talking.

"There's been an accident," Bud says. "Ned's nine -year -old daughter died last night from an uncontrollable asthma attack. Leonard is taking him to Denver to catch a flight back to New York." We all gasp and people start exclaiming what a tragedy, how awful for Ned. Two women near the front of the room begin weeping and hug one another.

Bud holds a hand up signaling silence. "Please, do not dramatize your sorrow. The death of a child warrants grieving, but that's Ned's business, not ours." This seems a bit harsh but what Bud says next makes sense. "Very few of you knew Ned and none of us knew Karen, his daughter. Sympathy for both of them is appropriate but indulging in displays of horror and grief is like feeding on someone else's deep personal loss. It's using a secondhand tragedy to fuel a heightened emotional state that makes you feel more alive. What we need to do instead is offer Ned, and Karen, some real help."

I'm wondering how we can help Karen if she's dead when Bud says, "If we can put our automatic emotional reactions aside, we can actually do something to ease Karen's passage, or voyage, or whatever you want to call the transition between the states we refer to, in our ignorance, as 'life' and 'death.'"

He pauses to give us time to absorb what he just said and then tells us that we're going to do a meditation that will help Karen's essence return to its source and also help Ned understand the continuity of life and death, which should bring him some comfort. Then he takes a step forward, holds one hand up, palm forward and waits. When the room is completely silent, he gives us the following instructions, which I hope I'm reproducing accurately.

"Close your eyes. Take a deep breath, from your abdomen, and see yourself breathing in a brilliant, clear light, a light that burns away your hopes, fears, and ideas about death." We all breathe in. "Now exhale and see the fine powdery ash of your annihilated delusions expelled through your open mouth." We all breathe out, open-mouthed.

"You are now empty, and with your next breath that emptiness will fill with crystalline light. You see in front of you a sphere of dazzling white light, brighter than a thousand suns. As you watch, it expands to fill all space and time. Fix your attention on that infinite brilliance and with every molecule of your being, visualize Karen's spirit speeding towards it, disappearing into that searing, blinding, beautiful illumination."

I don't know how long the meditation lasts, ten seconds, or ten minutes. It's like time gets suspended. But I feel like I myself am speeding towards some limitless white brilliance, leaving my body behind on a chair in a dilapidated shed on a Colorado mountain. I don't know how to describe it but I would swear I experienced some kind of self that is separate from my body and mind, kind of an impersonal point of awareness that can get detached from the conscious thoughts and physical organism I call myself. Wow!

Maybe that's why Bud says, at the end of the meditation, when everyone is sitting there looking stunned, that this exercise will help us as well as Ned and Karen. Maybe it will, because now when I think about Mom and Dad I don't get stuck on those awful memories of their funerals. I can see them as little points of light within some kind of enormous infinite light. I still miss them but it doesn't hurt as much.

• • • • • • • • ● • • • • • • • • •

Dorie dropped the journal on the floor beside the tub and slid down into the rapidly cooling bathwater so that her shoulders were covered. She turned the hot tap with her big toe and felt an influx of warm water swirl around her hips.

Why hadn't she remembered that exercise in the dining hall when she needed it eight years ago? An experience of non-corporeal existence would have helped her deal with Colin's death considerably more effectively than the bland platitudes offered by the Newton grief counselor. A live-in au pair to bear the brunt of Phoebe's outrage and misery would have helped too.

Dorie sunk an inch deeper into the water until it reached her chin. This line of thought was going to lead straight into the slough of despond. Best to invoke the Scarlett O'Hara defense.

"I'll think about that tomorrow," she muttered, and clambered out of the tub. She toweled herself off in front of the full-length mirror on the bathroom door. Forty-eight, she mused. This body has been in existence for forty-eight years. She turned from side to side, assessing the damage that time had wrought, and concluded that nothing had slid irreparably south. One of the few advantages of being small-breasted, aside from not needing to wear a hideous support bra, was a relative immunity to the forces of gravity.

So if I were ever again to have sex with anyone, she thought, I wouldn't have to undress in the dark. With that comforting possibility in mind, she went to bed.

## Nine

Saturday morning, the day of Phoebe's birthday party, Dorie woke from one of those generic anxiety dreams about running in slow motion after a departing train. She considered the various missed opportunities this might represent: failure to finish her book manuscript; putting off reserving a flight to a Boulder workshop on teaching multicultural literature; repeatedly rejecting Doug Brenner's dinner invitations. All were possibilities, but none produced a telltale "aha!" moment.

She flung back the covers and stumbled into the bathroom to brush the fur off her teeth and wash her face. Maybe the dream had something to do with Phoebe. Had she'd missed her chance to connect with her daughter before she left on Pastor Charlie's express train bound for glory.?

Dorie splashed warm water on her hair, which had arranged itself into punk rocker spikes during the night, and wrangled it into submission with a brush. No, the dream couldn't be about her relationship with Phoebe. Things had been better between them the past few days.

The previous Thursday, Phoebe's actual birthday, Dorie had picked her up at the coffee house and taken her to Pablito's Taqueria, a hole-in-the-wall eatery that Phoebe liked.

As they waited for their orders to come, Dorie announced, "I got a little something for you, babe." She took the exquisitely wrapped gift box from Weiss's Jewelry out of her purse and put it on the table along with the envelope containing a card she'd bought at the college bookstore. She'd spent twenty minutes looking for just the right one, bypassing the sloppy sentiments in the "To Daughter from Mother" section, as well as the crude jokes in the "Humorous Birthday" section. She'd settled on a Japanese print of pink peonies, Phoebe's favorite flower. There had been a peony bush in the tiny back garden of their Newton townhouse and, as a toddler, Phoebe liked to bury her nose in the big blooms, which she called "peepees."

"Oh, Mom, that is a beautiful box," Phoebe said. "I hope it's what I think it is."

"Open the card first," Dorie directed, "Let's prolong the suspense."

Phoebe slit open the envelope, pulled out the card, and smiled when she saw the peonies. Her smile widened when she read what Dorie had written inside: "To The WBD on her 16$^{th}$ Birthday. May you bloom as sweetly as these flowers." "WBD" was their private shorthand for "World's Best Daughter," an endearment Dorie had coined when Phoebe started first grade and deemed herself too old for her previous culinary pet names of "Pumpkin" and "Muffin."

"That is so lovely," Phoebe said. "Thank you, WBM."

Dorie was floored; she hadn't heard her counterpart nickname since Phoebe hit the rocky shoals of adolescence. She felt herself flush with pleasure. I hope she likes the cross, she thought. I hope the diamond isn't too much.

Phoebe undid the gold cord and tore the blue wrapping paper off the gift box. She saw the Weiss's Jewelry logo and looked up at Dorie, her eyes sparkling with delight.

"I bet it is what I think it is…" She opened the box. "Awesome!"

She dangled the cross from its chain and examined it closely "It's perfect," she said, "Exactly what I wanted."

"You don't mind the diamond?" Dorie said. "I was worried it might be…umm… inappropriate."

"No," Phoebe said, "it's beautiful. I've never had a diamond anything before." She put the chain around her neck and fastened the clasp. "Besides it's kind of symbolic, you know? Pure and clear, like Jesus' heart?"

Yikes, Dorie thought, but all she said was, "I'm really glad you like it, Phoebe." And so the evening had ended in a wash of warm feelings that spilled over into Friday.

Dorie ran a comb through her wet hair. The dream was probably just another manifestation of her chronic existential angst over the pursuit of some unobtainable whatever. She might as well forget it and do something productive.

She put on her house-cleaning clothes, comfortably loose worn-at-the-knees jeans and an old Harvard sweatshirt splattered with olive green paint, a souvenir from the redecoration of the Newton townhouse's dining room. She needed to exterminate the dust bunnies under the living room sofa because Phoebe and her sleepover guests, Kimberly and two other TFC girls, would be spreading their sleeping bags on the living room floor, the better to binge on DVD's and access the kitchen for snacks. Dorie suspected that Kimberly might consider domestic cleanliness next to godliness. She didn't want her slapdash housekeeping habits to embarrass her daughter.

Dorie was on her hands and knees brushing ashes out of the fireplace when Sharon Folsom rang the front doorbell. It was only nine o'clock on a weekend morning but Sharon's highlighted hair was sprayed into a country-western singer's flip and she was fully lipsticked, blushed, and mascaraed. She held a clipboard in one hand and one end of a bright blue propylene rope in the other. Her three-year-old twins, Stuart and Russell, were holding onto loops in the rope with one hand and swatting at each other with the miniature plastic tennis racquets in their free hands.

"It's my own invention," Sharon said, nodding towards the rope in response to Dorie's questioning look. "It's the only way I can keep track of them when we're out. We pretend we're mountain climbers. The racquets are supposed to be ice axes."

Sharon belayed her twins into the living room, settled herself on the sofa and waved the clipboard at Dorie.

"It's my Cosmic Cosmeceuticals product list," she said. "I know I said I'd just do makeovers on the girls and not try to sell them anything but I thought you might like to look it over in case there's anything you want. Russell, stop that."

Russell had dropped his rope loop and was trying to pry the battery cover off the television remote control. Stuart took advantage of his mother's diverted attention to disappear into the kitchen. Dorie collared him as he was heading for the under-sink cabinet with its cache of potentially toxic cleaning potions. She hauled him back into the living room, reattached him to the rope, and sat down to examine Sharon's product list.

"What are all these things you've circled?" she asked. "Wrinkle Eraser? Anti-Gravity Serum? Illusion of Youth Foundation? My God, Sharon, am I that bad off?"

Sharon looked at her appraisingly. "Not yet," she said darkly, "but if you don't take care of your skin now you'll wake up one morning and those little laugh lines will be creases and then the creases will turn into wrinkles and you'll look old."

"I believe that's the natural order of things," Dorie replied, "and I've accepted it. Along with hot flashes and insomnia."

"But you don't have to," Sharon said excitedly. "Not with modern technology. If you'd commit to a good skin care regime and stop dressing like that," she pointed an accusing finger at Dorie's sweatshirt, "you'd get asked out all the time."

"Who says I want to be asked out?" Dorie replied, wondering if she appeared to be one of those middle-aged women desperate to snag a man before the sweet bird of youth flew the coop.

"You don't?" Sharon asked, wide-eyed.

"Not particularly," Dorie said. "I've more or less given up on men."

"Really?" Sharon said, looking unsettled. She's probably wondering if I'm gay, Dorie thought.

"Look Sharon, I had a marriage that ended badly and a couple of disappointing boyfriends. I'm just not good at relationships."

"How come?" Sharon asked. "You're a nice person. A little snippy sometimes, but basically nice."

"Well, thanks a bunch," Dorie said. "I'll put that in my Women Seeking Men ad: SWF, 48, snippy but basically nice."

"Seriously, Dorie," Sharon went on, "you're too young to be a recluse. You just need to put yourself out there, you know? Give off some availability vibes?"

She reached out a hand to grab a wandering twin. "Sit, Russell. I mean Stuart. Mommy will be finished in a minute. So what happened, Dorie? To your marriage?"

Dorie hesitated. She hated this question because the answer always seemed to produce a flurry of embarrassed commiseration.

"My husband died. He was killed in an auto accident."

"Oh," Sharon gasped. "I'm so sorry. That must have been just awful."

"I got through it," Dorie said. "I had Phoebe. That's what kept me going."

Sharon smiled down at her twins, who had put the rope loops over their heads and were attempting to strangle one other.

"Yes," she said. "Kids. They're what it's all about, aren't they?" She looked up at Dorie brightly. "Hey! I've got a great idea. After I finish doing Phoebe and the girls this afternoon I'm going to do a megamakeover on you. I'm going to turn you into a babe. Just wait and see."

Dorie laughed. "Thanks Sharon," she said, "but I think I'll settle for aging gracefully. It's less traumatic."

$$Ten$$

At four that afternoon Kimberly's SUV rolled into the driveway. Phoebe, who had spent most of the day in her room doing something with digital photos and MP3 files that was completely beyond Dorie's comprehension, clattered down the stairs to the front door.

"They're here, Mom!" she shouted. "Where's Sharon? She's not going to be late, is she?"

"I'm sure Sharon will be here in a minute," Dorie said as she came out of the kitchen where she'd been scouring the sink with bleach just in case Kimberly decided to be helpful and wash the dishes. "She's probably just locking the twins in a cage or something so they won't destroy the house if Greg gets hypnotized by ESPN."

Kimberly and two other girls got out of the car. Dorie assumed the plump auburn-haired one was Amber Reilly, whom Phoebe had described as "sort of Kimmi's assistant." Right, Dorie thought, the Kimberlys of this world always have assistants, typically plump and plain. The slender brunette with amazing boobs, shown to great advantage in a rib knit tank top, was undoubtedly Nicole Chavez, who, judging from the way she tossed her head to resettle her glossy brunette mane, would never be anybody's assistant.

The girls unloaded their backpacks and sleeping bags and a big pink shopping bag with turquoise and pink tissue paper and curly ribbons erupting from the top. Phoebe skipped down the front porch steps to meet them. Dorie, watching from the door, almost teared up when she saw the girls hugging her daughter. They like her, she thought. I don't care if they speak in tongues and grow up to be rightwing Republicans. Phoebe's finally got some girlfriends.

Phoebe introduced Nicole and Amber to Dorie with the formality of a junior Emily Post as Kimberly nodded approvingly. She directed her friends to deposit their gear in the living room, then turned to Dorie. She looked worried.

"Do you think we should call Sharon? What if she forgot?"

"She won't forget," Dorie said. "She came over this morning and left me a list of products I'm supposed to buy. They came to $314. There's no way Sharon's forgetting."

A yodel came from the front porch. "Cosmic Cosmeceuticals calling! Are you ready to be beautiful?"

Sharon was armed with a large aluminum case of the sort used to transport expensive photographic equipment and a Wal-Mart shopping bag. The case was emblazoned with a logo: a diagram of a carbon-based molecule and the slogan "Cosmic Cosmeceuticals: Bio-Energized Skin Care." Sharon was wearing a silver Mylar lab coat with the same logo and a black plastic badge that identified her as "Sharon Folsom, Dermal Technician."

"Hi, everyone!" she said. "I'm Sharon and I'm here to show you how to bring out your inner beauty through the miracle of modern science."

She turned a bright professional smile on each of them in turn, including Dorie, who suddenly realized there was another dimension to this frazzled mother of hyperactive twins; she was born to sell.

"Follow me," Sharon ordered, "We're going to make Dorie's kitchen into our little laboratory for your personal transformation." Dorie and the girls trailed after her like the children of Hamlin following the Pied Piper.

Sharon placed the case on the kitchen table and opened it to reveal an assortment of glass jars, bottles, and vials nested in grey foam niches.

"Ta Da!" She swept her hand over the case like a stage magician waving his wand over a rabbit-filled top hat. "The Cosmic Cosmeceuticals line of skin care products and makeup, formulated by scientists with Ph.D.s from...uh..."she lost the thread of her spiel momentarily "...Stanford or someplace," she finished.

The girls clustered around the case examining the potions and lotions and questioned Sharon about their properties while Dorie arranged cotton balls, swabs and tissues on the table and brought over a stool from the breakfast bar.

"Okay, who's first?" Sharon asked. "The birthday girl?"

Phoebe took her place on the stool and Sharon draped her in a Mylar cape she whisked out of her case.

"First we cleanse and tone and then we moisturize," Sharon instructed. "I'm going to use this special set of products for acne prone skin."

"I don't have acne," Phoebe protested.

"You better use it on Amber," Nicole interjected. "She gets humongous zits."

"I do not get zits," Amber protested. "I just have sensitive skin."

"Nicole," Kimberly hissed, "that is not a charitable thing to say."

"Okay already," Nicole muttered. "Just trying to help."

Sharon finished prepping, as she termed it, Phoebe's skin, then brushed a pale peach blush on her cheeks, outlined her lips with a coral pencil, and finished them off with dabs of sticky gloss.

She stood back and examined her handiwork, head cocked on one side. "Got to do something about those eyebrows," she announced. "I'm going to pluck."

"Hey," Dorie broke in. "Hang on, Sharon. We don't exactly have a Frida Kahlo situation here."

"I'm just getting the strays, Dorie," Sharon said. "Trust me. Hold still, Phoebe, this isn't going to hurt."

"Ouch," Phoebe cried as Sharon extracted a particularly recalcitrant stray. "It does so hurt."

"No pain, no gain, "Sharon said. "Just wait til you get to be my age and have to do fifty situps a day to keep your stomach from pooching out."

"Or wait til you get to be my age," Dorie added, "and you hike 3000 vertical feet a week and your butt still sags."

"You don't need to worry, Mrs. Winslow," Amber interjected. "You're lucky you're so thin. My mother's done Jenny Craig and Weight Watchers and every diet you can think of and she's still has to buy her clothes at Total Woman. I just hope I don't end up like her."

"With the Lord's help and a little portion control you won't," Kimberly assured. "Just remember what I told you; Jesus wants you to be your best self and your best self wears a size 5."

Amber said she thought that was a bit of a stretch given her metabolism. Dorie, who had recently read an article on teenage anorexia at the dentist's office, pointed out that while Amber's best self might be a size 5, Jesus had done a number with loaves and fishes that suggested he did not advocate starvation.

Nicole snickered, but Kimberly looked miffed. "Of course he wasn't," she said, "and I'm certainly not telling Amber to starve herself or stick her finger down her throat after she eats or anything. I'm just saying that she needs to remember that Jesus is her number one support person. Then all she has to do when she's tempted with a cookie or something is to say a teeny little prayer.'

Dorie couldn't resist. "Like 'Get thee behind me, Oreo?'"

"Seriously, Mrs. Winslow," Kimberly said, "you'd be amazed at what the Lord can manifest in your life if you just give Him a chance. You know my parents? When car sales were off last winter they asked their prayer circle to pray for prosperity, if that was what the Lord wanted for them, of course, and they sold two Escalades the next month."

Sharon interrupted their theological discussion. "I'm going to do Phoebe's eyes now. They're her best feature and I really want to play them up. Now Phoebe, this is important. We curl first and then we put on mascara. Always in that order."

"Why?" Phoebe asked.

"Because if you do it the other way your eyelashes stick to the curler and get pulled out." Nicole offered. "By the roots. It's gross."

Sharon ignored her and continued to make up Phoebe's eyes, highlighting them with iridescent sand eye shadow as a finishing touch.

Kimberly whispered something to Amber who nodded and went into the living room. She returned with the pink gift bag and handed it to Kimberly.

"Okay, Phoebe," Kimberly said. "We went in together and bought you a group present. So we want you to go upstairs and put everything on and come down and do a reveal."

Phoebe blushed and took the bag. "Wow," she said. "I mean… I never expected this. You all are just great. Thanks."

"Go," Kimberly ordered. "We're dying to see how you look."

Phoebe started towards the hall and Sharon grabbed a hairbrush, blow dryer and a spray bottle out of the Wal-Mart bag.

"I'm coming with you," she said. "You can't leave one of my makeovers with your hair looking like that."

Ten minutes later, after Dorie had made polite small talk with Phoebe's friends by carefully avoiding anything to do with Teens for Christ or Pastor Charlie, Sharon appeared in the door to the front hall.

"Here she is," she sang, "Miss Sweet Sixteen America." She stepped aside and Phoebe entered the kitchen. Kimberly, Amber and Nicole applauded and cheered. Dorie was speechless.

Phoebe's hair, which usually hung straight from a middle part or was pulled back into an untidy ponytail, had been parted on the side and brushed into a gleaming swag that fell seductively aslant her left eye. And her eyes! The blue-green of her irises was accented by a fringe of lush black lashes. Her lips were full, pouty and moist with sparkly gloss.

My god, Dorie thought. She's stunning. She looks like a movie star. She looks like a…. woman.

The outfit her friends had assembled as a birthday gift completed the transformation: black Capri pants, black patent slides, and a gauzy fuchsia blouse over a matching camisole, both cut low enough to reveal the gold cross that Dorie had given her.

"Awesome," Nicole pronounced. "You are now an official hottie. Jared is going to freak when he sees you."

Dorie hoped the cross offered protection against human as well as were- wolves.

Kimberly, Amber, and Nicole took their turns on the stool and Dorie was impressed by Sharon's ability to create a "look" appropriate for each girl. Kimberly became an urban sophisticate, her blonde hair pulled into a casual topknot. Amber got a pre-

Raphaelite treatment, pale skin and eyebrows, with her red hair coaxed into a thousand wild ringlets. Nicole's Latina roots were emphasized with smudgy charcoal eyeliner and crimson lipstick.

"And now," Sharon turned to Dorie, "it's your turn."

"I don't know," Dorie said. "It's already 5:30 and the twins are probably driving Greg crazy." Besides, she thought, I'm too old to get tarted up like those kids. I'll just look ridiculous.

"It won't take long," Sharon insisted. "I know exactly what I'm going to do."

"Yeah, Mom," Phoebe chimed in. "Let her do you. She's really good."

"They're right, Mrs. Winslow," Kimberly added. "Let Sharon give you a new look. It'll make you feel better."

Feel better? What the hell does she mean by that? Dorie wondered as she allowed herself to be seated and caped.

Sharon took a small silver vial out of her box of tricks.

"This is from our Ponce de Leon line," she said, "designed especially for mature skin. It may tingle a little but it's only temporary."

She smoothed a syrupy liquid over Dorie's face. As it dried, Dorie felt her skin grow taut, as if it were being pulled up to her hairline by tiny invisible tractor beams.

"What is this stuff?" she asked uneasily.

"It's called 'Up and Away'," Sharon explained. "It gives you an instant face lift. Gosh, you look ten years younger already."

"That's lovely, Dorie said without moving her lips, which seemed to be paralyzed, "but if I smile somethings going to crack.."

"Don't worry," Sharon said. "It wears off in twelve hours."

"Great," Dorie replied. "I'll be sure to keep track of the time if I'm out on a date. I'd hate to turn into a withered pumpkin in public."

"Well, that's why you have to use the products I recommended to you this morning. They'll rebuild your skin from the inside out."

"That," Dorie said, as her lips began to regain their mobility, "sounds both painful and impossible."

"Stop complaining and let me finish," Sharon ordered. "Now I'm going to use a light reflecting foundation to hide the sun damage and a little sheer cream blush."

Dorie sat passively as Sharon finished patting and smoothing various pigments onto her cheeks and eyelids. She even endured the heated eyelash curler, after Sharon described its magical ability to "turn tired eyes into happy eyes."

"All done," Sharon announced. "And very nice, if I do say so myself."

"Cool, Mom," Phoebe said. "I've never seen you look like this."

"Way bad," Nicole added approvingly.

"Fantastic, Mrs. Winslow," Amber put in, "You don't look like a mother anymore."

Dorie took that as a compliment.

Kimberly examined Dorie's face, nodded thoughtfully, and then walked around her in a circle.

"Sharon, what about her hair?" she asked.

"Hey," Dorie broke in. "I do make an effort in that department. I use gunk to cover the gray."

"Uh huh," Sharon said. "But your cut's got no line. It's lumpy." She extracted a leather sheath containing a barber's shears from the Wal-Mart bag. "I thought I might need these," she said, advancing towards Dorie.

"Now just wait a minute," Dorie said hastily. "I can wash off the makeup but if you butcher my hair…"

"Dorie, I did graduate from the Front Range School of Aesthetics, you know," Sharon said indignantly. "With honors."

She grasped a section of Dorie's hair and applied the scissors. "I'm just going to shape it up so you have something like a style."

Dorie looked down as alarmingly large chunks of her short bob fell to the floor. She closed her eyes.

"That's much better," Sharon said, brushing stray hairs off the Mylar cape. "A touch of gel and we're done." She tugged and tousled selected strands of what was left of Dorie's hair and stood back to assess the result.

"Good," she said decisively. "I like this cut on you. It's very French."

"Go upstairs and look in the bathroom mirror so you can get the full effect," Phoebe urged.

Dorie did, and the full effect, while not so dramatic as Phoebe's transfiguration, was impressive. Sharon was right; she looked like a chic Parisienne, and if not exactly nubile, at least an indeterminate age somewhere between 30 and 40.

She bounced downstairs, unaccountably energized. She never suspected that face paint and a pixie cut could be such an upper. Kimberly, who was sweeping up Dorie's shorn hair, looked up and beamed at her.

"See what I told you?" she said. "When you look pretty you feel better about yourself." She turned to Amber, who was holding the dustpan. "Doesn't Mrs. Winslow look a zillion times happier than she did before?"

Amber nodded. "You look great, Mrs. Winslow. You should use those products all the time. There's nothing wrong with being pretty. You know how it says in the Scriptures, don't hide your light under a bushel? Well, it's like you're letting your light shine now."

"Amber," Nicole broke in, "Mrs. Winslow doesn't..." she stopped, but Dorie suspected the rest of the sentence would have been "read the Scriptures."

Nicole turned to her, "Mrs. Winslow, you look awesome. You should go out dancing or something. There's a great band playing at The Snakepit. And you don't have to have a date or anything. My mom goes there with her girlfriends sometimes."

Kimberly gasped. "Nicole, you know what Pastor Charlie said about places like that."

Nicole sighed. "Yeah, uh uh. I know. Demonic influences." She took the dustpan full of hair clippings from Amber and emptied it into the trash. As she brushed past Dorie she whispered, "My mom says it's a blast from the past."

Dorie smiled. "Thanks for the tip," she said, letting the reference to demonic influences pass even though she was tempted to point out that such beliefs were the vestiges of primitive mythologies left over from the Middle Ages.

The girls collected their jackets, a year-round necessity in the evening at 7,000 feet, in preparation for their evening on the town.

"You really do look amazing, Mom," Phoebe called over her shoulder as she and her friends flocked towards the door. "Sharon, thanks heaps for making my birthday so incredible." She blew a kiss to Dorie. "We'll be back by eleven, right after the movie. Don't wait up for us."

Sharon packed up the tools of her trade and headed for the door too. "Got to get home before the boys and Greg fill up on chips and salsa. I've got a chicken noodle thing in the crock pot."

Dorie thanked her profusely for her services and, motivated more by gratitude for the successful party than the promise of youth in a jar, handed over a check for the products needed to rebuild her skin from the inside out.

After Kimberly's car pulled out of the driveway and Sharon closed the door behind her the house was quiet. Very quiet. Too quiet.

Well, thought Dorie, here I am, all dressed up, facewise at least, and nowhere to go. She picked up the hand mirror left on the kitchen table and studied her reflection. Yes, this face was too good to waste. She needed to go out on the town herself.

She went to her study and found Doug Brenner's home number in the faculty roster. She took the handset from its cradle then hesitated, her finger poised over the keypad.

Is this really a good idea? she asked herself. What if Doug wasn't serious about dinner? She recalled the Post-it notes with their bits of doggerel. Were they not written invitations, in a manner of speaking? He must be serious.

"What the hell," she said aloud, and punched in Doug's number quickly before she lost her nerve.

When she heard the phone ringing on the other end of the line, she almost hung up but checked the impulse. Maybe he's not home and the machine will pick up and I can say I'm calling about the workshop in Boulder, she thought. There was a click and a groggy male voice said, "Hello?"

Dorie's mouth was suddenly dry as dust. "Doug? Is that you?" she croaked.

"Yeah, who's this?"

"It's Dorie."

There was a slight pause, barely discernable but enough to make her stomach clutch.

"Well, hey. What's up?" Doug asked.

"I'm hungry and I don't feel like cooking. Is it too late to take you up on your standing offer of dinner?"

"Gosh, Dorie," Doug said hesitantly, "that would be great but I..."

"Dougie, what's happening?" Dorie heard a female voice, very sleepy and very close to the phone. Her stomach sunk to somewhere around her ankles.

"Whoops," she said. "You've got company. Bad timing. Sorry."

"Dorie, it's okay. Hang on a minute," Doug pleaded.

Dorie heard the distinctive sound of creaking bedsprings before a hand was clapped over the receiver. Nevertheless, she heard Doug's muffled whisper "Don't. Not now."

"Talk to you later, Doug," Dorie said. "Got to run." She dropped the phone into its cradle. She could feel a flush of shame rising from her chest to her cheeks.

Dumb, dumb, dumb, she castigated herself. It's Saturday night. Of course he had a date. Someone young. A student maybe? No, Doug wouldn't stoop that low. It was probably a junior faculty member. Someone a decade younger than herself.

I should never have called him, Dorie admonished herself. I'm such a dork.

She wandered into the kitchen and fixed herself some comfort food, a peanut butter sandwich with mayonnaise, sweet pickles, and lettuce, and took it, along with a beer, into the living room. The only bearable thing on television was a Clint Eastwood spaghetti western, but it kept her from obsessing about interrupting Doug's tryst with a pathetic request for his company at dinner.

When the movie was over she went upstairs and removed her party face with soap and water. Her features resumed their usual position at half-mast.

"Bye bye Miss American Pie," she told the mirror. "And so to bed, perchance to dream... "

# Eleven

Dorie managed to fall asleep fairly easily even thought it was only ten p.m. But she woke up, tense and drenched with sweat, at midnight. She reconsidered her decision to avoid hormone replacement therapy; at the moment eight hours of sound sleep seemed worth the increased risk of stroke, heart attack, and breast cancer.

She could hear voices downstairs. The girls were home from the movies and doing what was normal at slumber parties: not slumbering. Dorie flapped the sheets in the air to cool herself and the bed. She turned the pillow over and punched it into a more comfortable shape. She still couldn't sleep. She got up and drank a glass of water from the tap in the bathroom. It was no use. As usual her body was wasted while her mind was on red alert.

"Tryptophan," Dorie muttered. "That's what I need." She didn't have any turkey on hand, but milk would be the next best source of that supposedly calming amino acid. She padded down the hall barefoot, listening idly to the murmur of girlish voices rising up the stairwell. She started downstairs, then froze. She held her breath so she could make out the words drifting her way.

Kimberly was speaking. "And one more thing, Jesus," she intoned. "We ask you to help Phoebe's mom to open her heart because she's lost and lonely and she really needs to feel Your love."

Phoebe chimed in. "Please dear Lord, please help my mother find You before it's too late."

There was a chorus of soft "Amens."

Dorie took two steps backwards up the stairs and slunk into her bedroom, closing the door quietly behind her. She stood in the middle of the room, besieged by a storm of mixed feelings, not sure whether to laugh or cry. A group of teenage girls were praying for her. Her own daughter was praying for her. In the course of one evening, she had become not only a middle-aged fool but also a lost soul.

Sleep wasn't even a remote possibility now. She picked up her journal from the bedside table. Given the way the present was shaping up, the past was looking better and better. Maybe she could soothe herself with another stroll down memory lane.

## Saturday, July 22

I must be getting over Roger-the-Bastard because I'm noticing men again. One man anyway. Colin MacKenzie, a Canadian who's just arrived to study with Bud. Rosa says he's some kind of scientist. He's tall, lean and handsome. Not at all nerdy and not wearing a wedding ring.

He also has a great Canadian accent, which got him stuck with the role of narrator in the stupid skits we're performing at the Boulder Theater in two weeks. They're based on Sufi teaching stories that, according to Bud, have an "earthy, timeless wisdom" that anyone can relate to. So we're dressing up as Arabs in India print bedspreads and turbans and acting out the plots of the stories while poor Colin reads them. All this hoo-ha will be accompanied by electronic rock music and a flashing strobe light that is supposed to create the impression of "moments frozen in time." Bud's idea, of course.

## Thursday, July 25

Everyone, including Bud, is in a foul mood at today's rehearsal. Colin-the-Canadian-hunk is annoyed because the narrator's lines aren't synchronized with the on-stage action. Bruce, who's in charge of the lights, gets a shock from the extension cord connected to the strobe and threatens to quit unless we use grounded outlets. Corinne's upset because the theatrical makeup she ordered from Denver got lost in transit. Bud finally calls it quits and slumps down in his director's chair with his head in his hands. (The back of the chair says "I.M. Budd, Impresario" and it has one of those rubber doughnut thingies on the seat. Could it be true that Our Esteemed Teacher needs a tube of of Preparation H? Maybe so, considering the supposed origin of The Watercloset Tapes.)

Bud broods darkly for nearly six minutes by my watch while we shift and squirm. When we're sufficiently uncomfortable, he delivers his lecture.

"The reason we are all gathered together in ...my name..." he says and we all laugh too loudly to show that we get the Biblical allusion "... is to realize some basic truths about human existence. You've been given certain exercises to practice during this creative project we've taken on. I've told you to control your outbursts of negativity, speak thoughtfully and sparingly, observe your outward manifestations and inner states, and so on. But you don't have to be so damned grim about it."

He adjusts his tushy cushion with a pained expression and the lecture continues: "You people have got to realize that no one can tell anyone else how to do their inner work. This is a do-it-yourself project. Neither a teacher nor a guru can do it for you."

Colin raises his hand and asks if that's the case, then what's the point of hanging around a guru? Why not just get a pile of books and a stack of tapes by a bunch of teachers and study on our own?

Bud smiles. "I figured you'd be the one to ask that," he says, "or, if not you, Dorie. Well, you can do it that way, in theory, but your chances of getting the experiences you need are increased if you hang around a guru. However, you have to hang around in a particular way." He takes a swig of his ever-present bottle of Perrier. "I'll give you a hint. Pay attention to me. Not just to what I say and do but where it's coming from. Align yourself with my inner state as best you can." He picks up an unraveled gauze turban from the prop box and winds it around his head, which makes him look like Johnny Carson as the Great Karnak. "This thing is really cheesy, isn't it?" he asks rhetorically. He unwinds it and tosses it to Rosa, then resumes his speech.

"Paying attention to me does not mean gossiping about me or imitating me. It's done through internal resonance and I can't tell you how to create that except to say that it involves being simultaneously aware of my inner state and your own."

He scans our intent, puzzled faces and smiles sadly. "But it won't work if you want something for yourself, like becoming enlightened. Or getting high on eternal bliss. Those foolish ambitions will just get in the way. One absorbs the condition of the guru simply because one is disposed to be with him. For no reason at all."

A few people try to get him to explain what he means, but he shakes his head and puts his finger to his lips to shush them. He looks exhausted, which isn't surprising considering the tiresome questions people ask. Then he suddenly gives us a big cheery smile and says, "Nighty night, don't let the bedbugs bite," and exits, Corinne and Polly in tow.

Colin catches up to me on the way out and says that Bud must have the two of us pegged as the skeptics in the crowd. I agree and ask him why he's here and he tells me that he was raised Catholic but left the church in his teens and has felt guilty ever since. "I'm looking for something to fill the void," he says. "Science can only take me so far. I tried zen but it was too abstract. Then a friend of mine told me about Bud. Said he was a good guru for intellectual types like me so I took a couple of weeks vacation time to come check him out."

"Vacation from what?" I ask, fishing for personal details. Turns out he's a microbiologist and works for a Canadian research firm that has a big grant to study mitochondria and aging. I don't know a mitochondria from a mouse turd so he explains they're like little power plants inside cells and they run down when we get old. But he doesn't sound condescending, which I like. Then he starts asking me questions about what I do and where I live and I can't manage to steer the conversation back to important things like how old he is and does he have a girlfriend. I'd ask Rosa to show me his registration form but I'm afraid she'll tell Bud and he'll create some sort of public drama about me having the hots for our foreign visitor.

I say good night to Colin, who has a lovely smile in spite of crooked front teeth, and drag myself to the bunkhouse to record the events of the day, which seem completely ridiculous in retrospect. I wonder if all this, the Community, the exercises in self-observation, the meditations, the silly projects we put so much work into, even being around Bud, makes any difference. It's kind of fun, but is it bringing me any closer to seeing the Face of God?

## Sunday, August 6

This has been the worst night of my entire life. A total, unmitigated, humiliating disaster.

The stupid theatrical performance took place as planned, in front of an audience of about two hundred people who must have believed the gullible reporter from the Boulder Camera who interviewed Bud and described him as "a Sufi master and performance artist who has recreated an ancient dramatic form laden with esoteric meanings." Gag me with a spoon...

The performance started out okay. The electronic score really did rock and the bursts of strobe light hid the tackiness of the homemade costumes. Everything's groovy and I think maybe we're going to pull this travesty off without getting pelted with rotten tomatoes. Then Corinne hunts me down in the ladies' room where I'm shucking the army blanket burka I had to wear to play a Middle Eastern bag lady in a bazaar scene.

"Emergency," she says. "You've got to do the belly dancer part in the last skit. Polly's sick." This is bad. Polly's got a big part. A part that requires writhing around in a rented harem dancer costume playing a Mary Magdalene type who's touched by baraka while performing for a guru in mufti as a traveling olive oil vendor.

"Sick how?" I ask. "Sick as in barfing all over the place," Corinne snaps. "Sick as in morning and evening and night sickness." "Sick as in pregnant?" I ask. "You bet your sweet life," Corinne shoots back. She is not a happy camper. Possibly we have had a little Tantric containment mishap and the balance of power among the guru's sweeties has shifted beyond repair. I don't have time to pry because Corinne hustles me into Polly's gold lame bra top and a bikini bottom with attached scarlet tulle skirt and I run onstage and do my best imitation of a Lebanese Barbie Doll, reminding myself that this too, like all temporal phenomena, shall pass.

Wrong. After the performance, the attendees who actually got something out of this comedy of errors are congratulating the cast and producer—the famous impresario I.M. Budd—in the lobby. Who to my wondering eyes should appear but the head of the CU English department, the eminent Dr. Harrison, along with his wife, who, it seems, is a fan of Idries Shah's Sufi tales and dragged him to our performance. Dr. Harrison makes it clear that my association with this motley crew is not what he expects of a recipient of the Hawthorne Studies Fellowship. I'm trying to convince him that I'm doing research into contemporary religious cults to deepen my understanding of Hawthorne' s transcendentalism when Bud grabs my elbow, demands an introduction to Dr. Harrison, and declares "Don't you think Dorie's on-stage performance reveals a hidden but deeply sensuous nature?" Dr. Harrison's eyebrows nearly hit his receding hairline and I want to sink through the floor of the Boulder Theater and never show my face in the state of Colorado again.

I'm furious with Bud. As we're driving back to Marmot Rock, I accuse him of jeopardizing my academic career. He replies, and this is an exact quote: " I was just trying to show you what dry husks scholars turn into in their old age in case you want to alter your course before it's too late."

I'm having second, third, and fourth thoughts about jumping out at a red light and hitching a ride to my apartment. Somehow Bud senses this and launches into a puzzling story that doesn't seem to have anything to do with the evening's events but somehow calms me down.

"I want to tell you about something that happened to me years ago, Cookie, " he says quietly, as we're winding up the canyon past Boulder Falls. "When I was young and had all my hair and a lot of questions, I went to a monastery to try to find some answers. When I got there, the monks took away all my clothes and my wallet and gave me a robe and a pair of sandals. I stayed there for a while and did as I was told and watched and listened, and then one morning I got up and found my clothes, shoes, and wallet outside my cubicle and I knew it was time for me to leave. So I did."

"And?" I ask. "That's all," Bud says. "I left. A long time later I understood what I had learned there."

I have a feeling Bud's giving me a clue to something. But I don't know what it is.

• • • • • • • ● • • • • • • • • •

Dorie sat motionless in bed, looking at the open journal in her lap. Bud had given her clues to a lot of things, including Colin. She'd remembered them for a time; she'd even tried to decipher their coded meanings and act on them. But as her vivid memories of that crazy, exhilarating summer faded, the habits of ordinary life had gradually and insidiously reasserted themselves. She'd gotten caught up in the pursuit of academic status, been thrown off balance by motherhood, then devastated by sudden widowhood. Yes, she'd singled-parented, and she'd published, but had she also perished?

And now look at me," she whispered to the dark, empty room. "An aging scholar. A dry husk. Just like Bud said."

# Twelve

Dorie slept late Sunday morning, but not as late as Phoebe and her friends, who were still cocooned in their sleeping bags when she tiptoed down to the kitchen. She put out breakfast makings for the girls, a pitcher of premixed pancake batter, applesauce, yogurt, and syrup, poured her tea into a travel mug, and snuck out the laundry room door to the garage. After the debacle of last night's disastrous phone call, she needed a New York Times fix. A quick scan of the front page alone would render her personal problems trivial in contrast to the political and ecological disasters exploding all over the globe.

By the time she got back from town with the paper, the girls were dressed and had rolled up their sleeping bags. They looked none the worse for their late-night gabfest and prayer meeting. Such is the resilience of youth, thought Dorie. Four hours of sleep, no problem. Unlike us dry husks. She did a slow neck roll to loosen the tightness in her shoulders. Her cervical vertebrae emitted decidedly dry huskish crackles and pops. She made a mental note to purchase glucosamine tablets on her next trip to the health food store. But meantime, there were hungry girls to feed.

"You all want pancakes?" she asked. "Everything's ready."

"Yum," Amber replied. "Absolutely yes."

Kimberly glanced at her watch and shook her head. "Thank you so much Mrs. Winslow but I don't think we've got time."

"Why not?" Amber protested. "It's only nine thirty and I'm hungry."

"I told my mom we'd pick up the doughnuts for the New Friends Forum and help her set everything up before the service begins." Kimberly looked pointedly at Amber's waistline. "Besides, remember what I said about eating carbs first thing in the morning?"

Dorie refrained from commenting on the carbohydrate content of the proposed church-sponsored refreshments.

Amber sighed and made do with a bowl of unsweetened yoghurt while the other girls had applesauce and granola.

"I'm sorry we don't have time for pancakes," Kimberly apologized, "but my mom will murder me if I don't bring her Krispy Kremes and the only place I can get them is on the other side of town."

"No problem," Dorie said. "The batter will keep for a day or two. Besides, I'll eat a bunch after my hike."

"That's great," Kimberly said, a little too enthusiastically. "Who do you go hiking with?"

The phrase "lost and lonely" from Kimberly's midnight prayer for her salvation came to Dorie's mind and for a moment she considered a face-saving white lie involving a fictional companion.

"I enjoy hiking alone," she said. "It's a good time to think about things. You know, contemplate the eternal mysteries. Like the meaning of life." There, she thought, let little Miss Sanctimony chew on that.

Kimberly took her juice glass to the sink and rinsed it. Then she turned to Dorie with her ultra-white smile at full wattage.

"I've got an idea," she said. "Why don't you come to church with us? Then afterwards you can go to the New Friends Forum. My mom's the steward and she can introduce you to lots of interesting people. I know she wants to meet you. I've told her all about you."

I bet you have, Dorie thought. Phoebe's mother, the godless widow stuck out in Rabbit Valley without a friend in the world.

"Thanks for the invitation, Kimberly, "she said. "But I think I'll pass. I'm looking forward to a lazy morning with the Sunday paper before I head for the hills."

Kimberly, Amber and Nicole thanked her profusely for hosting a birthday party they variously described as "fabulous" (Kimberly), "the funnest ever" (Amber), and "way cool" (Nicole). Phoebe pronounced it "totally perfectomento" and kissed her on the cheek. The girls left in a flurry of giggles and mutual teasing about boys; Dorie heard several references to Jared and Chris French, whom the Lord had evidently brought down with his celestial buckshot.

Dorie stretched out on the sofa. The Times was a comforting weight on her stomach; it would take her half the day just to skim the headlines. She could hike in the afternoon and then work on her Hawthorne manuscript. Or finish reading her old journal. Or maybe not. Her midnight excursion into its pages had been a bit of a downer. She wouldn't be up to dealing with the events chronicled in the remaining pages until she got over the Doug debacle.

In the end, she spent Sunday afternoon cleaning the refrigerator, reorganizing the kitchen cupboards, and weeding the flowerbeds. Anything to avoid facing her manuscript. The result was a tidy kitchen and yard and a mood so foul that when Phoebe came home after a post-church lunch with Kimberly, she snapped at her for leaving her backpack on the dining room table.

Phoebe looked daggers at her.

"You don't have to take it out on me just because you don't like your life."

Dorie flinched. Phoebe was right.

"I'm sorry. I'm having an anxiety attack because I should have been working on my book and instead, I cleaned the damn house."

"If you hate writing that book so much you shouldn't do it," Phoebe said. "It just makes you miserable and then you make me miserable and that's not fair."

She snatched her backpack and disappeared upstairs. Dorie heard the door to her room slam shut over the noise of the dishwasher, which sounded as if it were pulverizing the dishes rather than rinsing them.

Dorie went into the kitchen and aimed a vicious kick at its bottom panel. It was probably twenty years old, just like the rest of the house, and due to break down any day. Which meant another major dent in her bank account. She hoped Phoebe wouldn't mind forgoing an Ivy League degree for a mundane diploma from a Colorado state school. Although the way things were going, she might opt for one from Oral Roberts University.

Dorie stayed home on Monday and edited another chapter of her Hawthorne manuscript, but she needed to go to her office on Tuesday to collect her mail. Doug was teaching this session but since he rarely showed up in his office before noon the chances of encountering him were slim.

But not slim enough. She was returning to her car when Doug's Jeep pulled into the parking lot. She ducked behind a FedEx van but it was too late; she'd been spotted. Doug beeped his horn, turned the wrong way into a one-way lane, and braked to a stop in front of the van. He rolled down his window as she pretended to fumble with the clasp on her briefcase.

"Listen, Dorie, I'm sorry about last night. I..."

"No biggie," Dorie interrupted. She could feel her cheeks burning. "I just had this spur of the moment impulse to go out to eat and I thought you might be free." She hoped she sounded more composed than she felt.

"Yeah, uh, well, any other time I would have taken you on in a heartbeat but I just happened to be sort of tied up last night."

"Are you speaking figuratively or literally?" Dorie asked, on the principle that the best defense was a good offense. Besides, Doug seemed to be almost as embarrassed as she was and she liked watching him squirm.

Doug ducked his head and smiled ruefully.

The sheepish little boy act, Dorie thought. Cute but I'm not buying.

"It's not what you think, Dorie," he said. "I can explain... well, I could explain but this isn't the time or place."

"Good grief, Doug," Dorie said. "You don't have to explain anything. I'm a mature woman, remember?" If he's going to play the little boy card, she thought, I'm raising with the ace of big mamas.

Doug nodded. "Yup, right, but we both know you're not as tough as you pretend to be. We are going to talk about this, Dorie. As soon as possible. But right now I've got an appointment with Drescher. I'm already in hot water and I don't want to make things worse by being late."

Dorie pricked up her ears. Earnest Drescher was the Dean of the Liberal Arts division and it was common knowledge that he disapproved of both Doug's poetry and his egalitarian relationship with his students.

"What's going on?"

"I'll tell you after I find out myself. All I know is Drescher's uptight about the Western Interstate Poetry Slam finals we had this weekend. Tony and I emceed and it went well but someone in the audience thought the language was too raw and raised a royal stink."

"But that's the nature of poetry slams," Dory said. "Post-adolescent venting studded with four letter words."

"Yeah, but whoever we offended must have clout because Drescher called me yesterday afternoon and scheduled a meeting this morning. I mean to sort it out as quickly as possible."

"Be careful, "Dorie said. "You know Drescher would love to find an excuse to drop your contract. Especially after that anti-war tirade you published in the paper."

"It wasn't a tirade," Doug protested. "It was a prose poem. In iambic pentameter, too, in case you didn't notice."

"I don't think the meter was the problem," Dorie reminded him. "It was more likely the alliterative imagery. 'Bereft of brain, the baffled Bush relies/upon the addled wits of unwise men?' Crikey, Doug, it should have been censored on aesthetic grounds alone."

Doug chuckled. "Yeah, but it got everyone's attention, didn't it?" He drove off with a jaunty wave.

Dorie tossed her briefcase onto the passenger seat of her car. Doug, she mused, was like Br'er Rabbit. He courted disaster but always managed to emerge from the briar patch intact. She found she was actually looking forward to hearing him explain why he'd had some bimbo in his bed Saturday night. The storyline might be contrived but it was bound to be entertaining.


Dorie was mentally revising her lecture notes on Willa Cather while she drove home when her cell phone jangled the samba tune that she had assigned to Phoebe.

"Mom, I know you're really busy and all but you know, the car wash thing we're having Saturday?"

Dorie said that yes, she was quite aware of the car wash thing since Phoebe's computer-generated posters advertising it were plastered on every public bulletin board in town.

"Well, Kimberly's mother said we should have a bake sale along with it since people would be stuck while we're cleaning the inside of their cars so it would be, like, a good time to get them to buy food."

The entrepreneurial mind, Dorie observed, never misses an opportunity to score a buck. Unlike the dry husk academic mind, which never misses the opportunity to score an intellectual point.

"Good idea," she said. "Kimberly's got a smart mom, even if she does sell crappy American SUVs."

"So, can you make those gooey caramel square things?" Phoebe asked, ignoring the jibe. "Everybody loves them and we can wrap each one separately and charge a dollar each."

To atone for dissing the Medderlys' perfectly reputable means of livelihood, Dorie agreed to make two pans of caramel squares, deliver them personally to the bake sale, and purchase a complete car wash, wax, and interior vacuuming package for eight dollars. But then she had to ask, "What exactly is TFC raising money for?"

"It's to buy Bibles for our Golden Gate Ministry."

"Your what?" Dorie asked, picturing her daughter passing out New Testaments in a San Francisco flophouse.

"It's this deal where we go to nursing homes and talk to old people and give them Bibles and, like, talk about how important it is to get saved before...you know..."

"Before you croak?" Dorie supplied.

"Well, we don't say that, "Phoebe protested. "We say there's a golden gate to eternal life that Christ opens to anyone who believes in Him. And I know that's a metaphor so you don't have to tell me, okay?"

Dorie shifted the cell phone to her other ear as she negotiated a right turn. "Okay," she said. "But don't you think you're exploiting a captive and possibly desperate audience?"

"Oh, Mother," Phoebe said. "You don't understand anything."

"I'm trying," Dorie said, but all she got in reply was the silence of a terminated connection.

Dorie intended to work at home the remainder of the week, not because she was trying to avoid Doug, she assured herself, but because she wanted to use the days before the next summer session began to outline the final section of her Hawthorne book. But every time she confronted the stack of printout that represented eight years' worth of halting progress on her magnum opus all she wanted to do was lie down and take a nap. Did the world need yet another analysis of a dead American male writer? Even if it was from a post-feminist, post-deconstructionist point of view? The answer was obvious.

By Wednesday afternoon she was so depressed she had to go out and buy a flat of bright pink petunias to cheer herself up. When she got home, the message light on her phone was blinking. She punched the "play" key and heard Doug's voice: "Dorie, it's Doug. Call me when you get a chance."

Halfway through dialing his number Dorie stopped. Making Doug wait a bit before explaining himself would be satisfying. Besides, she didn't want to appear to be as interested in his explanation as she actually was. She'd put off returning his call for a day or two.

As it happened, she put it off so long that she couldn't reach him. She got a cryptic email from him on Thursday: "Gone to Moab to bike and ponder my fate. If I don't ride off a cliff let's get together when I'm back. Will tell all so you can stop hiding behind trucks when you see me coming. Hasta la vista, Doug."

Dorie pressed the delete key. The waiting game had worked. Her dignity was salvaged, her face was saved, and she was fully in control of the situation again. Doug had better arrive bearing flowers, wine, and the whole truth and nothing but the truth.

Phoebe had arranged to take Saturday off from her barista duties to help at the car wash but she declined Dorie's offer to drive her into town, saying she could ride her bike.

"You need to finish baking and then get dressed before you come, "she instructed, eyeing Dorie's faded tank top and running shorts. "Anyway, Jared will bring me back afterward. That's the great thing about his truck; we can just stick my bike in the back." She turned to go then looked over her shoulder. "In case you were wondering, Jared's dad bought it for him so he could get to school in the winter without freezing to death on his bike."

"I get the hint," Dorie said. "I'll buy you a new down jacket before the first frost. But no car."

After Phoebe left, Dorie wrapped the caramel squares individually, as requested, and packed them in a wicker basket lined with a red checked tea towel. As an afterthought she placed a fern and a spray of yellow snapdragons on top. Why am I doing this, she asked herself. To help Teens for Christ raise money to proselytize terminally ill old ladies? Or to make myself look like a nice suburban mommy so Mrs. Medderly will approve of me? She was assailed by an image of Bud laughing and shaking his finger at her. "It's not the deed that counts, it's the impulse, Cookie. Always question your motives, especially when they seem altruistic."

"And who are you to talk, Mr. Bigmouth Goo Roo?" she responded, but she couldn't help smiling. Having Bud's aphorisms pop into her mind was invigorating. They were a cheerful link to a time when nothing was predictable and anything seemed possible. Maybe reading the rest of her journal, uncomfortable as some of the memories might be, was a good idea after all.

Not now, though. She didn't want to disappoint Phoebe by delivering the cookies late. Or by showing up looking frumpy. She changed into a pair of neat khaki capris and a crisp white sleeveless blouse and, disregarding the voice of her inner Bud mocking her vanity, applied a discrete selection of products from Sharon's bag of tricks. Looking in the mirror, she was so pleased with the results that she added a coral heishi necklace and a pair of dangly silver and coral earrings as a finishing touch. Watch out, Mrs. M, she thought. The merry widow of Rabbit Valley is on the prowl. She did a bump and grind on her way out of the bedroom just to prove her point.

Thirteen

TFC carwash signs started to show up three blocks from Medderly Motors. At Dorie's suggestion, Phoebe had riffed on the rhyming Burma Shave highway signs from the fifties. A series of fluorescent orange poster board rectangles on wooden stakes read: "Dirty Car? Need a Nosh?; Don't Despair--Almost There; Yummy Sweets-- Great Car Wash."

The entrance to the parking lot in front of Medderly Motors was marked with a larger sign proclaiming "TFC Benefit Bake Sale and Car Wash" but that wasn't what caused the Chevy Blazer with the West Fork State decal and a load of young men to brake so abruptly that Dorie almost rear-ended it. It was Nicole, waving down prospective customers with a large American flag. She was wearing white shorts, a navy blue shirt tied at the waist, a red bandanna around her neck and a white cowboy hat, an outfit possibly inspired by the Dallas Cowboys cheerleaders.

"Great look," Dorie called. "Very patriotic. But isn't it a little racy for a church-sponsored event?"

Nicole grinned. "Not now," she said. "Kimberly made me pull the shirt down so my belly button wouldn't show. It was better before."

Dorie edged around the Blazer, whose occupants were all trying to talk to Nicole at once, and parked in front of the automobile showroom. She spotted the bake sale card table, strategically located at the far end of the car wash assembly line. As she sidestepped a puddle on her way to the table, someone called, "Hey, Mrs. Winslow! Over here!" She looked up to see Jared waving at her from behind a mud-caked sedan. Chris French, beside him, brandished a sponge and greeted her too. "Hi, Mrs. Phoebe's Mom."

These really are sweet kids, Dorie thought. And washing cars for Christ is no worse than selling fake Indian moccasins to keep the Community in beans and brown rice. Maybe they don't have someone like Bud prodding them towards self-knowledge, but maybe it doesn't matter. They're happy and productive. Even if they are terminally deluded, a Bud-voice in her head added.

"Mom! I'm over here." Phoebe was polishing the windshield of a station wagon while another girl vacuumed the interior and hung an air freshener from the rearview mirror. Dorie did a double take. The air freshener was not the usual cardboard pine tree; it was a pair of praying hands.

Both girls were wearing lime green tee shirts with "JC ROX" and a line drawing of a jagged mountain range printed on the front.

"What's with the shirts?" Dorie asked.

Phoebe looked down at her chest. "That's our band. JC Rox."

Dorie didn't get it.

"You know," Phoebe said. "Jesus Christ rocks. They're amazing. Especially Jared. He writes most of the songs."

"I'd like to hear them some time, "Dorie said. Really? The Bud-voice questioned. Or are you just saying that to make Phoebe feel good?

Dorie examined her motives. Yes, she actually did want to hear Jared's music. In fact, she was itching with curiosity about this gangly boy who seemed to have captured her daughter's heart.

"You can hear them tomorrow," Phoebe said. "They're playing before the service. You should come. They're doing Jared's new song. It's called 'Three Strikes.'"

"Three strikes? As in 'and you're out'?"

Phoebe laughed. "Not exactly. It's more like this." She waved her cleaning rag in the air as she sang, "Three strikes/you think you out/ Think you a loser, got no doubt." She twirled in a circle and the girl with the vacuum cleaner followed her moves. They sang in unison, "You think you got/ no more chances/ Think everybody give you/ judging glances." Phoebe looked over at Jared who grinned and made an OK sign with his thumb and forefinger.

"Way to go Phoebs," he called, and Phoebe beamed and sang louder as Jared and Chris started to clap.

"But you wrong/it ain't true. 'Cause Jesus never/ no, he don't never/ give up on you."

"No, no, no," chorused the girl with the vacuum and a second girl who was walking by with a bucket of soapy water. "Jesus he never give up on you."

Dorie, while appalled at their grammar, was amazed. She hadn't known Phoebe could sing, much less like this, in a strong clear soprano and with the spontaneous gestures of a natural performer.

"Hey, guys! Get with it. We've got cars lined up out the driveway," Kimberly admonished them from the bake sale table where she and Amber were doing a lively business in sweet rolls and doughnuts.

Dorie gave Phoebe a thumbs up and delivered her flower-bedecked basket of caramel squares to Kimberly who pronounced it "charming" while Amber peeked under the napkin, admired the contents and asked for the recipe.

"I love to bake," she said, "but I'm dieting so all I can do is collect recipes." She brightened. "But I've already lost five pounds and I should get to my target weight by the fourth of July. With the Lord's help, of course. I could never do it on my own."

Kimberly arched an eyebrow, but refrained from comment. Dorie was about to congratulate Amber on her self-discipline while surrounded by an abundance of sucrose when a cloud of lavender scent assaulted her nostrils. A woman's voice, loud and possessing an unmistakably crisp British accent, rang across the parking lot.

"Girls, this is brilliant. I absolutely love the way you've set things up. No one can possibly leave without passing your table. But where's the coffee urn? Everyone will want coffee at this time of day. "

A barely discernable frown shaded Kimberly's brow. Dorie turned around to see a tall slim woman in black slacks and a pink linen shirt bearing down on them.

"Sorry, Mum," Kimberly said. "I'll go borrow the one in the employee lounge."

"Yes, that's quite a good idea." Mrs. Medderly brushed past Dorie to inspect the baked goods. "Excuse me, dear," she said. "I just have to make sure there's nothing here that needs to be refrigerated. We don't want to give anyone food poisoning, do we?"

"Mum," Kimberly interrupted. "This is Phoebe's mother. You know, Mrs. Winslow."

Mrs. Medderly whirled around to face Dorie. "I had no idea. You look too young to have a daughter in high school."

Dorie thanked Mrs. Medderly for the compliment and vowed to adhere to Sharon's skin care regimen come hell or high water.

"Mrs. Winslow brought us this." Amber pointed to Dorie's decorated basket. "Isn't it gorgeous?"

"My goodness," Mrs. Medderly said. "How did you find time to do all that? You must be so busy with your job at the college. Plus taking care of that old house all on your own."

Patronizing bitch, Dorie thought. "I don't sleep," she replied. "Insomnia is a vastly underrated aid to productivity."

To Dorie's surprise, Mrs. Medderly laughed.

"You're so right. I revised our entire bookkeeping system in the middle of the night one horrible week when I was determined to get off Ambien."

Dorie reconsidered her prior judgment; possibly Mrs. M. was okay after all.

"Carry on girls, "Mrs. Medderly said, taking Dorie by the elbow and steering her away from the table. "I'm going to borrow Phoebe's mother for a minute."

Dorie felt herself being propelled by a force beyond her control. Mrs. Medderly had an unassailable self-confidence that practically guaranteed acquiescence; she was obviously the block from which Kimberly had been chipped.

"Now since our daughters are such great friends, I hope we will be too," she said. "I'm Evelyn but everyone calls me Ev. I don't actually care for it but it got tossed at me when I was a wee tot and it stuck."

"I'm really Dorothea," Dorie said, "but everyone calls me Dorie, which is an improvement on the original."

"Well, dear," Mrs. Medderly continued, "I'm hoping we can entice you to one of our services. They're really quite lively, not at all 'churchy', if you know what I mean. And Phoebe would be thrilled if you came."

"Ummm," Dorie stalled, trying to think of an excuse that wouldn't make her sound like a terrible mother. On the other hand, maybe she should give it a shot, if only to satisfy her curiosity about Jared and JC Rox. "Well, maybe..." she began.

"No maybe," Ev said. "You'll come tomorrow. And after the service you must go to the New Friends Forum. You have no idea of the interesting people you'll meet at our church. In fact..."

She steered Dorie towards the Toyota Camry that Jared and Chris were now hosing off.

"Yoo hoo, boys," she called. "Turn those hoses off for a minute. Viktor, I've got someone I want you to meet."

The driver of the Camry rolled down his window.

"Hold your horses, Ev," he called. "I'm still in the rinse cycle."

Jared sprayed the car's wheel covers free of suds and the Camry pulled out of the wash line and stopped. A short, well-muscled man dressed in jeans and a white polo shirt stepped out. He waved to Jared.

"Good job," he said. "Looks great."

"Thanks, Dad," Jared said. "Phoebe'll shine 'er up for you. Just like in that old Karate Kid movie, hey Phoebs? Wax on, wax off." Jared sparred with the air in clockwise and counterclockwise motions and Phoebe mirrored him in an improvised pas de deux.

They do make a cute couple, Dorie thought. Even if Jared will probably grow up to be a televangelist.

Ev dropped Dorie's arm, which she had been holding as if she expected Dorie to bolt, and greeted Viktor with a dignified, upper body hug, which, given their difference in stature, left his chin hanging over her shoulder.

"Viktor, this is Phoebe's mother, Dorie Winslow," Ev said. "Dorie, Viktor's been just dying to meet you."

Viktor looked down at his running shoes. Dorie could have sworn he was blushing.

"Well, Jared keeps talking about what a great cook you are, and how you're always going off hiking in the mountains and how you're writing a book. Sounds like you're some kind of superwoman."

"Hardly," Dorie said. "I'm just running in place trying to keep up." She wondered if Viktor worked out. The sleeves of his polo shirt barely accommodated his biceps. He was actually quite attractive, she thought. In a balding Eastern European sort of way.

There was an awkward silence that Mrs. Medderly made even more awkward when she announced that she would leave Dorie and Viktor to get acquainted while she went to help Kimberly set up the coffee maker.

Dorie cast about for a conversational opener that wouldn't lead to any theological topics. Geography seemed a safe bet.

"Phoebe tells me you and Jared came here from Chicago," she said. "That's quite a leap. I mean, big city to small town."

Viktor nodded vigorously. "Best move I ever made. I love it here and it's been great for Jared. He was a little screwed up back in Lake Forest, getting in with a wild crowd and all ,but after we came here he got his head on straight."

Lake Forest? Dorie thought. Viktor looked more South Side than North Shore.

"That's a surprise," she said, "Jared is such a gentleman I can't imagine him giving you any trouble."

"It was the divorce. Very ugly. Jared's mother and her family were old money. I wasn't. My wife's folks did everything in their power, including spoiling Jared rotten, to make sure their grandson stayed on the right side of the tracks where I couldn't afford to live."

"But Jared's with you. So it didn't work."

"Yup." Viktor shoved his hands in his pockets and rocked back on his heels. "Thanks to a really good divorce lawyer who convinced the judge that Jared needed a strong male influence more than he needed a two thousand dollar road bike and his own big screen TV."

"But why West Fork?" Dorie asked. She dimly remembered Phoebe mentioning some kind of family connection.

"Fresh air, fresh start. And my brother was already here. You know Ace Foreign Car Repair? Over on Montana Street? That's ours. I came in as a partner. Frank, that's my brother, he does the German cars and I'm the Japanese specialist. That covers all our bases."

The reference to Japanese cars diverted Dorie from admiring the way Viktor's polo shirt stretched tautly over what must be an impressive six pack.

"So that means you work on Subarus."

"Sure do. Great little cars. You got one?"

Dorie hesitated. Asking Viktor, whom she barely knew, about the strange squishiness that had developed in the Forester's brake pedal was probably the equivalent of cornering a cardiologist at a cocktail party and talking about your HDL/LDL ratio.

Oh, why not, she thought. At least it won't lead to a discussion of whether or not I've been saved.

When she described the Forester's symptoms Viktor insisted on having a look at it then and there. "Don't want the brakes going out on you," he said. "Not in these mountains."

He took Dorie's arm as they threaded their way through the now congested parking lot. She felt the tiniest little flutter in her tummy. The gesture seemed …she searched for a word…old world? Chivalrous? Whatever it was she liked it. It had been a long time since she'd been treated like a lady instead of a liberated wo-man.

Viktor started the engine, depressed the brake pedal, looked under the hood, and made a quick diagnosis.

"Low on brake fluid. Could have a leaky cylinder. You might want to top it up to get through the weekend. Then I'd have it checked out if I were you." He closed the hood carefully and wiped his hands on a folded white handkerchief that he pulled out of his jeans pocket.

Dorie was enchanted. She didn't know anyone carried actual cloth handkerchiefs any more.

"If you want," Viktor continued, "I could take a look at it on Monday. That is if you don't already have a car guy."

"I'd like that," she said. "The dealership charges a fortune for a routine service. I hate to think what fixing my brakes would cost."

"Well, don't you worry," Viktor said. "I'll take care of you and you can pay me off in caramel squares."

Dorie looked at him quizzically.

"I sneaked over and sampled one while you were talking to Ev. Wanted to see if Jared was right about your cooking."

Viktor excused himself to do his Saturday morning routine, which he described as "grocery store, recycling center, and fixing everything that broke during the week." Dorie watched him leave as she pulled the Subaru into the line for the car wash. He was definitely attractive. And such lovely manners. She found herself humming a little tune she couldn't quite place.

Then the words to the melody emerged: "No, no, no. Jesus he don't never give up on you."

Somewhere in the dim recesses of her mind she heard Bud laughing.

# Fourteen

At the first red light she came to, Dorie removed the praying hands air freshener from her rearview mirror. She examined it while waiting for the light to change. One side was inscribed with the ubiquitous John 3:16 verse promising everlasting life; the other side bore the phone number of the Circle of Friends in Christ and a website, pastorcharliepritchett.org. She stuck it in the glove box but the artificial spruce scent had already pervaded the interior of the car. A small price to pay for a spotless car and a happy daughter, she thought. She felt unaccountably happy herself. Phoebe's exuberance had been contagious and meeting Viktor was…well, if not promising at least intriguing. So, Dorie thought, I've got made-over skin, a cute haircut and I'm in town. It's time to shop.

Arabella's, a boutique that specialized in offbeat but stylish brands, was sandwiched between a candle shop and an internet café on the trendy south end of Main Street. Dorie had glanced in the windows and admired the displays of simple, natural fiber outfits in subdued colors, but she'd never gone inside. Her wardrobe of pants and tops in various stages of disrepair had been more than adequate for meeting her classes and stripping wallpaper. But now she had a hankering for a dress. Something soft, she thought, and not beige or black. Maybe coral. Some kind of happy color.

One step into the store, however, and her resolve wavered. She found herself pawing helplessly through a rack of ecru linen separates, practical, safe, and boring. The lone salesgirl, who had cheerfully instructed Dorie to "holler if you need help" and gone back to arranging a display of costume jewelry, came to her aid.

"I need a dress," Dorie announced.

"A dress?" the salesgirl asked dubiously. She was whippet-thin and clothed, barely, in a tiny denim skirt and a wispy lace blouse. "Like for a party?"

"No," Dorie said. "Nothing fancy. Just a dress. Something pretty."

The salesgirl guided her to a rack at the back of the store. "You can look through these," she said. "Is it for work?"

"Not exactly," Dorie said. "It's for, uh, church." She nearly choked on the words. What was she doing, buying a dress because she wanted to look girly for a born-again Polish auto mechanic? This is sick, she thought. I must be suffering from a hormone imbalance. Is there such a thing as estrogen flooding?

"Cool," the salesgirl said, as if dresses for church attendance were the latest fashion craze. "I've got something that will look great on you." She shuffled through the rack and pulled out a butter-yellow rayon dress with a tailored collar and buttons down the front. It had a vaguely 1940's air and Dorie liked it immediately.

"See, you can button it all the way to the bottom for church but then if you want to look sexy you can leave it open to above the knee," the girl said.

"I'm too old to look sexy," Dorie protested.

"No way," retorted the salesgirl, who looked decidedly sexy as well as too young to vote. "Look at Tina Turner. She's way older than you and she's still sexy."

Dorie bought the dress. Also a pair of strappy sandals, and some big fake pearl earrings to wear with it. She resolved to drop in on Arabella's and its exceptionally discerning sales staff on a regular basis.

Dorie had dinner alone that evening after Phoebe and Jared left for a post-carwash celebration at Kimberly's house. The Medderlys, Phoebe had explained, were treating everyone to pizza. "They've got a really big heated pool," she added. "And stereo speakers on the patio. It'll be awesome."

"That sounds like great fun," Dorie said, for once not envying the Medderly's affluence. Mrs. M. had surprised her by turning out to be a kind of British Christian yenta, and both she and Mr. M., whatever he might be, were certainly generous in sharing their resources with their daughter's friends. And she didn't have to worry about Phoebe experimenting with drugs or alcohol and ending up drowned. Not in a pool owned by God-fearing evangelicals who probably drank nothing stronger than iced tea.

While she was eating her supper of lentil soup and tomato and cucumber salad, Dorie flipped through a brochure for the Boulder workshop on teaching multicultural literature. It was scheduled for the coming weekend, which meant driving to Boulder on Friday since she'd waited too late to book a flight. She wondered if Doug was going, and if so, whether she wanted to share a ride with him. She might, but only if he came up with an inspired explanation for his little sleepover party.

She closed the brochure. Her faux pas with Doug didn't seem so humiliating anymore. She had an optionally sexy new dress and a secret admirer who could fix cars. Life was definitely looking up. Of course, the secret admirer probably had no more than a high school education and would try to convert her to his primitive religion, but she couldn't deny that Viktor radiated animal magnetism. She felt a little frisson of pleasure directly below her navel.

"Praise God," she thought. "There's life in the old girl yet." She wondered if the three-year-old bottle of Chanel No. 5 in the bathroom had gone bad and if it would be inappropriate to wear a dab of perfume to a church service.

A stern interior voice interrupted her reverie. Whoa, Dorothea. Do you really want a relationship with a man again? Keep your life simple. Finish your book. Get a new dishwasher. And a dog. That's all you need.

Nothing risked, nothing gained, a husky Tina Turner voice broke in. You go girl. Tempus fugit, carpe diem and all that jazz.

Sheesh, Dorie thought. What's the matter with me? I've gone all wishy-washy. I'm losing my nerve.

You used to have plenty of nerve, Tina admonished. Remember that summer of '78? You had balls, sister, and don't you forget it.

Dorie smiled. Yes, she did have balls when she was in her twenties. Balls and an indefatigable curiosity. The consequences of that combination hadn't been entirely bad. In fact, some of them had been priceless.

She fetched her journal from her bedroom, and, now that Phoebe was safely out of the house, fixed herself a stiff bourbon and branch. She settled into the sofa and prepared to reclaim another little piece of her past.


**Thursday, August 21, 5:45 a.m.,
somewhere up Shit Creek, paddleless.**

Oh say, I can see dawn's early light and not nearly soon enough. We're in the middle of an Outward Bound type exercise designed by Bud to create maximum physical discomfort and social friction. He pairs us off with people we can't stand and drops us off at various points in the woods with sleeping bags but no tents or food. We're supposed to observe our fears and fantasies as they arise and recognize their unreality. Of course, Bud sticks me with Herr Kommandant Omar, who evidently skipped his Hitler Youth lesson on wilderness survival as I have to build the pathetic little fire we huddle by all night.

Last night was awful. Omar can't sleep until I assure him I'll stand watch. Even then he has to perform some traditional Native American ritual to "cleanse the sleeping space" of evil spirits by blowing smoke from the fire in four directions. He also blows a shower of sparks into a pile of pine duff and I have to scuff out the resulting blaze to keep the Arapahoe National Forest and its fauna, including ourselves, from being incinerated.

So there I am, hungry, dirty, exhausted, lying on my bed of pine boughs. Then around two a.m. this weird thing happens. I must have dozed off because all of a sudden, I'm on my back with my eyes wide open but I can't move. It's like my mind is awake but my body is still asleep. And I'm having a terrifying attack of claustrophobia--in the middle of 500,000 acres of conifers. I feel like the night is going to last forever, literally, and that even if I could move my paralyzed body, there would be nowhere to go. I'm convinced that the forest, and the world itself, ends just beyond what I can see of the sky and treetops. It's as if space has contracted to my immediate sphere of sensations and the flow of time has stopped, freezing me in one moment.

I want to scream and run, somewhere, anywhere, but I know I can't because there is no place and no time except for this awful unchanging here and now that's going to go on forever. The tiny part of my mind that still works thinks: this must be what Hell is like.

After I don't know how long, the waves of panic fade away and I turn over and everything goes back to normal and I fall asleep and don't wake up until a little while ago. What a horrible experience. I hope it never happens again.

4:30 p.m. Back at the ranch at last. We manage to get thoroughly lost trying to retrace our steps back to the highway where Bud and the pickup crew are waiting for us. We'd still be wandering in circles if Colin hadn't blown a rescue whistle he had the good sense to bring along. When we stumble out of the underbrush Colin sweeps me off my feet in a bear hug, which I'm willing to prolong indefinitely except that Bud honks the horn impatiently and motions me in beside him.

"Since you and Omar didn't kill each other in the course of the night," he says "you must have learned something about enduring the displeasing manifestations of others." Omar, who is squeezed in between me and the door, says yes, he finally grokked the theory about how controlling your automatic negative reactions lets you to jump to a higher energetic plane where you can perceive a greater reality.

"Forget theory; that comes later, after you have some real-life data," Bud barks. "Concentrate on experiencing your experiences. The answers you're desperately seeking are so obvious that you overlook them a hundred times a day. God is staring you in the face, just waiting to be recognized." Bud turns the radio on and the nasal whine of a country and western singer fills the cab. He thumps the steering wheel in time to the music.

"And I can tell you it'll make your hair curl when it happens," he shouts. "All of a sudden the gestalt will jump out at you, like it does in those figure-ground pictures where you see first a vase and then two facing profiles, or vice versa, and you'll see the eye of God winking at you in the midst of the mundane phenomena of everyday existence, and you'll feel such a mixture of joy, gratitude, chagrin and disbelief that you'll laugh and cry at the same time."

Bud grins, as if at a private joke between Mr. God and himself, and I take advantage of his momentary good mood and ask about my claustrophobia attack last night. For some reason he finds it riotously funny. He whoops and hollers and I'm afraid he's going to lose control of the truck.

"Congratulations, Dorie," he howls. "You just had a little taste of eternity, the place, if you'll excuse my spatial imagery, where nothing ever happens. People wouldn't think life eternal was so desirable if they knew what it was really like: no time, therefore no movement, therefore no change. Eternity by definition is incompatible with organic life, which is essentially a process of change, of cycles of growth and decay."

He looks at me to see my reaction as we round another hairpin curve pulling about 2Gs. He downshifts to counteract the centrifugal force but doesn't pause in his lecture.

"Now I'm not knocking eternity. It has its role in the cosmic design, at a highly abstract level, but it's no place for the personal consciousness to hang out. There are better post-mortem destinations, but you gotta work damn hard to earn your ticket to them."

"What kind of destinations?" I ask. "The mind of God, for one," he says. "Becoming a brain cell in the mind of God. That's a good one."

An interesting chat but I don't think I understood half of it.

## Friday, August 25

Bummer. I've lost my favorite gold chain with the "D" pendant. I noticed it was gone when I looked in the mirror after I washed my hair last night, but I have no idea when it disappeared. Probably somewhere in the woods with Omar. First my wristwatch, which has never turned up, then my travelers' checks, and now my jewelry. I hope this completes some sort of triad.

This morning Colin and I sneaked out to have a private conversation on the dining hall porch without Bud picking up our converging blips on his radar. Colin tells me that word has gone around the Community that I'm a ballbuster. He says he's been warned to stay away from me.

I ask by whom, assuming this is another one of Omar's dirty tricks. "The Big Enchilada himself," Colin says. "You mean Bud?" I sputter, "Bud actually warned you off me?"

Colin tells me to cool it, I should know better than to take Bud at his word. He says Bud just wants to keep us from joining forces in an attempt to figure out his game. He also tells me Bud will try to hook me into the Community by offering me the opportunity to fulfill some fantasy I don't even know I have.

"The bait he dangled in front of me," Colin says, "was the ocean. Somehow he found out I like underwater photography so he describes this crazy plan to make a documentary of marine life in the Sea of Cortez. With me as director."

"Were you tempted?" I ask, banishing a momentary fantasy of my own: Colin and Dorie cuddling on a Mexican beach. "No way," he says. "Bud is just a summer project for me. I'm going back to Toronto and my serious research." He tells me he works for a biotech company that's developing a formula to pep up elderly mitochondria. It seems the potential market, baby boomers who want to keep jogging until they drop, is enormous. I ask him if he'd take the stuff himself. "Absolutely," he says, "I just turned thirty and I hear time's winged chariot drawing near."

A mature, ambitious man who can quote Andrew Marvell. I'm definitely smitten. I wonder what the airfare to Toronto is?

· · · · · · ●●● ● ●●● · · · · · · ·

The airfare to Toronto had been outrageous, as it turned out. Dorie closed the journal and put it on her chest. She slumped lower into the sofa cushions and stared at the ceiling. Well, Bud, she thought, we showed you, didn't we? You didn't manage to keep us apart. She smiled as she remembered the heady rush of romantic attraction that pulled her and Colin together like magnetically charged particles. She, for one, was sure she'd found her soulmate, her missing Platonic half, even while she told herself there was no such thing. Colin, always the practical one, had seen her as his intellectual equal, a partner with enough ambition and energy to keep up with his own inexhaustible drive to achieve.

She got up from the sofa and did a slow, forward bend to ease the cramp in her back. She had been so immersed in the lost world of her journal that she hadn't shifted position for half an hour. And she must have overdone the bourbon in her drink. While her head didn't exactly spin when she stood up, she did feel pleasantly floppy and warm. She searched for a word to identify the sensation. Relaxation? Peace? Not exactly. It was something more like acceptance.

Nothing turned out as I expected, she thought. Nothing. But maybe that's all right. Maybe it turned out just the way it had to.

She took her glass into the kitchen, rinsed all traces of bourbon from it, and put it in the dishwasher so Phoebe wouldn't find it. No sense in upsetting her on the eve of their mother-daughter religious bonding experience. Or whatever it was going to be.

"You just never, know, do you?" Dorie said aloud. "You can guess, but you never know."

Fifteen

"Mom, you look fine. Let's go." Phoebe was fidgeting in the doorway to Dorie's bathroom.

Dorie examined herself in the full-length mirror next to the linen closet. The butter yellow dress was skillfully cut and fit well. She kicked one leg out from the partially buttoned front closure. It had seemed a waste to do up all the buttons when her legs were so deliciously tanned.

"You don't think I'll scandalize anyone if I show my knees do you?" she asked Phoebe.

"No," Phoebe grumped. "It's not Circle of Prudes in Christ, Mother. Come on. We're going to be late."

"No, we're not," Dorie said. "It shouldn't take more than fifteen minutes to get there.'

"Yeah," Phoebe said," but Kimmi's saving us seats down in front so we can be close to the band and she can't hold them forever. So hurry up."

Dorie slipped on her new sandals and grabbed her handbag off the bathroom doorknob. She took one last look in the mirror. A new Sunday-go-to-meeting dress. Who would have thunk it? She was actually going to Sunday meeting. She felt a little shiver of anticipation as an image of Viktor in a Sunday-go-to-meeting suit came to mind. She smiled. Short, muscular Viktor- the- mechanic was certainly a contrast to cerebral, ectomorphic Colin. While she refused to take her visceral response to Viktor seriously, there was no harm in enjoying it. And she was looking forward to seeing Pastor Charlie do his charismatic thing, even though, according to Phoebe, it did not involve draping poisonous snakes around his neck.

"Hi ho, hi ho, it's off to church we go," she sang cheerily as she followed Phoebe down the stairs.

Phoebe stopped at the front door and turned around. "Mom, you are going to be nice, aren't you?" she asked. She looked at Dorie imploringly.

"Of course I'm going to be nice," Dorie said. "Why wouldn't I?"

"I mean, you're not going to get into an argument about evolution or something are you? Because if you do I'm just going to die."

Dorie promised to keep her mouth as well as her skirt buttoned.

The drive to the church, which was in a low-rent neighborhood on the east side of town, took longer than the anticipated fifteen minutes due to a fender-bender that blocked the bridge across the river. Just as Phoebe predicted, the parking lot was so full that they could only find an outlying space and had to scurry across the baking asphalt while Phoebe sputtered I- told -you -so's. Nevertheless, Dorie stopped to gawk on the walkway to the church. In front of the building, a large white circle was suspended by chains between upright posts. Fat black letters spelled out "Circle of Friends in Christ" in an arc over a smaller circle of three arrows chasing one another around a central cross.

"I don't get the arrow thing," Dorie said.

Phoebe explained. "It's supposed to show how our lives revolve around Christ and how we help each other stay in fellowship."

Dorie looked back over her shoulder as they dodged a family hustling four stairstep children towards the church entrance.

"Kind of looks like a recycling center symbol to me."

"You said you were going to be nice," Phoebe wailed.

A young Hispanic couple, the wife in a vivid floral print dress and the husband in a neat guyabera, murmured pardons as they brushed past Dorie and Phoebe.

"You've made us late," Phoebe complained. "We're going to be the last ones inside."

Dorie apologized, reiterated her promise to behave, and followed Phoebe toward the white-columned front porch of the church. It was a low, round yellow brick building, probably dating from the fifties, she thought, when this style of ecclesiastical architecture was in vogue among progressive Methodists. She wondered if the structure had inspired Pastor Charlie's choice of name for his congregation or if his choice of real estate had been a fortuitous accident.

She hadn't gotten more than three steps inside the foyer of the church when a tall, gaunt man in a blue blazer accosted her. The tag on his lapel read "Welcome Friends! Herbert Baskin, Greeter."

"Welcome, welcome, friend!" Herbert grabbed her hand and shook it vigorously. "Your first time here? Glad to have you with us. We love to have new friends. Let me show you to a seat. There's a pew with your name on it just waiting for you."

"Thank you, Mr. Baskin," Phoebe interrupted, "but Kimberly Medderly's saving us seats down front."

"Okey doke," Herbert was undaunted. "Betcha this is your Mom. Am I right?"

Phoebe nodded and tugged Dorie towards the double doors marked "Sanctuary."

"Hope to see you at the New Friends Forum after the service," Herbert called after them.

"They take this 'friends' business seriously here," Dorie muttered as Phoebe guided her down the center aisle between the packed pews. She noticed that the occupants appeared to be primarily white, with a scattering of dark Hispano heads, and dressed neatly but informally. Not a hat, suit or tie in sight.

Phoebe was scanning the congregation. "There's Kimmi and everyone! Down in the second row. They saved our seats."

Dorie edged past Kimberly, Amber, a plump red-haired woman and a balding man whom she assumed were Amber's parents, and sat down next to Nicole, leaving a space for Phoebe, who had lingered in the aisle whispering apologies for their tardiness to Kimberly.

"You're just in time," Nicole told her. "The show's about to start."

What's she talking about, Dorie wondered. We're having a show, not a sermon?

Suddenly the lights dimmed and the sanctuary went dark. A rainbow sequence of colored lights from an overhead projector flickered across the walls and a series of pounding electronic chords reverberated throughout the room.

Dorie, who had concentrated on avoiding treading on anyone's feet on her way to her seat, took a good look around. A raised stage ran across the semi-circular area that would have been the apse in a traditional church. A circular dais about six feet in diameter had been erected in the center of the stage. Four folding chairs, a drum set, keyboard and microphone were arranged behind it. An American flag hung on the wall to the left of the stage and a Colorado flag to the right. There was nothing like a pulpit, lectern or altar, and the floral decorations consisted of potted silk ficus trees adjacent to the flags. Dorie was thinking that the general effect was decidedly secular when a gigantic cross outlined in bright white LEDs began to pulsate on the rear wall of the stage area.

Phoebe slipped into the seat beside Dorie and nudged her shoulder. "Here comes the band.".

A spotlight illuminated a door to the right of the stage and Jared, followed by Chris French and two girls, one of whom Dorie recognized as the air freshener fairy from the car wash, bounded onto the stage. Jared was waving a ruby red electric guitar in one hand and the girls were carrying a lime green banner reading "JC ROX AND SO CAN U." The congregation cheered and clapped as the band members took their places at the rear of the stage. Chris sat down at the drums, the air freshener girl at the keyboard, and the other girl, whose black spiky hair and liberally lined eyes reminded Dorie of Phoebe's former goth buddies, grabbed the microphone.

Nicole was right. This was clearly a show.

As the band launched into an exuberant rendition of "Three Strikes," an oversized closed-circuit TV screen descended from the ceiling over the stage and the first lines of the song flashed into view. The congregation rose to its collective feet and shouted out the teleprompted lyrics, which, Dorie was relieved to see, were not accompanied by a little bouncing ball.

Dorie stood up reluctantly. She didn't dare remain seated, an obvious sourpuss Philistine among the true believers. Especially since Nicole was not only singing lustily but also executing impressive Watutsi-like vertical jumps in time to the beat, and the perfectly normal-looking middle-aged couple whom she took to be Amber's parents were waving their arms in the air with their heads thrown back. She sneaked a sideways glance at Phoebe.

Phoebe was swaying back and forth with her eyes closed and one hand pointing to the ceiling. Or possibly Heaven. Dorie had no idea of her daughter's state of mind but she was uncomfortably reminded of the twitching attacks of ecstasy that sometimes befell Bud's more devotionally inclined students, known in spiritual circles as "Bliss Chicks."

"Three Strikes" was followed, to Dorie's great relief, by a more sedate number, something about letting the Son shine in to the dark little corners of your heart. It was more of a ballad than the previous hard-rocking tune and Nicole modulated her leaps into a lateral sway that was taken up by her pew mates and then spread to the rest of the congregation. Dorie wondered if they would segue into an evangelical version of The Wave.

Mercifully, the band abandoned their instruments after one last chorus of "let the Son shine in/and set your heart aglow." The congregation reseated themselves and, after a ripple of chatter and laughter, fell silent. Dorie looked around. All eyes were fixed on the stage.

The expectant hush was broken by an electronic version of a football charge fanfare blaring from the surround sound system. A well-built fortyish man with a luxurious shock of sandy hair brushed into a hint of a mullet emerged from the door to the left of the stage.

Phoebe squeezed Dorie's arm. "That's him, Mom. That's Pastor Charlie!"

The pastor was extremely well put together, Dorie noted. He wore a pale grey summer suit and a yellow foulard tie and moved with the easy grace of a natural athlete. He leapt onto the circular dais at the front of the stage and stretched his arms wide as he broke into a toothy open-mouthed grin.

"Welcome, welcome, welcome, friends! Praise the Lord! What kind of day is this?"

"It's a good day to be alive!" chorused Dorie's pew mates and their brethren.

Omygod, Dorie thought. What am I in for now? The musical prelude had been entertaining but she wasn't sure she could sit through a tent revival call and response session.

Pastor Charlie continued, his resonant tenor amplified by a handheld cordless mike, "Yes indeed, it's a good day to be alive, alive not just in the body, not just in the mind, but alive in the spirit. In the spirit of Jesus Christ our Savior, who died to give us everlasting life."

There were scattered "Amens" and "Praise Gods" from the assembly. Dorie glanced at Phoebe. Her eyes were glued to Pastor Charlie and her lips were parted expectantly. Dorie had never seen her so rapt. It suddenly occurred to her that all this might be a daddy thing, that Phoebe's religious obsession was fueled by some deep need to replace the father she had lost. This thought was followed by a stomach-churning wave of guilt. It's all my fault, Dorie thought. All of it. First the accident and then all those years I was a lousy single parent.

She broke out of this black reverie by returning her attention to Pastor Charlie, who was charging into his sermon like a tackle into a line of scrimmage. The title, "God Wants You to Think Big", superimposed on a photograph of an expansive, star-studded sky, was displayed on the overhead TV screen.

"If God had thought small he couldn't have created the universe," Pastor Charlie shouted. "If God had thought small we would have been stuck with the void. If God had thought small we wouldn't have the oceans, we'd have some little old puddles of saltwater. You can't be a creator if you think small. "

The woman who was probably Amber's mother shook her head vigorously and murmured agreement.

"Well, friends, "Pastor Charlie continued, stepping off the dais and coming perilously close to the edge of the stage, "well, guess what! God doesn't want you to think small either. God made us in his image and he wants us to be creators too." He paced up and down the edge of the stage making intense eye contact with people in the first few rows. Dorie resisted the impulse to look down at her lap when he stationed himself in front of her pew but when she glanced sideways at Phoebe she saw her daughter's face turned upwards like a flower following the sun.

"Yes, friends," Charlie went on, "God wants us to create good health and loving families and satisfying careers and prosperity." Dorie felt Phoebe elbow her in the ribs. "The only thing that limits us is thinking small. Thinking 'I can't,' 'I don't know how,' thinking 'It won't work out.'"

Charlie flung one arm out and pointed his finger at the congregation. "God doesn't like that, does he?"

There was no immediate response and Charlie repeated, "Does God like that?"

"No," the congregation chorused obediently.
"That's right. That kind of thinking is based on fear, not hope, and we're not going there, are we?"

The congregation, now primed, delivered a resounding "No!"

When Pastor Charlie went on to outline a kind of twelve-step process for supersizing one's thinking by reading selected passages of scripture, Dorie's attention wandered to a rectangular plastic box affixed to the back of the pew in front of her. It was filled with multi-colored three by five index cards. She extracted several and discovered that they were color-coded for the various categories of prayers that could be requested by filling in some blanks and then depositing the card in the same color box in the lobby. Something called the Prayer Relay Team would then collect them and instant message the Lord on one's behalf. Dorie considered filling out a red card (relationships) and a green card (prosperity) just to see what might happen. The blue (health) and white (world peace) cards she'd leave for others less robust or more altruistic than herself.

Phoebe glanced at her with obvious disapproval and she replaced the cards and listened to the sermon, which was building to a finale.

"Remember "John 16:24," Pastor Charlie instructed. "'Ask and you shall receive.'"

The verse flashed on the overhead TV screen for the hearing impaired, or, considering the level of amplification in the sanctuary, the stone deaf.

"And when you ask, ask big. God's goodness is infinite, friends. You don't have to be polite and hold back like there's not enough food at the table. You don't have to plead and beg like you're asking for a loan from your tightwad rich uncle. There's plenty of prosperity and health and happiness to go around and God is just waiting to gift you with it. So think big. Ask God to help you create the abundant life He wants you to have. "

Pastor Charlie stepped down off the dais and came to the front of the stage, opened his arms, and gestured for the congregation to rise. Dorie braced herself; she sensed a prayer coming on.

"Now, my friends, let's join hands and bow our heads and everybody think big and visualize those special blessings that you want to manifest in your life while we say the Circle of Friends Prayer. And for you new friends who don't know the words, well, you folks," Charlie smiled benevolently, "you can keep your heads up and follow the video. "

Dorie joined hands with Nicole on her left and Phoebe on her right and looked around at the sea of obediently bowed heads.

Here and there a new friend's face looked up at the TV screen as the sanctuary lights dimmed and a brilliant rainbow was projected on the back wall over the illuminated cross. As far as Dorie could see, any resemblance to the First Presbyterian Church of Moline, Illinois, her only experience of institutionalized Christianity, was purely coincidental, if not completely nonexistent.

The Circle of Friends Prayer was brief, to the point, and heavily capitalized.

> "Heavenly Father, we thank you for
> sending us Jesus Christ Your Son
> To save us from our sins and
> give us Everlasting Life.
> We open our hearts to Jesus.
> We ask that He drive out the Demons
> Of Doubt, of Ignorance and of
> Temptation. We ask that He
> Keep us Strong in the Holy Spirit.
> We ask that the Circle of Friends
> Remain Unbroken. In Jesus Name, Amen."

The text disappeared from the video screen as Pastor Charlie intoned a sonorous "Amen." It was replaced by an image of humanoid figures resembling the aliens on tourist brochures from Roswell, New Mexico standing in a circle holding one another's upper appendages.

"It's meet and greet time, friends!" Pastor Charlie announced and an orgy of ritual hugging ensued. Nicole and Phoebe embraced Dorie, then turned to do the same to their outlying neighbors. Dorie felt a bit awkward hugging them under false pretenses but grateful that she could avoid full frontal contact with total strangers.

"Okay, friends, "Pastor Charlie beamed down upon his flock, "that's enough loving for now. The band's going to play another tune for you and our wonderful TFC volunteers are going to pass the plate and you know what that means. I'm thinking big here. I'm thinking building fund for that new sanctuary we need because we're growing so fast we're darn near busting out of this itty bitty meeting house."

Dorie put a dollar in the brown plastic basin as it was handed down her pew. The least she could do in payment for the son et lumiere extravaganza she had just experienced was to buy Pastor Charlie a brick or two. Phoebe followed suit with a dollar of her own. Dorie wondered if, as a wage-earning adult, she should have given more, but Phoebe didn't seem offended.

JC Rox played an upbeat instrumental involving tambourines and handclaps as a cadre of TFC volunteers, uniformly fresh-faced and neatly dressed, filed up to the stage and deposited their proceeds in a large metal cash box produced by a youngish man with a slick black pompadour. Dorie assumed he was the Circle of Friends version of a church elder but given his outfit, a white dress shirt and black slacks, she couldn't help thinking he bore more than a passing resemblance to a casino pit boss.

Pastor Charlie pronounced a final benediction:

"God bless, friends, and may the Circle be unbroken until we meet again."

"Amen," responded the congregation. Dorie joined in wholeheartedly, adding her personal thanks to whatever deity was in charge of the morning's proceedings for helping her get through them with a straight face.

*Sixteen*

Dorie's first impulse upon reaching the foyer was to bolt for the front door, but Phoebe, Nicole, Amber, and the couple who were indeed Amber's parents, clustered around her, effectively cutting off all escape routes. They pelted her with questions: did she like the band, what did she think of Pastor Charlie, wasn't the light show amazing?

Dorie was determined to be nice.

"It was very energizing," she said. "Really positive and upbeat."

Phoebe bounced a little on the balls of her feet. "See? "I knew you'd like it."

Dorie smiled benignly. Right now a little tactful hypocrisy was in order; maybe later she'd confess that the service struck her as a cross between a motivational psychology lecture and a rock concert. And, as far as she was concerned, Mr. God and His Son had left the building some time during the first set.

Phoebe, Nicole, and Kimberly excused themselves to visit the coffee bar in the south wing of the building. Amber and Mr. Reilly disappeared to collect Amber's two younger brothers from one of the Sunday school classrooms. This left Dorie in the enthusiastic care of Mrs. Reilly, who offered to guide her to the New Friends Forum in the north wing.

"I'm just so happy you decided to join us." Mrs. Reilly clutched her elbow and propelled her down a tiled corridor that smelt faintly of Lysol. "This is truly a life-giving church. We've got all these great special interest groups. I'm in the Cooking With Spirit group on Wednesday night. That's cooking with the Holy Spirit, of course, not with liquor." She ducked her head and giggled, "And then on Thursday I meet with the Home School Moms. Not that Amber's home-schooled anymore. She insisted on public school this year but I'm keeping the boys at home as long as I can. Boys are so much more vulnerable to sinful influences, don't you think?"

"I really wouldn't know," Dorie said, "never having been one myself."

"Oh, but I forgot. Phoebe's your only one, isn't she? Well, never mind, it's probably better that way, with you being on your own and all. Oh, here we are." Mrs. Reilly nudged Dorie towards an open door topped with a placard that said "Welcome New Friends" and left to join her family.

Dorie sighed. She had promised Phoebe to make an effort. She might as well go the whole nine yards. She stepped through the door into a large room spartanly furnished with a folding conference table and metal chairs. The Venetian blinds on the windows opposite the door were partially closed against the midday sun and she felt a surge of claustrophobia, followed by the urge to lie down on the carpeted floor and have a little nap until whatever was going to take place was over.

The seductive aroma of strong, fresh coffee revived her. The source was an urn on a long table at the far end of the room, where Ev Medderly was arranging the requisite Krispy Kremes on paper plates. Dorie made a beeline for the table; she was going to need both a caffeine jolt and a sugar high to deal with her New Friends.

"Dorie!" Ev exclaimed. "You made it. Good for you."

"You thought I was going to chicken out?" Dorie asked.

"It had occurred to me," Ev said. "But I wasn't going to hold it against you. Do you want coffee or would you rather have one of these wretched tea bags?"

Dorie helped herself to a styrofoam cup of black coffee and a chocolate frosted doughnut; the combination would send her blood sugar into crash mode in about an hour but until then she'd be soaring.

"So where is everybody?"

"It takes a while for people to get here," Ev explained. "The new folks usually mill around in the lobby meeting the regulars until Herbert Baskin shoos them back here. Herbert's our chief greeter. He takes his duties quite seriously."

"So I noticed."

"Once everyone's had a bit of a chat and gotten comfy, Pastor Charlie comes in and has a word. Explains what the church is about, answers questions, that sort of thing. It's quite informal so you can be perfectly open. Actually, it's amazing what some people say..."

"Here we are, friends," Herbert Baskin's voice echoed down the hall. "Starbucks Coffee, Krispy Kremes, and good Christian fellowship. All the comforts of home right here in the New Friends Forum."

Ev groaned. "Lord love a duck. I wish that man would put a cork in it."

An elderly man in a neat seersucker suit, accompanied by a matronly silver-haired woman, shuffled into the room, followed by a chemically tanned blonde stuffed into light blue polyester slacks and a matching sleeveless sweater. The new arrivals looked at Ev and Dorie questioningly.

"Come on over and tuck in," Ev encouraged. "You too," she added, beckoning to a small, bespectacled bald man hesitating in the doorway. "Somebody's got to eat these doughnuts so I don't."

While the newbies were helping themselves to coffee, Herbert Baskin, armed with clipboard, Sharpie, and a box of stick-on nametags, made sure everyone was identifiable.

"There you go," he said, handing the elderly couple a pair of tags. "Roy and Shirley Platz. In case you forget who you're married to, right?" He chuckled at his little joke. Roy and Shirley stared at him uncomprehendingly.

He moved on to Dorie, who was reading a leaflet listing the various resources available through Circle of Friends. It appeared that all one's human needs, from purchasing insurance to finding a podiatrist or a Pilates instructor, could be filled by members of the congregation.

"And I know who you are because of that charming daughter of yours," he said, inscribing a nametag and presenting it to Dorie.

Dorie looked at it. "I'm sorry," she said. "But my last name's Winslow not Ferguson."

"What?" Herbert said.

"Phoebe's a Ferguson but I use my maiden name," Dorie explained. Herbert frowned and she added hastily, "for professional reasons. And my first name ends in 'I E', not 'Y.' If it were a 'Y' I'd be a boat."

"What?" Herbert repeated. He looked bewildered.

"Never mind," Dorie said, taking pity on him. "I'll fix it myself." She took Herbert's clipboard from him, wrote herself a new tag, and pressed it onto her left lapel. "See? All better now." She returned his tools and he fled towards the blonde in the polyester pants, who looked as if she would be grateful for any sort of male attention.

"I guess this is your first time too."

A reedy voice drew her attention and she turned to see the small bespectacled bald man standing at her elbow. He had just suffered an unfortunate encounter with a jelly doughnut and a blob of red goo decorated the front of his white short -sleeved dress shirt.

"Do you know anything about the youth groups here?" the little man said. "I thought maybe I could help out with some of them. I'd really like to work with young people. Influence them in the right direction and all."

Dorie peeked at his nametag: Paul Greenberg. Dorie wondered if he were a Jew for Jesus or if he too were here under false pretenses.

"That seems like a very good idea, Paul." He needs to get that stuff off his shirt before it stains, she thought. "But do you know you've got jelly on your shirt?"

Paul tucked his chin into his neck and examined his chest.

"Oh dear. This shirt is almost new. Oh dear. I should do something about this, shouldn't I?"

Ev, who had been talking to Ray and Shirley Platz, overheard Paul's cries of distress and came to his aid with a handful of napkins. She scooped up the blob, dispatched Herbert to fetch some damp paper towels from the men's room, and instructed Paul to soak the shirt in cold water and hydrogen peroxide when he got home.

"Now don't you worry about a thing, dear." She patted him on the shoulder. "It'll come right."

"Thank you so much," Paul said. "I feel so silly, meeting the Pastor with a dirty shirt."

"Nonsense. He won't even notice. I guarantee it. And if he does he won't care. The only reason he dresses so well is because his wife picks out his clothes for him."

And she has damn expensive taste, Dorie thought. That suit didn't come from Men's Warehouse.

Ev looked at her watch. "Find yourself some seats at the table, people. Pastor Charlie should be here for the Forum any minute now. Your New Friends cards are in that basket over there," she motioned towards a cabinet at the other end of the room, "and you can pick up brochures on our small groups and our various ministries to take home and study."

Dorie passed on the brochures but took a New Friends card to be polite. She selected a seat as near the door as possible, just in case she managed to think of an excuse to leave early. The blonde woman, whose tan was two shades darker than her hair, sat down next to her.

"Hi! I'm Tracey Enright. Isn't this the most fabulous church ever? Can you believe how friendly everyone is?"

"Yes," Dorie said, "I can."

"I've been looking for a real God-fearing church for ages. My girlfriend told me about this one. I live in Sulfer Springs and it's such a one horse town we don't have anything. It takes me an hour to get here but it's worth it, don't you think?" She took a breath and rattled on. "My girlfriend told me they have a great singles group for, you know, people like us. Have you been yet?"

"No," Dorie said curtly. People like us? What was this girl thinking? She did not wear pastel polyester and she wasn't about to go trolling for trouser trout in a pool of Christian singles. With the exception of a mild flirtation with Viktor, of course. Viktor whom she probably wasn't going to get to flirt with now that she was trapped in this room full of people waiting for Pastor Charlie or the Messiah, whichever came first.

She swiveled around in her seat and tried to peer out the door, then looked at her watch. It was twenty -five minutes past noon.

"The Pastor should be here soon,"Ev said, "so why don't you fill out your New Friends cards while we're waiting?"

Dorie filled in the blanks on her card selectively. She was willing to provide name, address, and home phone number, but not her email address or cellphone number. And she didn't check any of the boxes next to the list of Friendly Groups that would be delighted to contact her to play bridge, hike, bike, make a scrapbook, or power walk through town praying for the unchurched.

"Helloooo New Friends!" Dorie looked over her shoulder. Pastor Charlie filled the doorway. He seemed bigger than he had appeared on stage and Dorie noted that the fabric of his suit had the subtle sheen of expensive Italian silk. However, his boyish grin and slightly disheveled hair mitigated what might have otherwise have been a somewhat overwhelming presence.

"I'm so glad to see all of you." He directed a personalized smile at each of them in turn. "I'm also so grateful to have the chance to talk about Circle of Friends and find out how we can serve you. And," he paused dramatically, "we've got a special friend with us today. My own very special, very best, friend, in fact." He stepped back from the doorway to reveal a petite woman in a peach linen pants suit. Her highlighted shoulder-length blonde hair was sprayed into immobility and her frosted lipstick matched her outfit.

"Hey, y'all. Ah'm Janelle Pritchett, Charlie's better half."

Wouldn't you know it, Dorie thought. A Southern Church Belle.

Charlie pulled out a chair for Janelle and seated her.

"And that's how we good Christian men treat our ladies," he said as he sat down beside her. "That's why they're so happy to let us be heads of the household, like the good Lord intended."

Janelle hesitated just a second too long before looking up at him with one of those wide-eyed adoring gazes perfected by the wives of presidential candidates.

"Well, let me say a word about our church here before we go around the table and get to know each other better. "Charlie tilted his chair back and spread his hands, palms down, on the table.

Uh oh, Dorie thought. He's a raconteur.

"Ten years ago, back in Shreveport I had a dream about a church in the mountains. I talked to my Daddy about it--I was assistant pastor in his church then--and he said, 'Son, you got to go West. That's where your dream's leading you. I'll sure miss you, but the Lord wants you out there in the Rockies.' And Janelle and I packed up-- I guess Janelle would say she packed while I supervised."

He winked at Janelle who responded with a head bob and demi-smile. "And so we came to West Fork. And I've got to tell you that we had to start small. We were thinking big but we had to start small. That's right, our first meetings were in our garage. Would you believe that? But the good Lord saw fit to favor us and look where we are now."

"And we aren't stopping here," Janelle broke in. "We're going to bring the Good News to all of Southern Colorado. We're planning a new sanctuary that will seat five thousand and we're going to have our own TV studio and..."

"Janelle, maybe you're thinking a little too big." Charlie held up his hand, interrupting her mid-sentence. "Maybe we better just concentrate on doing God's work right here in Ponderosa County."

Janelle pursed her lips. "Joel Osteen went national right away," she murmured.

"So folks, here we are, a God-loving church looking to grow and we'd be honored to have you  partake of our good fellowship." Charlie continued, ignoring her pout. "Now why don't you all tell us a little about yourselves and what brought you to us. Of course, I know it was really the Holy Spirit that guided you here, but I'd like to know what you personally hope to get from Circle of Friends." He smiled encouragingly at Mr. and Mrs. Platz.

"Well," Roy began, 'I'm Roy Platz and this is my wife, Shirley and we're sorta new kids in town. We just moved here from Ohio to be near our daughter. It's been kinda hard because we were real active in our church back home and we miss it. Especially the wife, here." He reached out and put his arm around Shirley, who nodded agreement. "But I told her not to worry, the Lord would provide and we'd find us a pastor that believed in the Good Book as it was written. And then I looked in the Yellow Pages and I saw that big advertisement for Circle of Friends and it said it was a Bible-based church. So here we are."

"It was like the answer to our prayers," Shirley said, her voice quivering with emotion. "Right there in the Yellow Pages."

"Just goes to show, "Pastor Charlie said, "ask and you shall receive. We're glad to have you with us." Janelle, reassuming her role as helpmeet, reached over and patted Shirley on the arm.

"And how about you, sir?" Charlie turned to Paul Greenberg, who identified himself as a semi-retired CPA and reiterated his interest in instilling sound values and moral principles in young people who might otherwise develop destructive habits and life-controlling issues.

Dorie wondered if Paul might have a tiny problem with a life-controlling issue himself, then chided herself for being mean-spirited when Pastor Charlie simply advised him to contact the youth pastor, who was always looking for volunteers to organize various character-building expeditions into the backcountry.

Tracey's turn for show-and-tell came next. She licked her lips nervously.

"I'm so full of the Spirit right now I could hug every one of you," she said in a choked voice. "I can hardly wait to join just about everything. I know I'm going to love Janelle's women's group, that one that gets together Tuesday nights for Bible study and dessert? I forget the name—"

"Heart of the Home," Janelle supplied, tapping a pearl-frosted fingernail on the tabletop before glancing at her watch.

"Yeah, that's it." Tracey rushed onward. "And I think I might try the FortySomething Fellowship." She giggled. "I mean I'm not looking to meet a man or anything but it would be fun to go out with some righteous Christian guys, you know? Instead of the creeps you meet through the Internet?" She blushed. "I'm sorry. That wasn't very charitable of me."

Pastor Charlie nodded approvingly. "That's okay, Tracey," he said. "We've got to support each other in our struggle to live a Godly life. Satan never misses a chance to tempt us off the path of righteousness. It's only prudent to choose friends who are strong in their faith. Friends who'll help guard your heart, mind and body from demonic influences."

Dorie folded her New Friends Card into little accordion pleats. At this point she had no intention of turning it in. She wondered what Ev, who seemed so down to earth and sensible, saw in all this. She glanced across the table, ready to exchange skeptical looks, but Ev appeared unperturbed by her pastor's reference to demons.

I've got to get out of here before I have to introduce myself, Dorie thought. She considered feigning an attack of acute gastroenteritis, complete with groans and stomach-clutching, but Ev would probably run after her with a bottle of Pepto Bismol while everyone else joined hands and prayed for her recovery.

It was too late, anyway. Pastor Charlie was looking directly at her, smiling broadly.

"Well, now, I am truly glad to see this lady with us today." He turned to the other people at the table. "Because this is an example of how the Lord works in mysterious ways. An example of how the little children can lead us." He looked back at Dorie. "Now I know who you are and how you were brought to us, but I'd like you to tell everyone what made you walk through our doors to a new way of life."

Dorie's mind went blank. What could she say? That she had come in hopes of understanding why her daughter had become a religious fanatic? And because she had the hots for the father of her daughter's boyfriend? A severely edited version of the truth would be required.

"I'm Dorie Winslow," she said, "My daughter belongs to Teens for Christ and I wanted to find out what she was so excited about."

"And?" Pastor Charlie said, leaning towards her.

"And what?"

"Did you find out? Did the Spirit touch your heart today?"

Oh, shit, Dorie thought. How am I going to answer that without insulting him or lying outright?

"Well," she hedged, "I can see why Phoebe enjoys your church but I'm not sure the Spirit got through to me."

Pastor Charlie took a moment to digest this. Janelle arched one meticulously penciled eyebrow and looked at her husband to see how he'd deal with this affront to his powers.

"Well, don't you worry yourself about that, Dorie," Charlie said. "The Lord is patient. All you have to do is say the word and Jesus' love will rain down on you like a torrent on parched earth."

"Amen," Tracey murmured. "Isn't that the truth."

"Phoebe tells us you're a professor up at the college, "Charlie continued. "And a writer, too. What's that book of yours about?"

"My book?" Dorie came back to the present. She had been mulling over Charlie's reference to parched earth, which was all too reminiscent of Bud's description of academicians as dry husks. Was there something about her that called up images of aridity?

"Oh yes, my book...uhhh..." She stalled for time as she formulated a severely abridged version of her standard answer to this always unwelcome query. "Uh.... it's about how some of the moral dramas in Nathaniel Hawthorne's fiction are still being played out today." She decided not to mention that it compared Hawthorne's betrayed heroines with Monica Lewinsky, Princess Diana and other contemporary ladies done in by powerful men.

"Hawthorne," Charlie said. "Hmmmm. Now isn't he that fellow who wrote that book about adultery? And how it's a mortal sin and leads to tragedy all around."

"Not exactly," Dorie said. "'The Scarlet Letter' is more about how hypocrisy, pride, and arrogance lead to tragedy all around. And how unfeeling male ambition can destroy naive, trusting women."

"Well, now that's a new one on me," Charlie said. "But maybe the men in that book weren't real Christians."

"They thought they were. That's the whole point."

There was a heavy silence.

"But adultery's still a sin," Janelle announced flatly. "The Bible says so. In the Ten Commandments. It comes right after murder."

"I don't think things are quite so black and white," Dorie said. Janelle was beginning to annoy her. "Adultery can be painful but I wouldn't put it on a par with murder."

"It defiles the sacrament of marriage," Janelle snapped. "That's a major sin. People don't take the sacrament of marriage seriously, but God does. The relationship between man and wife is a sacred trust. That's what I teach in Heart of the Home."

"I don't mean to disagree with you," Dorie said. The combination of caffeine and sugar had been a bad idea; she could feel herself becoming more irritated by the second. "I just think that real life moral dilemmas are too complex to be resolved by the literal application of a bunch of rules laid down for some Middle Eastern tribesmen thousands of years ago."

"Well, you're just denying the word of God then and I feel sorry for you," Janelle said, folding her arms across her chest. Charlie gave her a warning look and she quickly added, "But I'm going to pray for you anyway."

Tracey squirmed in her seat and Paul picked at the residue of the jelly stain on his shirt. Ev, looking bemused, pushed a plate of doughnuts to the center of the table so everyone could reach them but no one took any.

"Sounds to me like our friend Dorie isn't convinced of the inerrancy of the Good Book," Charlie said. "Would I be right on that count?" He winked at Dorie.

"You sure would," she assured him. "Given that this so-called Good Book was written by a committee, passed through multiple translations, and purged of anything that threatened the church hierarchy, yes, I have my doubts about its reliability."

Charlie leaned forward and looked at her without blinking. His charismatic intensity was disconcerting but Dorie resisted the impulse to lower her eyes.

"I'm not going to argue theology with you," he said. "No, ma'am. That's not going to get us anywhere. I'm just going to ask you to do one little thing. Can you do one little thing for me, Dorie?"

"Depends on the thing," Dorie said, anticipating a trap.

"I'd like for you to go home and open up a Bible--I know Phoebe's got one even if you don't--and read Psalm 121. That's all. Just read Psalm 121. Will you promise me you'll do that, Dorie?"

"Sure," she said. "I'll read it." By this point she would have agreed to read the entire Bible just to get Charlie off her case. She pushed her chair back from the table to signal imminent departure.

"Good," Pastor Charlie said. "And then maybe we'll talk some more. But now I expect you've all got places to go and people to meet. I know Janelle and I got to get our kids out of that Sunday School room before they tear it up. So God bless each and every one of you and I'll see you next Sunday."

He rose, pulled Janelle's chair out, and put his hand under her elbow to assist her. She shrugged it away and got up on her own. She smoothed the wrinkles out of her jacket and turned on a Homecoming Queen smile.

"It's been great meeting y'all," Janelle said. "Bye bye now, and y'all remember, every home needs a heart and that heart is Jesus Christ." She gave a little Homecoming Queen fingertip wave and followed Charlie out the door.

Tracey, Paul and the Platzes filtered out after her. They bid Dorie cordial goodbyes from a safe distance. Only Ev seemed inclined to talk to her.

"You found some of this a little hard to take, didn't you?" Ev began removing the folding chairs from around the table and stacking them against the wall. "I'm not surprised."

Dorie gathered up stray coffee cups and napkins. She felt vaguely nauseated. She'd blown her promise to be nice. She had just publicly attacked one of the fundamental precepts of evangelical Christianity. Phoebe would be horrified if she found out.

"I'm sorry I made a scene," she said. "But I can't handle this biblical inerrancy thing. It doesn't make sense."

"Don't worry about that." Ev added another chair to the stack and turned to face Dorie, who was relieved to see that she appeared amused and not at all offended. "Do what I do. Focus on the essentials."

"What do you mean?" Dorie returned the leftover doughnuts to their box. She vowed to swear off refined carbohydrates for the indefinite future; they had a deadly effect on her ability to practice common courtesy in the company of strangers.

"The love and humility and forgiveness parts," Ev said. "That's the core of Christianity. And the promise that if you admit you're lost, you'll be saved, in some sense or other. I don't bother with the details but I do believe that a firm faith in Jesus and what He taught will get your life in order. Besides, Circle of Friends is more fun than any other church I know."

She handed Dorie a spray bottle and a roll of paper towels so she could clean the crumbs off the conference table. Dorie made sure it was spotless; maybe she could atone for her lack of godliness with a surfeit of cleanliness. Nevertheless, she couldn't resist one more question.

"So do you believe that Jesus was really the Son of God?"

"My dear old dad set me straight on that. He was a Presbyterian minister in Norfolk and when I was going through my adolescent religious rebellion he made me read C.S. Lewis. Lewis argues that if someone claims to be the Son of God he either has to be delusional or the real McCoy, because why else would anyone make such a crazy claim? And the historical Jesus was clearly sane. And very wise. So, I think he was what he says he was."

Dorie considered this argument. It actually seemed reasonable. "You have a point there," she said. "I'll have to think about it."

"Dorie! So here's where you've been hiding."

Dorie turned to see Viktor in the doorway. He raised a hand in greeting. "I missed you after the service," he said. "I had to help fix a glitch in the audio system."

Viktor was wearing Sunday clothes, a blue oxford cloth button-down shirt and and neatly creased khakis. Dorie again felt the involuntary visceral, or more accurately, venereal, thrill of incipient lust. The rapid response capabilities of the human endocrine system are truly amazing, she thought.

"Hi," she said. "I've been busy making friends. Or maybe enemies would be more like it."

Viktor looked at her and shook his head. "What's she talking about?" he asked Ev.

Ev chuckled "She challenged Charlie on biblical inerrancy."

"You are a feisty one, aren't you?" Viktor grinned at Dorie. "Hang around a while though and we'll get through to you." He cocked his head on one side and looked at her appraisingly.

"You may be a heretic but you look great. Not that you didn't look great yesterday too, but I do love to see a woman in a dress."

Dorie smiled demurely, as befitted a woman in a dress. Her $129.95 had not been wasted.

"You two run along," Ev said. "I'll finish up in here."

Viktor guided Dorie towards the door with his hand resting lightly on the small of her back. She could feel the heat of his palm through the thin fabric of her dress.

"You hungry?" he asked.

Dorie admitted that she was in fact starving to the point of shakiness.

"Then you need lunch," Viktor said. "How about Renee's? You can get something healthy. They've got great soups and salads. All organic."

Dorie would have said yes to a Big Mac if Viktor had suggested it, but she had to find Phoebe before she could go to lunch.

"I have to take Phoebe home," she said.

"No you don't," Viktor replied. "I just saw her. She said to tell you that she was going to the mall with Kimberly and Jared. The girls are forcing him to buy some new clothes. He's outgrown everything he owns."

Dorie wondered if some karmic force had her in its grip. These encounters with Viktor seemed to be happening too easily. She resolved to proceed with caution. Karma, in her experience, was a mixed bag of tricks.

## Seventeen

Dorie was pleased with Viktor's choice of restaurants. Renee's had a European ambience that was a welcome contrast to the Tex-Mex cafes that dotted West Fork's Main Street. Its façade was lined with French doors that opened to create a sidewalk café and the cuisine was a Gallic-Californian hybrid that was both light and flavorful.

Viktor steered her to a table by the doors, pulled out a chair, and seated her. She wasn't sure whether this was a manifestation of Old World good manners or Christian chivalry, but she liked it.

A youth in a white shirt and black pants set menus in front of them and filled their water glasses with a flourish. "Would you care to see the wine list?" he asked, producing a glossy folder embossed with grape leaves.

"Certainly," Viktor said. Dorie's eyes widened. Viktor looked at her and smiled. "I may be a Christian but that doesn't mean I don't enjoy a civilized glass of wine with meals. Besides, if you've got the hunger wobblies this will settle you down while we wait for our food."

Dorie requested a glass of a modest but reliable domestic Chardonnay but Viktor suggested they have a New Zealand Sauvignon Blanc that she had never heard of. "You'll like it" he assured her. "It's crisp, with a hint of grass and gooseberries."

"You sound like a wine aficionado," she said. "I thought you were just an expert on Japanese cars."

Viktor laughed. "I'm hardly an aficionado. I took a wine tasting course right after my wife dumped me. Someone told me it was a good way to meet women. I didn't get a single date out of it but I did get hooked on good wine."

"That's better than I did," Dorie said. "After my first serious boyfriend dumped me I spent the summer at an ashram."

"Interesting. The ashram part, I mean. Not getting dumped. Everybody gets dumped. But not everyone goes to ashrams."

Dorie shrugged. "Hey, it was the seventies. It was like discos. That was what we did."

"There must have been more to it." Viktor observed. "Weren't you looking for God? In your own way?"

"Yes. I suppose I was. Although I wouldn't call what I was looking for 'God' in the sense that the Circle of Friends uses the term."

Viktor looked at her quizzically and Dorie hoped he wouldn't ask her to explain just what she was looking for; telling him that she was seeking "the truth" or "what's really real" was more or less accurate but would sound impossibly pretentious.

Fortunately, the waiter arrived with their wine, and made a show of offering Viktor a taste before pouring full glasses for them. Viktor sniffed, swirled, sipped and pronounced it fine.

Dorie lifted her glass, sipped, and said "Wow!" Just as Viktor predicted, it was excellent.

"This tastes like...." she searched for a description, "...like a summer day in the mountains."

"Which is exactly when and where we are," Viktor said, raising his glass to hers. "To many more of the same."

Dorie was beginning to feel giddy but she couldn't tell if it was the result of alcohol on an empty stomach or cascading hormones. This is insane, she told herself. Viktor is completely unsuitable. Besides, we could never get married because Phoebe and Jared might commit sibling incest.

"Yes," she said, meeting Viktor's eyes, which were the color of melted chocolate, "to summer days in the mountains."

"And to us," Viktor added.

"Possibly." Dorie took a sip of wine to calm herself. She was flattered by Viktor's interest but his intensity made her uneasy.

"So, tell me about yourself, Dorie Winslow." Viktor leaned forward with his elbows on the table and rested his chin on his interlocked hands. "Why West Fork? Aren't you a big city kind of gal?"

Dorie chose to overlook his use of the term "gal" and obliged him with a bland explanation of wanting a simpler life. Telling Viktor that she wanted to escape a house haunted with bad memories would have invited questions she wasn't prepared to answer. A partial truth would have to do.

"I moved here for Phoebe. She wasn't exactly flourishing back in Boston but she's really blossomed in the past year."

"Probably because of TFC. It gives the kids a structure, something to hold on to what with all the craziness in the world." Viktor said. "It pretty much got Jared on track. Actually, that's how I got involved in Circle of Friends. Through Jared and my brother. They kept working on me until I caved and went to a service."

"So have you been born again?" Dorie asked, figuring she might as well find out just how Christian Viktor really was.

Viktor laughed. "I resisted at first," he said," but yes, I did have what you could call a conversion."

"And what was it like?" Dorie probed.

"Life-altering," Viktor said. "You should try it." He offered Dorie a breadstick and took one for himself. "Don't worry. I'm not going to lecture you about getting saved. I'm just looking to get a date with you for Thursday night."

"What's happening Thursday night?"

"FortySomething Fellowship. We're going bowling this week and I need protection."

"From what?"

"Angela Chavez." Viktor sighed. "Nicole's mother. She's got her eye on me. She's an attractive lady but I'm not interested and I don't know how to discourage her."

"How about 'just say no'?'"

"Angela doesn't do 'no'. She's one of the top real estate brokers in town and she's never met a deal she couldn't close. She's too high-powered for me. I'm just a simple mechanic."

Not so simple, Dorie thought, not by a long shot. She waffled half-heartedly about not knowing how to bowl but Viktor said he would be delighted to teach her and without any further protests she agreed to an excursion to Riverside Lanes in four days' time.

"You needn't come out to Rabbit Valley to pick me up," she said, when he asked for directions to her house. "I may get hung up with work so it's better if I come under my own power."

This was a bit of a lie; she really wanted her own wheels in case bowling with a bunch of middle-aged Christian singles turned out to be as awful as it sounded. What we do for lust, she mused, as she attacked her Caesar salad.

Lunch proceeded amicably with talk of movies, books-- Viktor's taste ran to political thrillers but at least he read-- and Pastor Charlie and Janelle, whom Viktor described as "a good team considering that both of them want to be the quarterback." Lunch ended with a brief above-the-waist embrace that conveyed, Dorie thought, mutual good feeling without overtly sexual overtones.

She drove home in a happy glow. The sky seemed unusually blue, the leaves exceptionally green, and even the lingering odor of ersatz spruce from the praying hands auto air freshener was unexpectedly pleasing.

At home, however, storm clouds had gathered.

"Hi, honey, I'm back," Dorie called as she entered the house. Phoebe came out of the kitchen. She had a can of Diet Pepsi in one hand and a bag of tortilla chips in the other and her face was tear-stained and scowling.

Dorie"s heart sank. Had Jared dumped her? Did she and Kimberly have a falling out?

"Baby, what's wrong?" she asked, rushing towards Phoebe to embrace her.

Phoebe fended her off with the Pepsi can.

"You," she wailed. "Mother, how could you?"

"How could I what?"

"Say the Bible wasn't true. In front of Pastor Charlie and everybody. And you got into a fight with Janelle Pritchett. I am so embarrassed. I'll never be able to face Pastor Charlie again."

"I didn't say the Bible wasn't true," Dorie said, shaking her head a trifle too emphatically. "I just sort of said it was heavily edited. And I didn't get into a fight with Janelle Pritchett, who, by the way is a bossy little prig. I just disagreed with her. How do you know all this anyway?"

"Kimmi," Phoebe said, trying to push her way past Dorie, who quickly moved to block the stairway.

"Kimberly wasn't there. What does she know?"

"Her mom told her all about it. While we were in the mall. We called Mrs. Medderly to see how you'd liked New Friends Forum because we really hoped you would and she told Kimberly what you did. On the speakerphone. I just about died."

"Phoebe, Phoebe, you're making a big deal out of nothing. Ev wasn't upset by what I said and I don't think Pastor Charlie was either." Dorie put a comforting hand on Phoebe's shoulder. Phoebe shrugged it off.

"Leave me alone," she said. "You're hopeless." She slipped sideways past Dorie and ran upstairs. Dorie heard the door to her room slam shut, a clear message to keep out.

Dorie sighed. Just when things seemed to be getting better, she thought, I screw up big time. Now it looks as if the only way I can placate Phoebe is to pretend to believe something I don't.

She undid the buttons on her new dress as she retreated to her own bedroom. Why couldn't she have kept her mouth shut at the New Friends Forum? A lot of people found comfort in what Pastor Charlie preached. She should be more tolerant. Live and let live. Except the evangelicals didn't believe in live and let live. They believed in live like us or be damned. She changed into shorts and a shirt and flopped down on her bed. The world, she reflected, would be better off without its major religions. All they did was cause strife. From the Crusades to the Twin Towers.

"It's not the teachings, Dorie." She heard a ghostly echo of Bud's voice above her left ear. "It's the fools who misuse them." She rolled over on her side and extracted her journal from the drawer in her nightstand. It was time for another visit with her old guru.

# Eighteen

**Wednesday, August 30, 10 a.m.**

Three hours on the road and we're at a rest stop on I- 70, taking a pee break on the Continental Divide. (I don't mean that literally; there are public restrooms.) Bud stopped at Polly's request, I'd guess, because she was into the ladies' like a shot.

We're going to Vegas. For "life lessons" in the casinos, which Bud says provide perfect laboratory conditions for the study of attention. I'm excited and nervous at the same time. Excited because of the promise of bright lights and big city pleasures, like hamburgers. Nervous because I don't know anything about gambling and I'll probably make a fool of myself.

Bud has toned down his kamikaze driving because he's in a Winnebago nearly as long as a Greyhound bus. It belongs to his parents, who, I'm told, cruise the highways of southern Arizona from November to April to escape the harsh winters of Pasadena, where the temperature sometimes plummets to a chilling 60 degrees.

I wonder if they know their boy is using their RV as a traveling bordello. In addition to Corinne, Polly, and Rosa, Bud's got Jill, a ready, willing, able, and, incidentally pretty, blonde, on board. I'm not sure when Jill officially joined the harem, but this morning she made sure everyone in the Community knew exactly which vehicle she was assigned to for the Vegas trip.

Omar is following Bud in his Chevy van with the Boulder study group. Omar's sure to do his guru's apprentice number, expounding on his version of the dharma. Thankfully, I'm riding with Colin and Leonard in Rosa's VW van. It's plastered with stickers imploring everyone behind us to save whales, redwoods, and baby seals, and to honk if they love Krishna. Riding with Leonard and Colin has given me a chance to pry, discreetly of course, into Colin's past. He's never been married and recently broke up with his girlfriend because she was too emotionally needy. I can see how that would bother him. He's highly focused and rational. Just my type!

## Thursday, August 31, 8 a.m.

After last night at a KOA campground, we're having breakfast in a Grand Junction Denny's. Bud roused us from our sleeping bags at 7 a.m. I don't know what he did last night or with whom, but he's full of vinegar this morning. Corinne and Jill have dark circles under their eyes and aren't saying much to anyone, and even Rosa's subdued. Polly is all smiles and good cheer, but that could be due to second-trimester progesterone levels. It must have been a hot time in the old Winnebago last night.

I myself had a horrible night. I had a dream that scared me so much that I woke up with my heart pounding. Mainly because it wasn't my dream. It definitely did nott come from my subconscious. It had this strange, foreign, intrusive quality, nothing like an ordinary nightmare

I was in a closed room with a large rectangular window looking onto a bank of electronic control panels. Bud and Rosa and several faceless women were there. We were all bareass naked, lying around on large velvet pillows. Bud was stroking my hair and murmuring that I should relax and enjoy myself. That's when I woke up in a cold sweat, feeling violated. I don't know what's going on but I'm afraid things are getting out of control.

## 1 p.m. Somewhere along I-70 in Mormon Territory

We're making a rest stop at a freeway turnout designated as a "Scenic Overlook" where an awesome panorama of multicolored buttes and canyons is flawed by the presence of two international orange portable toilets.

Department of Utter Confusion: Later this morning, as we were finishing our breakfast in Denny's, Bud stops at my table. He puts his arm around me and asks if I had an interesting night. Then he walks away. I think he was referring to that dream I had. I've heard about gurus who tamper with their devotees' minds in order to speed up their spiritual evolution. Nevertheless, I don't want anyone mucking around with brain without my express permission. In writing and notarized.

## 10 p.m. Sunset Oasis Camperland, Las Vegas

It's 80 degrees—three hours after sundown—in this RV park and the interior of the VW bus is like a sardine can with central heating. Bud says don't worry, we're not supposed to sleep, we're supposed to Work. Our mission, and we have no choice but to accept it, is to penetrate the esoteric secrets of the casino, which Bud claims is a microcosm of the phenomenal world.

More specifically, we've been instructed to hang out in Caesar's Palace and observe the play of Lila. Bud told us to take careful note of the sensory assault designed to whip the hypnotized patrons into a frenzy of greed, lust and egotism: the flashing lights and electronic siren songs of the slot machines, the female waitpersons scantily clad in abbreviated togas, and the great Plexiglas box filled with One Billion Dollars in Uncirculated Bills and Protected by A Pressure Sensitive Security Device.

Bud is completely serious about this exercise. He gave us a stern lecture before he took the first group, Omar, Colin, Carole, Ianna and Bruce, into the casino about two hours ago. The gist of it was that two things would screw us up: the desire to win and the fear of losing. They're two sides of the same coin, attachment to the outcome. He also told us to be aware of our hunches but in a detached way so we don't distort them with our opinions. "Dispassionate interest" he says. "That's the attitude you want to cultivate." Easier said than done when you've put your bus fare home on the "Don't Pass" line at the craps table.

## September 1, 2 a.m. Coffee Shop in Caesar's Palace

Bud just gave me a gambling lesson that I'll never forget. He grabs me away from a slot machine where I'm slowly and steadily losing my allowance and takes me to the blackjack tables. I tell him I hate blackjack. I can't add without counting on my fingers and they don't go to 21. He says don't worry, he'll coach me.

So I sit on one of the high stools at a table where everybody but me obviously knows what they're doing and he whispers instructions. "Alert detachment, Dorie. That's the mark of the professional gambler. Practice that throughout your life and eventually you'll wake up. Maybe." His advice is sound but he acts like the fate of the civilized world hangs on every hand I play. If I lose even one dollar, he draws in his breath with a hiss, and pummels my back. I keep my head though, because I know he's trying to get me rattled. Finally, he shuts up and lets me play on my own. When I've doubled my money, he tells me to pocket my original stake and play only with my winnings.

I ask if we can switch to roulette because I'm mathed out. Bud shrugs. "Suit yourself," he says. "This is your learning experience, not mine."

We case the roulette tables. By now I've caught on to the finer points of casino etiquette and have adopted the disdainful, lizard-lidded stare of the high rollers. Bud hangs back, forcing me to choose a table. I try to ignore the chatty voice of reason telling me that a certain dealer looks friendly, or that a big win on the part of one player signifies a lucky table, and attend to the "subtle bodily inclinations" that Bud has directed us to follow. My bodily inclinations guide me straight to a table presided over by a handsome croupier with a welcoming smile. Too much sexual static on the intuitive channel.

I buy fifteen chips and manage to stay in the game for an entire five minutes by placing low-risk bets on the outside of the table, using a primitive precognitive visualization technique that works just well enough to keep me from going broke.

I'm getting up my nerve to put a couple of chips on one of the numbers, which will net me a thirty to one windfall if it hits, when Bud leans over and whispers urgently in my ear. "Quick. Put it all on twenty-eight." He sounds so certain that I shove my entire ten chip fortune onto the designated square in the middle of the table just as the little ping-pong ball is skittering around the circumference of the wheel. I'm hyperventilating so fast my hands tingle; I stand to win $600 if the gods of centrifugal force smile on me. The wheel slows, the ball bounces indecisively off the pins separating the numbered slots, and finally plops into the double zero. Caesar takes all.

The croupier sweeps my pathetic little stack of chips, representing a potential set of snow tires and a pair of cross-country skis, into the house winnings pile. I lay into Bud, who's standing behind me with his hands in his pockets looking at the ceiling. "Why did you tell me to put all my money on twenty-eight?" I demand. "I trusted you."

"Who told you to listen to me, sucker?" he says cheerfully. Then he winks at me and puts his arm around my shoulders. "Think about it, Cookie. Sometimes those little voices in your head lie." He walks away, leaving me standing in the middle of Caesar's Palace in a high funk. Finally, I get the point. I responded to Bud's prompting automatically, without stopping to evaluate it. I'm just as guilty of blind obedience to authority as the rest of his mutton-headed devotees. E.F. Hutton spoke, and I not only listened, I saluted and threw money.

### September 5, 4 p.m. Cleopatra's Barge Bar.

Colin and I hid out in here for an hour or so getting chummy before Corinne tracked us down. Bud's hosting a big dinner tonight in the Forum Dining Room. "He's making a Major Important Announcement," Corinne says. "And he says I have to lend you something to wear. He likes his women to dress up when they go out."

Colin snorts and says "what do you mean by 'his women'?" and Corinne looks daggers at him and tells me to meet her upstairs in the room Bud's rented for Polly in deference to her delicate condition. Colin says he'll come too but Corinne makes him go round up the guys and herd them to the campground showers.

As Colin leaves he tells me to watch my back. Does he know something that I don't? Anyway, I'm thrilled that he's being so protective of me.

• • • • • • • • ● • • • • • • • • •

Dorie put an emery board into her journal to mark her place and turned over onto her stomach. Going to the casino with Bud had been a hoot. She'd forgotten the incident at the roulette wheel and the flash of insight at her own naiveté that had followed. And Bud's uncanny skill at the craps table had been almost supernatural. Colin had told her later that he had watched him carefully and while he didn't seem to be doing anything illegal, the dice fell in his favor way more than the laws of probability allowed.

She scrunched her pillow into a more comfortable shape, sat up, and re-opened her journal. Her memory of the summer of 1978 was admittedly spotty but she knew what was coming up in the next entries. It was going to be interesting, if cringe-worthy, reading.

# Nineteen

Dorie had read only two sentences of the next journal entry when Phoebe interrupted her.

"Mom," she called from the hallway. "I'm still not talking to you but I need to borrow your hair gel. So I'm only coming in to get it, okay?"

Dorie hastily shut her journal and tucked it under the pillow. "Help yourself," she said. "Mi bano es tu bano."

Phoebe stalked past the bed into the bathroom and emerged with the hair gel with nary a glance in Dorie's direction. She was wrapped in a green bath towel that matched her eyes; her dark hair, still damp from the shower, curled in graceful tendrils down her back. She looked as fresh and innocent as a young fawn, and Dorie's heart ached for the inevitable loss of that innocence, a loss that would occur sooner or later despite everything she might do as a mother to delay it. Not that she was helping matters with her attacks on Phoebe's newfound faith.

"Phoebe," she said, "I'm really sorry I embarrassed you this morning. It was the last thing in the world I wanted to do."

Phoebe stopped in the doorway but didn't turn around "You think you know everything," she said over her shoulder. "But you don't even know what you're missing."

Dorie sighed. She could guess where this conversation was going. "What am I missing?" she asked.

"Love," Phoebe said, turning around and looking at her intently.

"But Phoebe, I love you. And even though you're mad at me half the time I think you love me too."

"That's not what I mean," Phoebe said, stamping her foot. "I know you love me and I do love you too. But I'm talking about a different kind of love. The kind where you just feel like you're surrounded by God's love and you want to..." she searched for the right words, "...you want to wrap your arms around the whole world and everything in it."

Dorie was taken aback. Phoebe could have been describing the kind of expansive joy she herself had experienced when she was with Bud. She was gratified that Phoebe, at her tender age, was capable of such emotional depth. If only she weren't being brainwashed into thinking Jesus Christ had a monopoly on transcendent love.

Dorie got up and walked over to Phoebe. She grasped her daughter's shoulders and held her so they were face to face.

"I do know what you're talking about, Phoebs. I don't believe in the Bible like you do, but I do know that feeling you describe." Even though, she admitted to herself, I haven't had it for a long, long time.

Phoebe shrugged but she didn't turn away. "Then why aren't you happy?"

Dorie dropped her hands and took a step back. "What do you mean? I'm happy. As happy as most people."

"No you aren't," Phoebe said. "Not really. You act cheerful and make jokes all the time but I see how you look when you think no one's around. You look sad. You think being funny hides it but it doesn't."

Dorie was floored. Everyone always described her as high energy, creative, and witty. Why was Phoebe so focused on the few times she was down in the dumps?

"I'll bring your hair gel back when I'm done with it," Phoebe said and padded out of the room leaving a trail of damp footprints.

Dorie was scraping the dinner dishes that evening when the phone rang. She punched the speaker button on the wall phone with a sticky index finger as she dumped the remains of Phoebe's salad in the garbage. Dinner had featured spinach omelets and long stretches of Phoebe-induced silence punctuated by very small talk. She was relieved to be alone in the kitchen.

"Hello? Dorie?" It was Doug.

"The wanderer returns," Dorie said. "How was Moab? Or are you still there and on your cell?"

"I'm home. But you sound like you're at the bottom of a well."

"Speakerphone." Dorie switched to the handset. "What's up?"

"I am calling," Doug said with exaggerated formality, "to request the honor of your company at dinner tomorrow evening. You may RSVP instantly and black tie will not be required. Because I'm only taking you to Joe's Cantina for burgers and beer."

"I'll have to consult my social secretary but I think I can fit that into my schedule. In fact, I'm sure I can if you promise to tell me who you were shacked up with last weekend when I called."

"That's the plan. I intend to wheedle my way back into your good graces. I'll even come out and pick you up like a real date."

Dorie thought about it for a minute and decided that this was another situation in which she wanted the option of leaving under her own power. Doug was saying the right things, but if the evening went south she didn't want to be trapped in a car with him all the way back to Rabbit Valley.

As she hung up she realized that she had two actual dates lined up. Which was two dates more than she had booked in the last year. Was it Sharon's cosmeceuticals or some massive realignment of planets in her house of relationships? She did a little boogie step as she put the butter back in the refrigerator. Life was good. Phoebe was wrong. She was perfectly happy.

"At the moment," added the unmistakable voice-of-Bud that had taken up residence inside her head. "At the moment."


The next morning Dorie woke up before the alarm went off. Viktor had said to bring the car in first thing on Monday so he could check the brakes and she intended to take advantage of his offer.

She parked outside the white concrete block building that housed Ace Foreign Car Repair. The overhead doors to the two-bay garage were open so she went in. The place was immaculate. The concrete floor was swept, tools were arranged in stainless steel caddies, and the back wall was lined with metal cabinets concealing the paraphernalia required to restore cars to health. She remembered her father telling her that you could you could pick a good mechanic by the way he took care of his tools. If that were true Viktor must indeed be an ace.

There didn't seem to be anyone around and she wondered if Viktor had forgotten their appointment. Maybe she'd arrived too soon, even though she'd delayed only a few minutes to apply blush and lip gloss and locate a flattering shell pink t-shirt in a basket of clean laundry. Or maybe he had second thoughts after their lunch and was going to renege on his offer.

She opened a side door that led to a small waiting room furnished with a wicker settee and chairs and an assortment of old magazines, mostly Field and Stream and Popular Mechanics. Another door, which was standing ajar, led to an office. On the wall to the left of the door a varnished wooden plaque adorned with decoupaged yellow roses proclaimed: "Believe on the Lord Jesus Christ and thou shalt be saved. Acts 16:31." Oh, give it a rest, people, Dorie thought. I'm just here to get my brakes fixed.

She heard the rustle of paper and the sound of a chair being pushed across the floor. A short woman with a round face framed in brown curls emerged from the adjoining office. She was holding a bunch of invoices in one hand and a coffee mug in the other. She smiled broadly when she saw Dorie.

"You must be Dorie," she said. "Viktor's told us all about you."

Dorie smiled and nodded as if this made sense. Viktor told his office staff about her? How odd.

"I'm Nancy," the woman said. "Frank's wife." Taking note of Dorie's obvious incomprehension, she added, "You know. Frank. Viktor's brother."

Dorie remembered that Viktor had said he was in partnership with his brother; he hadn't mentioned his brother's wife. Evidently the garage was a family business. But still, he'd told his brother and sister-in-law about her already? Dorie didn't know whether to be flattered or dismayed. She'd only had lunch with the man; they barely knew one another.

"Am I too early?" she said. "Viktor said to get here before eight."

"Oh no. He's expecting you. He's back in the parts room unpacking a UPS shipment. I'll call him."

"Don't bother. I'm here." Viktor appeared in the doorway from the garage. He had on work clothes, grey pants and a matching shirt with "ACE" embroidered in red on the pocket. He enveloped

Dorie in a bear hug that unnerved her until she remembered that hugging was the default Circle of Friends greeting.

"Good morning, sunshine," he said. "Good thing you got here early. We've got a full house. But don't worry. Your brakes are my number one priority."

He turned towards the doorway. "Frank, come on over. You got to meet Dorie."

Dorie heard a clatter of metal on concrete and a muffled exclamation.

"Oh oh," Nancy said, "Frank's dropsy strikes again."

"My baby brother is the world's clumsiest mechanic," Viktor explained. "We tease Jared that he takes after his uncle. But don't worry," he added. "I won't let Frank touch your car."

Nancy nudged Dorie "He's joking. Frank can fix anything. He just tries to do too many things at once."

Frank, a taller, younger, and more hirsute version of Viktor, entered from the garage, wiping his hands on a paper towel. "It's called multi-tasking," he said, "and you have to do it to get ahead." He extended a relatively clean hand in Dorie's direction.

"Glad to meet you. Viktor said you were a class act. I can see what he meant." He turned to his brother "Bout time you found yourself a real lady, Vik."

Dorie heard Nancy draw in her breath sharply. Viktor frowned.

"You guys better get to it," Nancy said quickly. "We'll be backed up until nine o'clock tonight if you don't get a move on."

What was that all about? Dorie wondered. Did Viktor usually date skanks? She didn't have time to pursue this disconcerting line of thought because Nancy was offering her a choice of coffee, tea, or orange juice, all of which she declined, and instructing her to make herself comfortable in the waiting room. She sat down in one of the wicker chairs and realized that, in her rush to leave, she'd forgotten to bring anything to read. She picked up a Field and Stream, which, having a photo of a handsome German Shorthaired Pointer on the cover, seemed marginally more interesting than Popular Mechanics.

Twenty minutes later she knew more about training bird dogs than she ever expected to, but she was spared from learning how to tie flies irresistible to cutthroat trout when Viktor opened the door to the waiting room.

"All fixed." he said. "You had a bad gasket in the master cylinder. Not a big deal after all. I replaced it and topped up the brake fluid. Should be just fine now." He had rolled his shirtsleeves above his elbows and he was wiping his hands with a paper towel.

Dorie was as impressed as if he were a surgeon coming out of the operating room to announce the successful excision of a malignant tumor. The inner workings of automobiles were a complete mystery to her. A man who could deal with all those complex, potentially dangerous moving parts was someone to be reckoned with. She looked at Viktor's grease-stained fingers, imagining them sliding down her back, caressing her buttocks. Get a grip, girl, she told herself. This isn't going that far.

"What do I owe you?" she asked Viktor.

"Not a thing," he said. "You can buy me a drink Thursday night. After we go bowling."

"Good enough," Dorie said, "but I think I'm getting the better part of the bargain."

Viktor smiled. "I wouldn't say that. I wouldn't say that at all."

Dorie paid careful attention to the behavior of the brakes on the way home. Viktor had told her to call him immediately if they got spongy again and he'd order a new master cylinder but so far they worked perfectly. It was a huge relief to have found a good mechanic in West Fork. "The Lord doth indeed provide," she said aloud. She wondered if Viktor would still be willing to take care of her car if they didn't develop a relationship. Surely his Christian principles would preclude leaving a lady in peril. Well, she'd deal with that problem when the time came.

Meanwhile, she had a bigger problem that required immediate action. The workshop on teaching multicultural literature was next Saturday. She'd waited too late to book a Denver flight so she'd have to drive to Boulder, which wasn't that distant as the crow flies but required a circuitous route by land due to the mountainous terrain. This meant departing Friday morning to arrive for the opening dinner and returning Sunday afternoon after the conference to avoid the expense of booking a room for an extra night. She'd have to call the student employment office and line up someone to stay at the house so Phoebe wouldn't be on her own for an entire weekend.

Suddenly she missed Colin. For all his faults he'd been a devoted father, willing to take Phoebe off her hands so she could prepare her classes and work on her book. More than willing, really. Much as she hated to admit it, Colin had preferred Phoebe's company over her own. Phoebe had been an unabashed Daddy's girl and Colin thrived on her adoration. She fed his ego, Dorie thought. I didn't. I couldn't bring myself to encourage his arrogance.

Distracted by this discomfiting memory she swerved into the left lane to avoid a cyclist and narrowly missed sideswiping a low -slung sports car. Its driver honked and gave her the finger. She felt her cheeks flush with embarrassment as she mouthed "sorry." My fault, she thought. As usual. Everything's been my own damn fault.

Dorie spent a few hours at her office working on next quarter's courses, then stopped at the natural foods market on the way home to pick up a few essentials: a supposedly sleep-inducing herbal tea for her insomnia, and some Dong Quoi capsules. She'd used up an entire bottle already with no discernable effects on her perimenopausal symptoms but maybe the herb was just slow to take effect. She added some baked cheese puffs to her basket. Phoebe loved them and a peace offering was clearly in order. Phoebe had gone to bed last night with no more than a curt nod in response to her own "good night" and "I love you."

When she got home she found Phoebe sprawled on the living room sofa reading a MacWorld. She didn't look up at Dorie's studiously cheerful greeting but turned a page and continued reading. Dorie took a deep, calming breath, put the grocery bag on the floor, and perched herself on the edge of the coffee table where Phoebe couldn't possibly ignore her.

"Okay my darling daughter. This sulking has gone on long enough. I've apologized for embarrassing you and I've come bearing gifts." She extracted the cheese puffs from the grocery bag and dangled them in front of Phoebe. "See? Junk food. Tangible proof of your mother's love. So snap out of it already."

Phoebe closed the magazine and took the bag of cheese puffs, holding it between her thumb and forefinger as if it contained toxic waste. "You have to promise me you won't do it again."

"Right. I promise. I will not trash the Bible to Pastor Charlie or any of your friends. And I won't ever mention evolution or stem cell research or, God forbid, abortion in front of them. Anything else?"

"Oh, Mother," Phoebe sighed, "could you just try to respect my feelings for a change?"

Dorie realized she had been inappropriately flippant. Phoebe's faith, and the friends that came with it, were dear to her heart. It wasn't okay to make fun of them.

"I'm sorry," she said. "That was mean of me."

She tossed the car keys to Phoebe and got up to take the groceries to the kitchen. "You can drive my car to work this afternoon. But you've got to come home by five because I need to go into town. I'm having an early dinner with Doug Brenner at Joe's Cantina."

Phoebe raised her eyebrows and opened her mouth in mock astonishment. "You've got, like, a date? With that cute guy at work?"

"Well, sort of. He invited me and he's paying. But we're just going to talk about stuff that's been happening at the college." And, she thought but didn't say, stuff that's been happening in Doug's bed. "So it's not a real date."

Phoebe rolled her eyes. "Whatever. Sounds like a real date to me."

Evidently mollified, she opened the cheese puffs and followed Dorie into the kitchen to help unpack the groceries. She also proposed an alternative when Dorie explained her plan for the weekend.

"Mom, I'm sixteen. You don't need to get a babysitter for me. But if you're really that worried I'll sleep over at Kimmi's. Mrs. Medderly likes for us to hang at their house. She says it makes her feel young."

"What about Mr. Medderly?"

"Oh, he does anything Mrs. Medderly tells him to."

"Somehow that doesn't surprise me."

"You don't have to be sarcastic. At least they don't fight all the time like you and Daddy did."

Dorie folded the paper grocery sack into a neat square and tucked it under the sink.

"We did not fight all the time. We had frequent and spirited discussions."

"You yelled. And sometimes you threw things. Don't think I was too little to remember because I do."

"Maybe you remember," Dorie said, trying to sound calm and reasonable, "but you don't understand. Your father was a complicated man. He wasn't easy to get along with."

"He was for me," Phoebe said and stalked out of the kitchen.

Dorie leaned her forehead against a cupboard door and closed her eyes. Oh no, she thought. Here we go again.

because of its proximity to the campus, rock-bottom prices, and gigantic TV to a sports channel. A collection of serapes and sombreros flanked the mirror behind the bar and the walls were plastered with autographed photos of the West Fork Wildcats, the CU Golden Buffs, and the Denver Broncos.

Dorie squinted in the dim light as she entered the long narrow room. She didn't see Doug at the bar or any of the tables. Just like him to be late, she thought. I should have made allowances.

"Dorie! Back here!"

She spied a hand waving from a booth at the rear of the room, then caught a glimpse of Doug's curly grey hair. When he stood up she saw was wearing jeans and a gaudy Aloha shirt printed with hibiscus blossoms and palm fronds.

"Nice duds," she said.

"Yeah. I dressed for dinner." He looked down at his shirt "Half of me, anyway."

"I didn't," Dorie said. She was still in the pink t-shirt she'd selected to impress Viktor with her femininity. "But I put on mascara." She batted her eyelashes. "See?"

"You look delectable, as always, my little Dorito." Doug sat down as she slid into the booth opposite him. "Excuse me, that should be Dorita."

"How was Moab?"

"Hot, dry and full of yahoos in Jeeps. But Tony and I had a great time once we got out of town onto the slickrock trails."

Why does he go biking with students, Dorie mused. Doesn't he have any friends his own age?

Doug poured her a glass of pale ale from the pitcher on the table. She took a long swallow. It was icy cold, faintly bitter, and instantly refreshing. She hadn't been to a bar for so long that she'd forgotten how good draft beer could be.

"Let's order now," Doug said, "so I can confess my sins without being interrupted."

"Good idea. I wouldn't want some innocent young waitress overhearing the sordid details."

They both ordered Joe's specialty, half-pound charbroiled burgers on sourdough rolls, plus sweet potato fries and coleslaw to share. Student food, Dorie thought. Doug probably lives on this kind of stuff. She pictured her refined bistro lunch with Viktor. New Zealand Sauvignon Blanc. Caesar salad. Tarte tatin for dessert. Grown-up food.

"So you want to know what was going on when you called me last week?" Doug said.

"Well, yes. I mean, you keep asking me to have dinner and then I call to take you up on it and you're having an intimate moment with some female person I don't know anything about. I think an explanation might be in order."

"Fair enough. The woman…"

"Woman? She sounded like she was about fourteen."

"The woman…" Doug gave the two syllables an exaggerated emphasis, "was a poet…"

"Well, that explains everything, doesn't it?"

"Will you be quiet so I can speak in something other than sentence fragments?"

Dorie clapped her hand over her mouth and nodded.

"The woman was one of the referees at the poetry slam. She was also an old girlfriend whom I hadn't seen for years. We had a completely unpremeditated intimate moment, as you call it. Your basic auld lang syne fuck."

Dorie laughed. Doug's confession was so straightforward and relaxed that he must be telling the truth. Or part of it. She wasn't going to let him off the hook just yet.

"If she's a poet she must be a child prodigy. I could actually hear her whining over the phone."

"Good grief, Dorie, she's in her thirties."

"How far in?"

"Not very. But what does it matter? I had a brief and uninteresting relationship with her. I can see the possibility of a long and extremely interesting relationship with you but you keep putting me off. You've got to get over your obsession with your age."

"I can't," Dorie said," I get these hot flashes that tell me the egg factory's shutting down. From a Darwinian point of view I'm obsolete."

Doug groaned.

"What did I say?" Dorie asked.

"Darwin. It reminded me of the other thing I need to tell you about."

Their burgers arrived and they stopped talking to doctor them with condiments and to discuss salting the French fries.

"I don't use much salt," Dorie said. "It makes me thirsty."

"I don't either," Doug said. "See? We're more compatible than you think. Where do you stand on sleeping with the window open?"

Dorie redirected the conversation into neutral territory. "What's the other thing you wanted to tell me about?"

Doug set his beer glass down and shook his head. "It's this mess with the Dean. I told you Drescher was ticked off about the poetry slam, didn't I?"

Dorie nodded.

"Well, I found out what got to him. A formal complaint from the Campus Christian Coalition. It wasn't just the street language that offended them. They didn't like the topics of the poems."

"These Christians are coming out of the woodwork," Dorie said. "We lions don't stand a chance. What was it they didn't like?"

"A couple of pieces were celebrations of being gay. You know, kids discovering their identity and proclaiming it to the world. Then there was the usual railing against ethnic injustice with four letter epithets hurled at authority figures. And last, but not least, a really sophisticated piece by a skinny little girl from Fort Collins called 'The Revolution of the Species.' About how humans are probably going to self-destruct because we're more violent than the apes we're descended from."

Dorie wiped a bit of beer froth off her upper lip. "I wouldn't disagree with that. But what do these Coalition people want Drescher to do?"

"Ban the poetry slams. They claim they're offensive to good Christian students and a bad influence on impressionable freshmen."

"What does Drescher say to this?"

"You know he's as conservative as they come. He more or less agreed with the Coalition. He says the slams are unnecessarily controversial and since non-students participate, the English department has no business sponsoring them."

Dorie squirted a puddle of ketchup onto her plate and dunked an especially crispy French fry. She bit off the end with more force than necessary. Drescher was a prick, an ambitious administrator who probably dreamt of ascending from his deanship to the provost's office. He wouldn't want any controversy blotting his record.

"This stinks," she said. "What are you going to do?"

Doug poked at his coleslaw with his fork. He looked as angry as Dorie had ever seen him.

"I'm not giving in. The poetry slams get a lot of kids turned on to reading and writing. Especially minority kids who'd never go near a book otherwise. And writing poems, even if they sound like hip hop cliches, helps them sort out their feelings."

He pushed his plate away. "I don't know what I'm going to do. But I'm not going to let these kids down."

This was a side of Doug Dorie hadn't seen before. He was, she realized, more than an activist poet; he was a dedicated teacher.

"Good for you," she said. "What's the point of public education if it doesn't reach the public?"

"Speaking of which," Doug said, "are you going to that multicultural thing at CU?"

Dorie confessed that she'd procrastinated about getting a plane ticket until it was too late. "So now I have to drive, which is a royal pain in the butt."

"No, it isn't. It's a scenic road trip. I'm going up Friday and coming back Sunday. Why don't you ride with me?"

Dorie thought for a second; if she rode with Doug she could leave her car for Phoebe so she could drive to her barista job. On the other hand, if she rode with Doug they'd be together in a very small enclosed space for a very long time. What if they ran out of things to talk about? They couldn't fill the silence with NPR and country-western music because there were too many dead spots in the mountains without radio reception. And what if he made a pass at her? She couldn't very well jump out of the car and hop a cattle truck back to West Fork.

"Thanks," she said, "but I better drive myself in case I have to get back early."

Doug shrugged. "Okay. But if you change your mind let me know. I'm an excellent traveling companion. I know all the words to 'Bobby McGee' and I never fall asleep at the wheel." He tapped his head with his forefinger. "It's all a matter of paying attention."

Dorie smiled; he sounded like Bud, who was always reminding everyone to be attentive. Maybe a road trip actually might be fun.

"Okay," she said," I'll let you know."

When Dorie got home she was surprised to see Jared's red truck parked in her driveway. She assumed the sound of the garage door opening would announce her arrival so that Jared and Phoebe wouldn't be caught in a compromising position on the living room sofa. Or, worse yet, in Phoebe's bedroom. Although it was more likely they'd be eating popcorn and watching HBO while saving themselves for marriage.

Nevertheless, maybe she'd better have another facts-of-life discussion with Phoebe. She'd done the birds, bees and disease talk years ago but it might be time for a review of the emotional pitfalls of premature sexual activity.

She was relieved to find Jared and Phoebe in the kitchen making Toll House cookies. The aroma of baking chocolate filled the room, along with the staccato beat of rap music issuing from Phoebe's boom box. Dorie caught a scrap of the refrain: "burn it, turn it, gotta learn it, God's way to-day, ain't no othah way."

Christian rap, she observed, was just as ungrammatical as the secular variety.

"Hello, Mrs. Winslow," Jared said. "We've kind of taken over your kitchen."

"No problem. Mi cocina es su cocina. And I love your outfit." Jared was wearing a red and yellow floral print calico apron that she'd bought at a crafts fair back in Newton.

"I made him put on your apron," Phoebe said. "So he wouldn't mess up his new clothes. Look what Kimmi and I picked out for him yesterday." She pulled the apron aside.

"Very spiffy," Dorie said, taking in the oversize black cargo pants and black and grey camouflage print shirt that hung off Jared's shoulders like a collapsing duck blind. She didn't understand this craze for voluminous clothing; drooping wide-legged pants and elbow-length short sleeves made the wearer look like a hairless orangutan.

"Jared doesn't like to spend money on himself," Phoebe said, "do you J. J.?" She put her arm around his waist and leaned into his side. "But we told him he owed it to the band to look good."

Jared looked dubious. "Maybe, but there are lots of people who need new clothes way more than I do."

"That doesn't seem to worry Pastor Charlie," Dorie said. "That suit he wore yesterday cost a bundle."

Phoebe shot her a warning look.

"Sorry," Dorie said, and busied herself with rinsing the remnants of cookie dough out of the mixing bowl. She really had to remember to mute herself whenever anything remotely related to Circle of Friends came up.

The timer on the oven buzzed. Jared grabbed a potholder and took out the cookies. They were nicely browned and their cracked tops revealed satisfyingly sticky interiors. Phoebe took a spatula from the crockery pot of utensils by the stove and began transferring them to a plate to cool.

Dorie felt an uncomfortable hollowing in her gut. The scene was so cozily domestic. She could see Phoebe as a young wife, if not Jared's, then some other man's. A man who would supplant her as the primary person in her daughter's life.

Jared broke off a bit of warm cookie and turned to Phoebe. "Sweets for the sweet. Open wide." He popped the morsel in her mouth. Phoebe smiled up at him and then offered the plate to Dorie.

"These are excellent," Dorie said. "Even better than my caramel squares. My compliments to the chefs." She might as well start practicing being a gracious mother-in-law.

"Oh, Mom, I almost forgot "Phoebe said. "I can't stay with Kimberly this weekend 'cause they're all going to see her grandmother in Salt Lake and they won't be back 'til Sunday night."

Dorie considered the alternatives. Phoebe couldn't stay with Viktor and Jared without straining the boundaries of Christian propriety. Amber's family lived in a semi-rural area east of town, too far to drive Phoebe to work and back on Friday.

"How about staying with Nicole?"

Phoebe hesitated. "I guess I could."

Dorie sensed reluctance. "But you'd rather not?"

"Uh huh. Nicole and I aren't that close, you know? And her mom is,like, a major neat freak. None of us really like going over there. Why can't I just stay home? It's only two nights."

Dorie thought a moment. Maybe her daughter was old enough to survive a weekend on her own.

"Phoebe, would you really be okay staying home alone? I can ask Sharon to check in on you every day and I'll catch a ride with Doug and leave you my car so you won't be stranded."

Phoebe nodded vigorously. "Like I said, I'll be fine. I'll just use the car to get to work. And I'll even water your plants."

"Don't worry, Mrs. Winslow," Jared said. "I'll make sure Phoebe's all right. And if something goes wrong with the car or house or anything my dad can fix it."

Dorie considered his proposal. From what she'd seen of Viktor this morning she had no doubt he could cope with anything from a broken pipe to a bear raid on the garbage can.

"Okay," she said. "We've got a plan. I can trust you both to behave yourselves, can't I?"

"Muh-ther, of course you can," Phoebe said. "But what about you?"

"Me?"

"Well, yes. You just came home from a date with this Doug guy. So now you're, like, doing a road trip with him?"

"Phoebe, it wasn't a real date. Doug's a colleague, not a boyfriend. And this trip is strictly business."

"Uh-huh." Phoebe raised an eyebrow. "Whatever you say. But you better call me every night so I know you're okay."

Dorie stifled a smile. Just who was the parent here?

"Sure thing, babe," she agreed. "I'll check in a couple times a day. Leave your cell phone on."

It's a good thing, she thought, as she left the kitchen, that Phoebe doesn't know I have a real date with Viktor Thursday night.

## Twenty-One

Dorie was rudely awakened Wednesday morning by the strident ring of her bedside phone. She'd been up late the night before editing chapter five of her Hawthorne book, in which she compared Rappacini's doomed daughter to Lisa Marie Presley, and she intended to sleep in as a reward.

She fumbled for the handset, jammed it against her ear without raising her head from the pillow and mumbled hello.

"Dorie, it's Doug. I'm truly sorry to bother you this early but I've got a problem and through no fault of your own you're part of the solution." He sounded so distressed that Dorie's irritation at being awakened vanished instantly.

"What's going on?" she asked.

" Drescher and I had a blowup over the poetry thing and I'm persona non grata on campus for a while. Actually I've been suspended. Drescher wanted me to cancel the upcoming poetry circus and I refused. Said I'd hold the damn thing in the quadrangle if I wasn't allowed to use the auditorium. And I'm afraid I delivered a little lecture on the moral responsibility of publicly funded colleges, too. He didn't take it well."

"Probably not the best move, Doug. So how do I come into this?"

"Someone's got to take over my classes these last two weeks of the term and the head of the English department suggested you might pitch in since you're not doing anything."

Dorie sat upright in bed. "I am so. I'm trying to finish my stupid Hawthorne book."

Doug groaned. "Sorry about that. I forgot. Anyway, it's only two classes. Expository writing this morning and contemporary American poetry tomorrow afternoon. And I really am sorry you got dragged into this. I just don't want to leave my kids in the lurch."

Dorie felt a twinge of guilt for her outrage.

"No worries. I'll do it. I might even learn to like rap, or whatever you pass off as contemporary poetry."

"I'm more conventional than you think," Doug said. "Tomorrow's class is on Charles Simic."

He instructed her to stop by his office where Tony would give her the class rosters and course outlines. He apologized again for getting her involved.

"I don't have the patience for academic politics," he said. "At least not the way Drescher plays the game. I might have to look at some alternatives."

"You're not going to quit are you?" Dorie was unaccountably alarmed at the prospect of Doug's leaving West Fork. No one else in the English Department shared their irreverent outsider view of the world. Her impromptu interoffice visits with Doug were the sole spice in her otherwise bland workdays.

"I don't want to leave West Fork. The biking's world class out here and I love my students. But I need a stable situation and I'm not sure that will ever happen under Drescher."

"Since when is the renegade poet worried about stability?"

"Since that last trip in Moab," Doug said. "My back hurt so much I had to take two Advil just to get out of bed. I'm getting old, Dorie. I want a steady paycheck and a nice wife to take care of me when I'm sixty-four. Think about it. Inside this hunky semi-young body beats the heart of a potential codger."

Dorie smiled. Doug's creative declarations of romantic intent always gave her a lift.

"Speaking of trips," she said. "I need a ride to Boulder after all. Are you still going to the workshop?"

"Of course. Why wouldn't I?"

"Well, "Dorie weighed her words," I sort of thought you might be so pissed at the system that you'd boycott it."

There was a moment of silence on the other end of the line. Then Doug spoke. "I'm one of the presenters for the poetry section. I'm hardly going to pick up my marbles and go home just because I had a run-in with a narrow-minded administrator."

There was an edge to his voice and Dorie realized that she'd insulted him.

"Sorry," she said. "My fault. I always see you as this free-wheeling Bob Dylan type."

Doug laughed, apparently mollified. "The only thing I have in common with Dylan is big hair, you ninny."


Dorie dropped Phoebe and her bike, which fit neatly into the back of the Subaru, at the coffee house on her way to the campus. Phoebe's shift didn't begin for an hour but she was happy to leave early and skip four miles of pedaling to get to town.

"Mom, you look half dead," Phoebe said as she unloaded her bike. "Wait a sec and I'll make you a latte."

"'Not a morning person' doesn't even begin to describe me," Dorie said. "Make it a triple shot." She leaned back against the headrest and closed her eyes.

Phoebe returned with a tall paper cup and thrust it under her nose. She inhaled the fragrant steam. "Mmmm. The elixir of life."

"Since when are you getting off on coffee?" Phoebe said, leaning on the open window. "You're the world's biggest tea freak."

"This is an emergency, "Dorie said. She took a sip of her latte. The hot, milky brew was both bracing and comforting and her mood improved instantly. "I've got to face Doug's writing students in an hour and talk about creating dramatic structure in essays. About which I know nothing. So I've got to fake it, which requires being awake."

"Why are you teaching Doug's class?"

Dorie saw an opportunity to make a point. "Because a bunch of high school kids used four-letter words in a poetry slam and offended some college Christian group."

Phoebe looked puzzled and Dorie realized she hadn't answered her question.

"The Dean asked Doug to cancel his poetry slams because the Campus Christian Coalition finds the content offensive. Doug refused and the Dean suspended him. So now I have to take over his classes for the rest of the term."

Phoebe shook her head slowly. "I don't understand. What was so bad about the slams?"

Dorie cradled the coffee cup in both hands. Its warmth soothed her stiff fingers.

"According to Doug, nothing more than some street language and expressions of gay pride. And a poem about how the apes we're descended from are nicer than we are."

Phoebe fingered a strand of hair as she considered this. "Maybe that Christian group is right. I mean, going on about that stuff in public kind of glorifies it, you know? If I had kids I wouldn't want them seeing other kids getting prizes and everything for swearing and dissing everything."

"Well then you could just keep them at home, couldn't you? We're talking about censorship of free expression. In a public forum. You Christians …" Dorie hastily corrected herself. "I mean some Christians think they've got a monopoly on the truth."

Phoebe stiffened and pulled back from the car window.

Dorie put her hand on her daughter's arm. "I'm not trying to knock your faith, baby, I just don't want to see a replay of the Spanish Inquisition in my own backyard."

Phoebe stared at her impassively. "I bet you wouldn't like it if it was me up there yelling 'fuck' and 'shit' and talking about blowing up everything I was against."

"Maybe not, but I'd defend your right to do it. Especially if your free verse scanned."

She handed Phoebe the empty coffee cup. "Thanks for the pick-me-up. Have a good day. And remember, your mama loves you, even if she's a heathen."

Phoebe sighed and shook her head. "Mom, what am I going to do with you?"

"Just use your head," Dorie said. "Think critically about what people tell you. Then take your leap of faith. That's all I want."


Tony Gomez was sitting in Doug's office chair with his feet up on the desk when Dorie arrived.

"Tony!" she said. "You look downright professorial."

"Thanks, Dr. W.," Tony shot her a sly sideways grin. "I'm developing a taste for the academic life style. It sure beats herding sheep."

Dorie chuckled. She loved Tony's deadpan humor. She could see him succeeding Sherman Alexie on the literary lecture circuit in the near future.

Tony extracted some folders from an untidy pile on the desk. "Here's everything you need to wing it through the next two weeks. The expos class is a piece of cake but the poetry kids can get rowdy. Just stay loose with them and you'll have a ball."

Dorie gave him a thumbs up.

"No problem. Believe it or not, I too can be a with-it-happening kind of prof. Even if I wasn't a hippie ski bum like Doug. I have a more colorful past than you think." She was tempted to tell Tony that she'd hung out with one of the more outrageous gurus of the seventies but restrained herself. The TAs were notorious gossips and her image might end up a little too tarnished.

Tony tapped a pencil against his teeth.

"Interesting, I'll pass that on to the boss."

"What's the boss up to, anyway? Now that he's got all this free time."

"Working on an illustrated narrative poem he's been playing around with. He's already got a publisher lined up."

Dorie felt a twinge of professional jealousy. "What's it about?" she said, trying to sound pleasantly interested rather than enviously curious.

Tony swung his feet off the desk and sat up straight. "It's a kid's book. A take-off on the Odyssey showing how heroes aren't always fearless and invincible. Half the time they're scared shitless—pardon my language—and the other half they're crazy egotists who start wars that don't solve anything."

Dorie nodded. She had to hand it to Doug; he really did put his money where his mouth was.

"Who's doing the illustrations?" she asked.

"Doug, of course."

"You're kidding me."

"You didn't know he painted?"

Dorie confessed that she didn't.

Ton tilted back in the desk chair.

"Well, he does. In egg tempera. Tried to get me into it but, man, that stuff is tricky to work with. Doug's really good though."

"Wow," Dorie said. "I'm impressed. Guess there's a lot about Doug I don't know."

Tony nodded. "You got that right, Dr. W. You might consider taking the time to find out."


Dorie got through the expository writing class with minimal effort by having the students pair up and critique each other's essays. The topic Doug had assigned, "What I Didn't Do Last Summer," seemed to have inspired a certain amount of soul-searching regarding contemporary political issues. Dorie suspected Doug might have prefaced the assignment with a lecture on the civic responsibility of social activism rather than simply emphasizing the importance of critical thinking and logic.

She got home by noon, intending to go straight to her study and work, but as she pulled into her driveway she saw Sharon unloading grocery bags and twins from her minivan.

"Sharon," she called. "Hold up and I'll give you hand."

Dorie sprinted across the lawn and grabbed a package of Fig Newtons from Stuart, who was trying to bite through the plastic wrapping while Russell flung himself on the ground in a heel-pounding tantrum after an unsuccessful attempt to wrest the cookies from his brother.

"Kiddos, you don't really want these," she said. "They'll rot your teeth and make you even more hyper than you already are." She pulled Russell to his feet with one hand and took the last grocery bag out of the car with the other.

"Listen to Dorie," Sharon said. "She's a doctor."

"Not that kind that helps people," Dorie said. "What's in this bag, anyway? Lead bricks?"

"Couple gallons milk. We should buy stock in Meadow Gold. Come on in. I'll make you lunch if you don't mind leftover tuna salad."

Dorie followed Sharon to the kitchen via the garage, which was littered with red, yellow, and blue plastic trikes, scooters, and wagons. She helped Sharon stow the groceries and clear bowls of congealed cornflakes and puddles of orange juice from the kitchen table while the twins entertained themselves by building towers with the canned goods.

"Would you believe I used to keep a clean house?" Sharon asked as she set out a loaf of sliced bread and a plastic container of tuna salad. "I had no idea how kids were going to change my life. Maybe if I'd had 'em one at a time like normal people do it would have been easier."

"That reminds me," Dorie said, "I need you to keep an eye on Phoebe this weekend if you can. I've got to go to Boulder on Friday for a conference and I won't be back until Sunday night. I have a ride so I'm leaving the car for Phoebe to drive to work. I told her to call you if anything goes wrong."

Sharon whistled. "You leaving her alone all weekend? Aren't you worried about a bunch of kids coming over and drinking your booze and smoking joints and burning the house down?"

Dorie shook her head. "Not Phoebe's friends. They don't do mind-altering substances. They all belong to Teens for Christ."

"What's that?"

"The youth group at that Circle of Friends in Christ church over on the east side."

"Oh, yeah," Sharon said, nodding vigorously. "We've been there. They have this amazing child care program. You walk in the door and they give your kids an ID badge and log 'em in the computer and whisk 'em away and you get a whole hour and a half to yourself. You can go to the service and then have coffee before you see the little monsters again. It's great. Greg and I are thinking about joining."

Dorie swallowed a bite of tuna salad sandwich and washed it down with a swig of instant iced tea. Someone at Circle of Friends, she thought, knows what sells to parents and I'll bet that someone is Janelle.

Sharon wrote her cell phone number on the back of the grocery store receipt and assured Dorie that Phoebe could call her any time of day or night. "And if something goes really wrong," she added, "I'll send Greg over with a softball bat."

"I'm sure everything will be fine," Dorie said. "The worst thing that ever happens in Rabbit Valley is when the power goes out during Monday Night Football."

# Twenty-Two

On Thursday afternoon, Dorie was finishing the footnotes to chapter five of her Hawthorne book when Phoebe called to say she wouldn't need a ride home. Jared was picking her up so they could catch an early half-price movie.

"We're going to meet Chris and Kimmi for Mexican food afterwards so you don't need to worry about dinner, Mom. I'll be home about nine."

"No problem, Phoebs. I've got plans tonight too."

"I bet you're meeting Doug, aren't you?"

"Uh, no." Dorie thought fast. She didn't want to say she was going out with the FortySomething Fellowship. She knew Phoebe would ask why, which would require some verbal subterfuge to avoid mentioning Viktor.

She settled on a partial truth. "I'm trying to broaden my social horizons. I'm going bowling at Riverside Lanes with some people I met at your church."

"Mom, that's great. Maybe you'll make some friends."

Phoebe sounded so genuinely delighted that Dorie almost regretted her deception. She hoped Viktor had been discreet enough not to say anything about their date to Jared so she could get this flirtation out of her system with Phoebe none the wiser.

"I should be home early, Phoebs," she said. "It's not likely I'll be hitting the afterhours clubs with this bunch."

Phoebe laughed. "I won't wait up. Just don't do anything I wouldn't do."

At six p.m. Dorie shut down her computer and went upstairs to take a shower and get dressed. She had no idea what constituted proper attire when bowling for Jesus. A Roseanne Barr combo of sweatshirt and baggy pants? A polyester shirt with a nickname embroidered on the back? She settled on her favorite khaki pants and a black sleeveless turtleneck that bared her taut triceps, a byproduct of digging thirty pounds of soil amendments into her perennial bed. Viktor should be impressed.

Her stomach felt a bit unsettled so she stopped in the kitchen to drink a glass of milk before she left. *Why am I so nervous,* she wondered. *I'm just going bowling. With a completely unsuitable man to whom I'm irrationally attracted and his provincial fundamentalist friends with whom I have absolutely nothing in common. There's no reason to be nervous.*

*Unless you're thinking about doing something you shouldn't,* whispered the voice-of-Bud from somewhere near her left temple.

"Of course I'm not," she snapped. "I may be horny but I'm not stupid."

Riverside Lanes was in a strip mall on the south side of town. Dorie had passed it on her frequent trips to Home Depot's garden department, but she'd never really looked at it. Bowling alleys, along with pool halls, roller rinks and bars with shiny tile facades and oval windows, were relegated to a shadowy category in her mental yellow pages best described as "lower class hangouts."

As she searched for a parking space, she observed that this particular lower class hangout was relatively upscale. "Riverside Lanes" was spelled out in neon lights: hot pink art deco letters flanked by glowing green bowling pins. The double entry doors were fashionable brushed stainless steel with a surround of glass brick.

She spotted Viktor standing in the recessed entryway as she made her way up the walk from the parking lot. He was leaning against the wall with his hands in the pockets of his faded jeans. A big, welcoming smile brightened his face when he saw her. That was reassuring, but Dorie was more impressed by the way his navy polo shirt stretched tautly over his well-developed pecs.

I'm sure he lifts weights, she thought hazily, as she approached him. No way he could get those muscles from tightening lugnuts.

As Viktor opened his arms to envelop her in the de rigueur Circle of Friends greeting hug, she noted the glint of a small silver cross in the tangle of dark chest hair peeping through the open placket of his shirt. Her heart thumped erratically. He was such an enticing mixture of sacred and profane. A Christian wine buff, a tradesman from the wrong side of the tracks with European savoir faire and an educated palate. Perhaps, just perhaps, they could bridge their cultural and social differences.

Or maybe not. Viktor's neck reeked of an aftershave that smelled suspiciously like Old Spice. She pivoted to the side but allowed his arm to remain around her shoulders.

"How's the car running?" he asked.

"Just fine. Better yet, it's stopping. The brakes haven't gotten squishy at all. I really appreciate what you did."

"No problem. It was a good excuse to get to know you better."

Dorie felt a pleasant flush warm her cheeks. Viktor was so mature and straightforward, such a contrast to Doug with his boyish jokes and flirtatious banter.

Viktor took her arm as they walked across the parking lot and her skin tingled at the light pressure of his fingertips. She moved forward in a kind of liquid daze; she felt as if she were floating in warm water. I wonder, she mused, if he's a good dancer. An image of herself and Viktor plastered together crotch-to-crotch in an Argentine tango flickered through her mind.

Her reverie ended abruptly when Viktor opened the door to Riverside Lanes. She was assaulted by a mélange of rumbles, echoing crashes, loud voices and pulsating music, accompanied by the aroma of deep-fried junk food and beer.

She blinked in the glare of the fluorescent lights, trying to focus. The blonde wood bowling alleys gleamed under an even brighter array of overhead spotlights. Vividly colored balls clattered down the alleys while electronic displays flashed animated replicas of the ensuing collisions with pins. The sensory bombardment reminded Dorie of Bud's description of one of the lower Bardo states; the only missing element was smoke, which undoubtedly would have been present if it weren't for the anti-tobacco lobby.

"Wow," she said. "This is a little overwhelming."

"You've never been bowling?" Viktor sounded surprised.

"I've led a sheltered life," she said. "Trapped in an ivory tower."

She surveyed her surroundings. To her left a young man with a gelled pompadour presided over a counter backed by racks of multi-colored leather shoes. Shoes that had been occupied by the possibly unwashed feet of many strangers.

"Do you have to wear those things?" Dorie eyed them dubiously. She'd come in her running shoes, assuming that they would supply whatever traction was required to heave a plastic ball at a cluster of wooden clubs.

Viktor patted her shoulder.

"My, my, my, you are an innocent. But don't worry. I'll teach you everything you need to know."

Dorie slid her eyes sideways and looked up at him with a half smile. "Okay. I defer to your expertise."

"I like the sound of that." He gave her shoulder a little squeeze that sent an electric shock directly to the pit of her stomach.

"Viktor! We're over here." Someone hailed them from one of the semicircular booths lining the lounge area. Dorie did a double take. The booths were upholstered in acid green vinyl so authentically retro it must have been left over from the seventies.

"Hey, Rick, we'll be there in a sec." Viktor waved a greeting in the direction of the unseen speaker." I've got to get my date some shoes."

He called me his date, Dorie thought. Does that mean he's going to pay? And if so, what might that entail? She reached into her shoulder bag to locate her wallet. She didn't want to incur any undefined sexual obligations by letting Viktor pay her way. Although surely in evangelical circles the tacit rule that if the man pays the woman puts out wouldn't apply.

The issue was resolved by allowing Viktor to take charge of shoe selection. He rejected three pairs as too worn and ordered the pompadoured youth to find a new pair. "The best for the best," he insisted. Dorie took advantage of this diversion and placed a twenty dollar bill on the counter. Viktor protested, but Dorie pushed the money at the clerk.

"Here," she said. "This is for the shoes and whatever it costs to bowl."

"Okay, be a liberated woman if you have to," Viktor said. "But for sure I'm buying the drinks afterwards."

Dorie did a quick calculation as she received her change. If her drink cost less than the shoe rental and bowling fee she'd still be social-debt free at the end of the evening. She made a mental note to have only one glass of wine in order to keep it that way.

Viktor insisted on carrying her newly acquired footwear to the booth where the FortySomething Fellows were waiting. The man who had hailed them was sitting on the near end of the semi-circular bench next to a brunette in a metallic knit tank top that clung to her shapely bosom. To her left sat two grey-haired women, decidedly more Something than Forty.

The man unfolded himself from the booth and extended his hand to Dorie. He had the rangy physique of a college basketball player topped by a freckled face and rust -red hair.

"Hi, there," he said. "I'm Rick Tibbetts. Welcome to our fellowship. Hottest bunch of God-loving singles in the world. We're glad to have you even if you did come with this ol' booger here." He grinned and punched Viktor lightly in the biceps. Viktor returned the favor by pounding him on the back.

When the male bonding rituals were concluded, Dorie introduced herself to the other occupants of the booth. The two older women, Edith and Barbara, greeted her warmly. The brunette stifled a yawn.

"Scusi," she said. "Late night. I'm Angela Chavez. I think my daughter Nicole is friends with your little Penny."

"Phoebe," Dorie said. "Her name's Phoebe."

So this was Angela, neat freak, power broker, and mother of precocious Nicole, who would probably be jail bait if she weren't a Teen for Christ.

Angela ignored Dorie's correction. "Hey there, Vik," she purred. Her crimsoned lips parted to reveal the tip of her tongue caught between her teeth.

This woman is about as subtle as Mae West, Dorie thought. No wonder Viktor's running scared.

Viktor, however, appeared anything but intimidated. He stepped forward and leaned over the back of the booth to nuzzle the side of Angela's head in a masculine version of an air kiss. Angela reached up and put one arm around his shoulders, sliding a languid hand over the back of his neck. This, Dorie reflected, was not your standard Circle of Friends greeting hug.

"Dorie!" A high-pitched shriek emanated from the adjacent booth and Tracey Enright popped into view. "I thought it was you. Look guys, it's Dorie. You remember Dorie, don't you?"

The two men sharing Tracey's booth swiveled towards Dorie. She recognized one immediately: Paul Greenberg. Paul, thought Dorie, was just the kind of perennially lonely guy who always showed up at singles groups.

The other one, much to her surprise, was Herbert Baskin. She'd assumed he was married. At any rate, he was hardly the type to be out on the town looking for a hookup.

"My goodness, what a pleasure!" Herbert extended a boney arm and beckoned to her. "Plenty of room here, right by me."

Dorie smiled weakly. She didn't want to sit in Herbert's booth, much less by Herbert. She wanted to sit by Viktor and Angela Chavez so she could figure out what was going on between them.

Tracey intervened. "You guys should sit together." She winked conspiratorially at Dorie and Viktor. "I'll go next door." She got up and moved to Rick's booth as Paul Greenberg gazed at her like a hungry dog watching his dinner dish being taken away.

"Scootch down, Rick," Tracey said, edging her jeans-clad rump onto the bench next to him. "This is your lucky night. You're the meat in a girl sandwich."

Rick scootched to his left, towards Angela. Angela frowned but accommodated him by moving towards Edith and Barbara, who looked increasingly ill at ease, perhaps sensing their position on the precarious end of the age continuum as well as the bench.

With everyone properly seated, Rick distributed soft drinks, pretzels and chips and instructed them to "get to know your neighbors before the games begin."

Dorie managed to control herself during the chitchat about families, home towns, and Circle of Friends activities by nodding politely and uttering benign platitudes that couldn't possibly challenge anyone's core beliefs. No sense in making a mess of things for Viktor the way she had for Phoebe.

Anyway, as far as she could tell, the FortySomething Fellowship wasn't that different from the various singles meet-up groups she'd sampled during the early years of her widowhood.

Then Rick rose to his feet and addressed the occupants of both booths. "Okay folks," he said cheerily, "Time to have a word with the Lord before we get out there and smoke up those lanes." He bent his head, revealing a spot of shiny pink scalp on the crown of his head. Everyone promptly assumed prayer position while Dorie looked on in amazement.

"Dear Lord," Rick began, "we thank you for the opportunity to gather together in good Christian fellowship. We thank you that we are sound in body and can enjoy this wholesome recreation. Especially since there are some who can't on account of they've lost limbs and such in the defense of our country. In Jesus' name, Amen."

Viktor nudged Dorie. "Rick's an ex-Marine," he whispered. "He feels very strongly about the war in the Middle East."

"I see," Dorie said, and added politics to her list of taboo topics. At this rate she'd be reduced to conversations about movies, restaurants, and the weather.

"Time to rock and roll," Rick said. "Let's choose up teams and get going."

Teams? Dorie hadn't expected an evening of competitive sport. She was flooded with shameful memories of being the last one chosen for volleyball in junior high. While she was no couch potato, activities involving speeding balls had never been her forte.

Viktor must have sensed her discomfort as he intervened.

"Good enough, Rick. Why don't we split up by tables? Your table against mine."

Rick considered this. "Okay, but we need to shuffle folks around a little. To kind of even things out, you know? Cause Edith and Barbara told me they've only bowled a couple of times. So I shouldn't have to take them both for my team."

"I've never bowled at all," Dorie said, "so two of them should equal one of me."

"Here's what we'll do," Viktor said, sliding out from the booth. "I'll trade you Herbert for Edith. Then it'll be me and Dorie and Edith and Paul versus you and Angela and Barbara and Herbert."

"What about me?" Tracey asked. "Which team am I on?"

"You can be on our team," Paul said. He looked at Viktor for support.

"But that makes the teams uneven," Herbert said. "There are five people on yours and four on ours."

"Nine people don't divide equally, Herbert," Angela said. "The teams have to be uneven. You adjust the score at the end with a little simple math."

"How do you do that? "They'll have more points than we do."

"You add a blind score for the missing player, Herbert. One twenty for a woman and one fifty for a man." Angela said. "That's the way it's always done." She turned her back on him dismissively.

Dorie decided that should the occasion arise to sell her house she would refuse bids from any and all buyers represented by Angela; the thought of negotiating a business deal with her was terrifying.

After a small commotion involving the disposition of shoes, purses and sodas, Team Rick and Team Viktor assembled at Lanes Eight and Nine and prepared to do battle.

"Okay, everybody," Viktor said. "Choose your balls and let's show those guys what this game's all about."

Paul, Tracey and Edith sorted through a cluster of multi-colored balls on a metal rack, picking and rejecting various ones. Dorie reached for a relatively unscuffed ball in an attractive shade of electric blue.

"This one's pretty," she said. "I guess it'll do." Viktor put his hand on her wrist to stop her.

"You can't choose by color," he said. "You go by weight and the position of the holes. Let's get you a ten pounder to start."

Dorie allowed him to insert her fingers and thumb into various balls until he found one that he considered a good fit.

"How does that feel?"

"Like I've got a ski boot on my hand," Dorie said. "What if my fingers won't come out? Am I going to go sliding down the alley attached to this thing?"

"That only happens in cartoons. Just straighten your fingers and the ball slips off." Viktor turned to Paul and Tracey, who had balls in hand and were waiting in front of Lane Eight. "You all go ahead and start. Dorie needs a quick lesson."

"You bet she does," Dorie said. She saw Rick, in Lane Nine, gracefully release his ball, sending it in a slight arc that resulted in a sequential collision felling all ten pins. Rick pumped his fist in the air and hooted while Barbara and Herbert applauded. Angela nudged Viktor with her shoulder.

"Catch us if you can, hotshot," she said.

"Don't worry, I'll be on your tail," he said. "So to speak."

"Really?" Angela's glossed lips parted in a half smile.

Predatory bitch, Dorie thought. And Viktor's encouraging her. What is it with him?

Viktor turned and winked at Dorie, apparently indicating some complicit understanding regarding Angela, and guided her to the unused lane on their left.

"Time for Viktor Lepawski's Bowling 101," he said. "I'll show you my perfect form--just kidding--and then you try it."

Dorie tried to imitate his easy stride and fluid arm movement as he demonstrated something he called "the approach" but all lines of communication between her upper and lower body seemed to have been cut and she couldn't synchronize her feet with her arms.

"Count it out," Viktor said. "Step one, two, three, four. Arm out, down, back, release. And relax, for heaven's sakes. It's a bowling ball, not a hand grenade."

On the tenth repetition Dorie managed to end up with her right leg sliding correctly behind her left and her right hand extended in something approximating the proper release position.

"Not too bad," Viktor said. "Might work better if you tried breathing."

"I can't," Dorie said. "I'm too busy trying to relax."

Paul, who had finished his turn, came over to watch.

"How's she doing?" he asked Viktor. "We need all the help we can get. Rick just racked up 200 points but I only got 130. Edith's up now and she's all over the place. It doesn't look good for the home team."

"No problem, "Viktor said. "I can mop the floor with those wusses. We'll give 'em a run for their money."

Dorie watched the computer screen that was tallying the scores by some mysterious electronic process. Numbers and symbols appeared in little boxes but the logic of the scoring system was as incomprehensible as a bookie's tote board. She didn't dare ask Viktor for an explanation as he was watching Edith so intently that the muscles in his jaw were twitching. When Edith's final score, 67, flashed on the screen he slapped his knee and shook his head. Paul groaned.

"Why don't I go next?" Dorie asked. "The anticipation of disaster is killing me."

"Go for it," Tracey said, patting her arm. "Don't worry about messing up. It's just a game."

"They don't seem to think so." Dorie inclined her head towards Viktor and Paul who were huddled together like football coaches discussing the next play.

Viktor broke free and took Dorie by the elbow. He steered her into position in front of Lane Eight.

"Aim at that little arrow on the lane like I showed you. And for God's sake don't throw the ball. Just let it roll."

Dorie took a deep breath and repeated her mantra of "out, down, back, release" as she stepped towards the little dots on the floor that Viktor had identified as the foul line. But the pendulum action of her arm got out of control on her last step and the ball hit the lane with a resounding thud, bounced into the air and ricocheted into the gutter.

"I told you not to throw it," Viktor hissed. "Just let it drop. Loosen up. Go with the flow."

"Sorry," Dorie mumbled. "I won't do it again." Jeez, she thought. I should loosen up? What about you?

"Don't worry," Tracey said. "I used to loft the ball too. You'll get the hang of it."

"Not in this lifetime," Dorie replied. "I feel like a total klutz."

Herbert Benson, who was up for Team Rick, interrupted his play to reassure her.

"Now don't you say that, Dorie. You just need to have faith. You'll catch on. Let the Lord guide your hand. And remember, you're among friends. We're all rooting for you."

Not quite all, Dorie thought, as Angela gave her a snarky smile and sat down beside Viktor in front of the computerized scoreboard mounted on the little table in front of Lane Eight.

"So, Viktor," she said, leaning against him, "you going to start moonlighting as a bowling instructor?"

Viktor looked down at her and grinned. "Only if you beg me, sweetheart," he said.

He disengaged himself from Angela as Dorie got into position for her second try.

"Listen, baby, you're standing way too far to the left. Line your foot up with that second dot." He put his hands on her shoulder and shifted her into place. "And remember what I told you. Don't throw the ball. Just let go of it."

Oh, shut up, Dorie thought as she moved into her approach. This time she managed to keep the ball sufficiently on course to topple one of the outlying pins.

"Whooeee!" she called out. "Progress! Praise the Lord!"

There was a resounding silence, then Paul said, "Good job, Dorie. Now take out the rest."

"Get your left leg back in position," Viktor pointed accusingly at the offending limb. "That's why your angle was off. And aim for that second arrow. You still need to hit the one pin."

"All right already," Dorie growled. Viktor was really getting on her nerves. Who did he think he was, ordering her around like a drill sergeant?

She missed the critical one pin but took out two side pins and, feeling increasingly reckless, bowled the rest of her set with abandon, actually scoring a strike in the process.

"How did I do?" she asked, as she peered at the computer screen.

"Could be worse," Viktor said. "But not by much. Hate to say it but you really dragged us down."

Angela pointed at the screen. "Your grand total," she said, "is 46."

"Lovely," Dorie said, smiling sweetly at Viktor, whose sex appeal was rapidly evaporating under the harsh overhead lights. "I owe it all to you, coach."

<h1 style="text-align:center">Twenty - Three</h1>

In the end, Team Rick triumphed over Team Viktor by a substantial margin, which required handshakes all around to dissipate any residual competitive friction. That done, Dorie quickly returned her rental footwear and was lacing her running shoes when her hopes for a quick getaway, preferably minus Viktor, were dashed.

"Okay guys," Rick said. "Circle time."

He spread his arms wide and wiggled his fingers invitingly. Barbara took one hand, Edith the other. Paul and Tracey linked themselves to Edith.

Dorie glanced at the exit but decided that making a break for freedom constituted inexcusably bad manners. She inserted herself between Tracey and Paul in order to evade Viktor's outstretched hand. Angela promptly grabbed it and dragged him into position beside Herbert Benson and Barbara.

Circle complete, Rick cleared his throat and bowed his head.

"Hey there, Lord, just checkin' in upstairs after our great evening together. We wanna thank you for teaching us to compete in a spirit of love and righteousness. We ask you to sustain us in our search for God-fearing Christian partners and guard us from the demonic influences that tempt us to look for love in the wrong places. "

That's me, Dorie thought, looking for love in the wrong place. But I have seen the light and now I am saved. From Viktor the Christian pig. Thank you, Lord.

Rick pronounced the ritual benediction, "May the circle be unbroken until we meet again," and a squeeze pulsed through the joined hands. Dorie didn't want to be rude so she dutifully passed the squeeze from Paul on to Tracey, but the minute the circle dispersed she grabbed her purse and bolted for the door, saying goodnight and thank you for a wonderful time to everyone she passed, including Viktor.

"Wait up." Viktor grabbed her elbow and escorted her out the entrance door. "Aren't we going for a drink? I've been looking forward to it all evening."

"Sorry, but I'll have to opt out," Dorie replied. "Bowling was more stressful than I expected."

She strode toward her car, hoping to dislodge Viktor but he remained firmly affixed to her arm.

"Come on. We could go to Renee's. You like Renee's. Or, if you're really that tired, back to my place. I'll break out my vintage port and fix us a cheese plate. Better yet, I've got some great Spanish sparkling wine. Ever had cava? You'll love it. We can celebrate our official first date."

He slipped his arm around her waist and pulled her close to him. Dorie stiffened.

"I honestly don't feel up to it. I've got to go to Boulder tomorrow for a conference and I need to get to bed early." She pressed the unlock button on her car's electronic key and the Subaru's headlights flashed in response.

Viktor drew back and looked at her intently. "Did I do something to tick you off? Tell me. I want to make it right."

Dorie hesitated. It would be easier to walk away from Viktor and never see him again than to list the multiple ways in which he'd acted like a jerk.

"Come on, Dorie," Viktor said, "you can't just cut me off like this. Tell me what's wrong."

His brown eyes were soft and pleading. He seemed so sincere that Dorie relented.

"Okay then. I didn't like the way you got on my case in there. You were totally caught up in winning. And you couldn't keep your hands off Angela."

"I'm sorry," Viktor said. "I guess I got carried away." He shook his head and produced a contrite smile. "I'm a pretty competitive guy. And I know I can be too blunt sometimes. But trust me, I'm working on it."

"What about Angela?"

"Not what it seems. It's a delicate situation." Viktor pointed at her car. "Why don't we sit down so we can talk?"

Dorie almost said no, but curiosity got the better of her. A delicate situation involving Angela sounded interesting. Viktor opened the driver's door for her before getting in on the passenger's side. He slid the seat into a semi-reclining position and stretched his legs out.

"That's better," he said. "I'm a little beat too. Like you said, bowling is more strenuous than you'd think."

"About Angela…" Dorie prompted.

Viktor sighed deeply. "I met her through the Friendly Circle Business Alliance and I listed my house with her. We had a couple of dates. It was okay at first but then she got too intense. So I broke it off. Problem was, Angela didn't want it broken off. She keeps calling me. I hoped that being with you tonight would give her the message that I'd moved on."

"The message would have been clearer if you hadn't just sat there while she was all over you like white on rice."

"Angela doesn't like rejection and I can't afford to get her mad right now. I've got an offer in on one of those new condos down by the river and I need to sell my house in town to close the deal. I want her working for me, not against me."

Dorie considered this explanation. It almost made sense.

"So are we friends again?" Viktor cocked his head to one side and smiled at her. "You going to give me another chance?"

"I guess," Dorie said. Maybe she shouldn't write Viktor off just yet. In the close confines of the car she could almost smell the testosterone through his cheap aftershave.

"Excellent. So why don't you reconsider coming over to my place? That cold bottle of cava's waiting for us. And I could give you a nice back rub, get rid of all that tension, hmm?"

He leaned towards her and cupped his hand under her chin, turning her face to his.

Dorie started to decline the offer of a back rub but her words were smothered by Viktor's descending mouth. She tried to twist her head to the side as his tongue probed its way between her lips and teeth but he tightened his grip on her chin. Panicked, she jerked away and her elbow hit the horn button on the steering wheel, triggering a deafening bleat. She freed herself and shoved Viktor in the chest with both hands so forcefully that he fell back against the passenger side window.

"What do you think you're doing?" she said, wiping her mouth with the back of her hand. The traces of his saliva on her lips repulsed her. She wanted to grab the water bottle she kept in the cup holder and douse her face with the contents.

"I was just kissing you," Viktor protested. "What's wrong with that? You were giving me signals. I assumed you were interested."

"Not that interested. I hardly know you, for heavens' sake."

"But our kids are buddies."

"That's no reason to stick your tongue down my throat in a parking lot." She wiped her lips again, recalling the forceful invasion of her oral cavity.

Viktor shrugged. "Okay, point taken. I'll do better next time."

She shook her head violently. "There's not going to be a next time. Please get out of my car."

"Hey," Viktor sat up straight and glared at her. "You can't brush me off like that."

"Oh yes I can." Dorie inserted the car key in the ignition. "Out. Now."

Viktor didn't move. A teasing smile flickered across his face. Dorie felt a twinge of anxiety. If he moved on her she'd pound the horn to summon help. Or jump out of the car and take refuge in the bowling alley.

Wait a minute, she told herself. You're overreacting. He's not going to rape you. He's a Christian.

"Come on now, Dorie," Viktor said. He settled deeper into the car seat and propped one knee on the dashboard. "Admit it. You like me. I can tell by your body language. We've got chemistry."

Dorie banged her fist on the steering wheel in exasperation. She should never have let Viktor get in her car. She felt as violated as if he'd forced his way into her bedroom. But she didn't want to anger him; for all she knew he might be one of those church-going secret wife-beaters.

"I like you fine," she lied, "but we do not and are not going to have any sort of relationship now or in the future. So goodbye. I need to get home." She turned the key in the ignition and started the motor.

Viktor removed his knee from the dashboard. His smile had vanished and his lips were set in a hard line.

"I thought you were the finest lady I'd ever met." His voice was harsh. "Guess I was mistaken."

Dorie flushed. She had encouraged Viktor's interest, that is, up until tonight when her romantic fantasies were shattered by seeing him way too up close and personal. She couldn't think of anything to say that wouldn't sound like an admission of guilt so she just looked straight ahead with her hands clutching the steering wheel, willing him to leave.

After a long silence, Viktor got out of the car, slowly and deliberately. He hesitated by the open door and Dorie was afraid he was going to get back in but he merely bent down and looked at her. Amazingly, he was smiling.

"No hard feelings," he said. "I forgive you."

What? Dorie thought. You jumped me, not the other way around. I'm the one who should be doing the forgiving. She put the car in gear and inched forward, forcing him to retract his head and close the door. She started to pull away, then braked and lowered the passenger side window. "Do give my best to Angela. You two make a lovely couple."

On the way home Dorie replayed her earlier contacts with Viktor, cataloguing the hints of sleaziness that she had overlooked. All that ostentatious vinology should have been a tip-off. And his toast at Pierre's, "To us," when they'd only just met. Viktor had come on too hard and fast. She should have known he was a player.

When it comes to men, Dorie thought, I am one lousy judge of character. I really better get a dog before I fall for a full-fledged sociopath out of sheer loneliness.

As she pulled into her driveway she noticed that lights were on both downstairs and up in Phoebe's bedroom. She was unaccountably relieved that her daughter was home from her date with Jared. The apple, she thought, does not fall far from the tree of good and evil. What if Jared's wholesome exterior masked a junior version of Viktor? She better have a talk with Phoebe right now.

Dorie stopped in the kitchen to wash her hands with antibacterial soap to annihilate the skin-borne bacteria that undoubtedly lurked in bowling ball holes, then went upstairs to find her daughter.

Phoebe was sitting on her bed painting her toenails bright coral.

"Hi, mom. Did you have fun?"

"It was interesting," Dorie said. "I learned to bowl. More or less. Mainly less."

"Did you see Mr. Lepawski? Jared said he was going to FortySomething tonight."

Dorie wondered if her cover had been blown, but Phoebe's question seemed innocent enough. Evidently Viktor hadn't said anything to Jared about their date.

"Sure did," she said. "He gave me some pointers on bowling. I actually got a strike." She quickly changed the subject. "How was your evening?"

"The movie was great. We both love Johnny Depp. Jared's going to rent us the DVDs of all his old movies. He says I'll really like 'Edward Scissorhands.'"

Dorie sat down on the end of the bed and sent up a trial conversational balloon. "It seems like you and Jared have a good relationship."

A slow smile illuminated Phoebe's face. "Ummmm." She shook the bottle of nail polish until the mixing ball clicked against the sides. "Jared's the best."

"Does he treat you right?"

Phoebe looked at her as if she were daft. "Well, of course. What are you talking about?"

Dorie cast about for the right words. She didn't want to be intrusive but she had to be sure Phoebe wasn't getting taken in by a junior philanderer. "I mean, he respects your wishes and doesn't try to control you. Or make you uncomfortable by flirting with other girls."

Phoebe laughed. "Are you crazy?" she said. "Jared is so not like that. Why are you so uptight?"

"It's a mother thing," Dorie said. "We worry." She peered at Phoebe's toenails. "Nice color," she observed, then added, as casually as possible, "I get the impression Jared's father is a bit of a ladies' man."

Phoebe applied a second coat of polish to the big toe of her left foot. "I dunno." She wiped a smudge of coral off the cuticle. "I mean, Mr. Lepawski's basically okay but Jared did tell me he had some problems before they moved here, you know? Jared gets along with him pretty well now but he didn't used to."

"Oh?" Dorie said, inviting further revelations.

"Yeah. Jared was really mad at his dad for a while. I think the divorce was pretty much his dad's fault. He had a girlfriend or something. Jared's mom got fed up and moved back to her parents' house and took Jared with her."

Interesting, Dorie thought. That's not the story I got from Viktor.

"So how did Jared end up with his father?" she asked

Phoebe dabbed polish on her little toe and pointed her foot in the air to survey her handiwork.

"Jared's mom got remarried and Jared, like, couldn't stand his stepfather. So the judge said he could go live with his dad."

"Sounds like Jared's had a pretty rough time. It's amazing that he's turned out so well."

Phoebe recapped the bottle of polish and smiled at Dorie. "No, it isn't. He found Christ."

Later that evening, after taking a hot bath and donning her pajamas, Dorie smuggled a bourbon and branch up to her bedroom. She hadn't gotten back to her journal since Phoebe interrupted her Sunday afternoon and she was determined to finish it tonight. After all, she thought, I'm going to Boulder tomorrow. Back to where it all began. Before it ended in Boston. In the worst way possible.

She got into bed, set her drink on the bedside table and flipped the pages of her journal until she came to the entry for September 1. Here we go, she thought. Into the heart of darkness.

# Twenty-Four

**Friday, September 1, around midnight,
Room 417, Caesar's Palace**

I'm really in the poo now and it's just like Bud says. The only way
out is up it and through it.

The trouble started a couple of hours ago at Bud's fancy dinner
party in the Forum Room at Caesar's Palace. We're there in our
best clothes (I borrowed a silk broomstick skirt and a camisole from
Corinne) and we're as high as kids at a birthday party because of the
gilded setting and the wine that Bud's ordered to celebrate. Bud
looks spectacular, in a vulgar sort of way. He's dressed like a Mafia
Don, black shirt with white tie and a white sports jacket. His over-
the-top dramatics don't even seem out of place here. Las Vegas is
Bud's kind of town.

I sit next to Colin but of course Bud notices and demands that I
come sit by him. Colin warns me not to go, that I'm being set up for
something, but I don't want to miss the action so I move up to the
head table. Bud starts flattering me like mad. Tells me I remind him
of some starlet he used to date and hints that Corinne doesn't meet
his need for intellectual stimulation. He feeds me asparagus tips by
hand and keeps topping up my glass of cabernet. I wink at Colin to

show him I'm not buying this bullshit. Colin draws a finger across his throat and shakes his head. I wonder if I'm as in control of the situation as I think I am but I don't want to cut and run yet.

Bud throws out his usual mix of quips, aphorisms and personal insults all through dinner but saves his Major Important Announcement for dessert, which is baked Alaska, a big hit with this sucrose-deprived crowd. (We're into heavy substance abuse this evening: the meal began with oysters Rockefeller and progressed to rare roast beef. Bud says we need to eat "profane" foods periodically to ground ourselves.).

The big announcement is that Bud is going to write an autobiography. "I'm sacrificing my treasured privacy," he says, "to set a few matters straight. Someone needs to dispel all the spiritual fluff floating around and I can't think of anyone better qualified for the job than myself." Then he says he needs an editor for this project and fortunately there is a qualified individual amongst us tonight. And he gives my shoulder a sharp squeeze indicating that I'm about to be anointed official scribe.

I'm thrilled. For about ten seconds. What a great way to hang out with the guru and find out what he's all about. But it would be the end of my life as I know it. I'd have to defer my fellowship and resign my teaching assistantship.

Bud doesn't give me a chance to object. He grabs my hand and hoists it in the air in a victory salute and everybody, except Colin, applauds and cheers the literary partnership of the decade.

"Th...th...th...that's all folks, " Bud calls out, in a Porky Pig stutter. "Rosa's taking care of the bill. See you in the morning. Be in the coffee shop at 8."

He's got a death grip on my wrist as he walks me out of the dining room. I do not like being man-handled so when we get to the foyer I tell him to take his book and stuff it. He just laughs at me and says, "You don't have to do anything you don't want to do. You must know by now I never force anyone to do anything against their will." He says the announcement was all a trick, designed to stir up gossip and jealousy in the community, which is good for everyone's inner Work.

I'm confused and ask him if he is or isn't going to write his life story. Now that I'm off the hook I'm interested again. He says of course he is and I should consider the benefits of helping him. "You want to find out if I'm a fraud or the real thing, don't you Cookie?" he says. "Don't deny it. We're too smart to play games with each other. So here's your big chance."

Colin steps out from behind a pillar where he's been listening to us and says, "Her big chance for exactly what?" Bud doesn't miss a beat. "To find what she wants to know," he says, "by working very closely with me." Colin is getting red in the face and looks really mad but I can't tell if he's mad at Bud or me. He stares at me and says I should be careful because I may not realize the implications of Bud's offer.

I feel like I'm being pulled in half. I'd like to grab Colin and run away with him into the night, far away from Bud and his tricks and the Community's craziness. But then I remember the strange and amazing experiences I've had in the past weeks--looking through Bud's eyes into a void when we first talked in the kitchen; feeling my consciousness detach from my body during the meditation for Ned's daughter; the terrible interlude of being frozen in time and space that night in the forest-- and I decide I have to find out the truth about Bud no matter what. If I don't I'll be I'll always be wondering if I missed my chance for a once in a lifetime spiritual transformation.

Colin tells me to come with him to the bar to talk. Bud says fine, go if you want, then adds that he's already had a typewriter sent to Polly's room and Rosa's waiting to take notes while we have a little brainstorming session "while our energy is high from tonight."

I can't resist that. I tell Colin I'll meet him later at the van. He walks away obviously upset and I feel like a heel. Bud watches him leave and says, "An interesting young man. But too smart for his own good." Whatever that means.

So Bud and I end up here in Polly's room, along with Corinne, Jill, and Rosa. There's no typewriter and we don't talk about Bud's autobiography. I should have known. Bud changes his mobster outfit for a shirt and shorts and says he's going to the Winnebago and anyone who wants can come with him. Polly is already asleep, as usual, but Corinne, Jill, and Rosa say they'll go.

Then they all do a kind of wink, wink, nudge, nudge thing and Corinne says, "Well, Dorie, since Polly isn't able to play her part these days, there's a temporary vacancy in our ranks in case you'd care to fill it."

I don't answer. Bud is leaning against the bathroom door watching me with a knowing smile that makes me want to crawl under the bed to hide.

"It's only temporary," Corinne repeats. "There's no commitment or anything."

I still can't answer. I desperately want to know what goes on in the Winnebago but I don't want to participate in a group grope, even if it produces instant enlightenment. I'd like to sit on the sidelines and watch Bud do his thing, whatever his thing is, but I don't think lurking in the background as an anthropological voyeur would be socially acceptable. Bud ends my dilemma by telling me to stay with Polly, who's been suffering intermittent bouts of nausea.

So here I am, writing in my journal while Polly lies in a heap on the bed snoring like a walrus. I could walk away, but I know I won't. I'm going to go against my feminist principles and better judgment in order to find out for once and all whether Bud's a genuine Enlightened Being or a supremely talented charlatan. I'm so nervous I could puke.

· · · · · · · · ● · · · · · · · · · ·

Dorie felt a wave of heat cascade from her head down through her body. Little prickles of perspiration dotted her face and chest. Another damned hot flash, she thought. Really? inquired her inner Bud-voice. How about anticipatory embarrassment?

"Shut up," Dorie said aloud, "And get out of my head."

In either case, her bedroom was suddenly unbearably stuffy. She folded down the page of the journal to keep her place and flung off the light quilt covering her legs. Even that wasn't enough. She got up and opened a window and inhaled the cool fresh mountain air. She could see the outline of the eastern peaks against the starlit sky. They looked pristine, distant, and enduring. Impartial witnesses to the endless petty human dramas that took place below them.

What the hell, Dorie thought. So I had to break a few eggs to make an omelet. In the long run, does it really matter? She returned to her bed, stuffed a pillow behind the small of her back, and began to read the final entries in her journal.

Twenty - Five

## Monday, September 4, Boulder

I'm home, I'm alone, the sun is shining through my bay window and it's a relief to be back in the ordinary world. Now I need to make sense of what happened in Las Vegas, the grand finale of my ashram adventure, before I forget the important details.

So there I am, dozing in the hotel room while Polly sleeps. It's around two in the morning when Rosa shows up with a "Bud Says" message: "Bud says to tell you he'd really like you to join us tonight. But you don't have to if you don't want to." Time to fish or cut bait. I pick up my backpack and follow Rosa to the Winnebago. My stomach is churning. I feel like I'm being swept along by some kind of karmic tidal wave that I can't escape.

As we thread our way through the darkened RVs in Sunset Camperland, I realize that my knowledge of Tantric fooling around is strictly theoretical. What if I do something wrong and set Bud's spiritual evolution back a couple of millennia? I confess my doubts to Rosa. She laughs and tells me not to worry, that Bud takes care of everything. This implies a complete loss of control on my part that really makes me nervous.

We find the Winnebago and the dim glow seeping through the drawn shades is ominous, like the light up at Dr. Frankenheimer's place in The Rocky Horror Show. Rosa raps three times on the door, it opens, I step in, blink and sneeze. There are votive candles flickering amid a cloud of musky incense. To my left, Corinne is reclining against a big velvet pillow on a bed under the large rectangular rear window. She's stark naked. For some reason I'm having a major flash of deja vu.

"Hello, Dorie. Glad you could drop by." Bud's voice drifts into my ear from somewhere above me. For one insane moment I think he's levitating, but when I look up I see him, along with Jill, in the elevated sleeping area over the front seats. Bud is lying on his back with his arms folded under his head. He's looking directly at me and smiling, which isn't too surprising considering that Jill is giving him what appears to be a highly professional blow job. Needless to say, they, too, are naked as jaybirds. I notice that Rosa, who has slipped in behind me and closed off my escape route, is shucking her clothes. I'm beginning to feel a tad overdressed.

Bud tells me to make my self comfortable. I wonder how he can speak so calmly under the circumstances. But if I'm going to play the game, I've got to wear the uniform so I take off my clothes and put them on my backpack, which I stow by the door so I can make a quick getaway.

Meanwhile, Jill is moaning and writhing around, completely out of her mind. Bud, however, is lying absolutely still with his eyes closed thinking of England or Buddha or the Voidness of the Void. He either has complete control over his autonomic nervous system or suffers from terminal impotence. He appears completely relaxed except for intermittent spells of rapid, shallow breathing.

Rosa and Corinne don't pay a bit of attention to what's happening upstairs. They're talking about a snack break. Rosa suggests cheese and crackers. Corinne says they don't have enough. "You know how hungry Bud gets when he's been Working," she whispers. I look up at Bud's inert form. That's work? What about Jill? She's going to need a rare steak and a bottle of stout when this is over.

Not knowing what else to do, I sit down on an upholstered bench opposite the door, almost impaling myself on a burning joss stick stuck in a small bowl of rice grains. Then I suddenly understand my flash of déjà vu. I've seen this place before!!! In the alien dream that invaded my sleep our first night on the road. The rectangular window in the "recording studio," the big pillows, the nude bodies, including my own. All the little hairs on my arms stand up.

As I'm trying to digest this, Jill shrieks, flings herself backwards on the elevated bed and lies still. She's gasping for air, like a goldfish ejected from its bowl. Bud yawns and props himself up on one elbow, ignoring Jill. He looks directly at me, crooks his index finger and beckons.

I'm practically hyperventilating at this point so I tell myself to focus on my goal: the truth about Bud. I take a slow deep breath and a miraculous calm pervades me. (I guess I have learned something about regulating my inner states.) My body moves toward the ladder to the upper berth as if I'm directing it from a distance. In fact, I'm in such a state of detachment that I don't even recoil as Bud reaches over the edge and helps me onto a large mattress covered with ivory satin sheets.

The ceiling of the sleeping area is so low I can barely sit upright but I'm not ready to stretch out and relax. Bud is sure relaxed though.

He's semi-reclining on his side, his head supported by his left hand. Jill is either asleep or in a protracted post-orgasmic swoon on the far side of the bed. Bud reaches behind him with his free hand and shoves her towards the wall like a sack of flour. She smiles blissfully without opening her eyes.

"Uh, what now?" I whisper. "Anything you want," Bud murmurs, with a heavy-lidded smile. He runs his free hand through my hair; his touch is delicate, but despite my mental detachment the muscles in my neck are so tight they ache.

"Relax, Dorie," Bud croons. "Nothing's going to happen that you don't want to happen. Trust me." He cups his hand around the back of my neck. His fingers are extraordinarily warm. The tension in my neck melts, and I sink back onto the mattress. I feel like I've been shot with a massive dose of horse tranquilizer.

"There, there, that's good," Bud says soothingly. "See, this isn't so strange after all, is it?" For just a moment, I silently disagree. I am voluntarily—I think—participating in a Tantric orgy in a Las Vegas RV park. This is hugely, enormously strange. The dim light of reason flickers out almost instantly. "No," I say in a voice that sounds weak and far away, "it's not too strange."

"Of course it isn't," Bud says. "We've known each other for a very long time, haven't we?" He turns my head towards him so I'm forced to look into his eyes. They are dark pools of infinite depth; it's like looking through a black hole to the beginning of time. I can't manage to speak. I can barely nod my head.

He takes my hand and guides it down his muscular, compact body towards his groin. I've lost all capacity for resistance. I note idly that his torso is quite hirsute. "Esau was a hairy man," I think dreamily. Slowly, gently, he moves my hand onto his penis, which is completely flaccid. He closes his hand over mine and sets it in motion; his cock comes to life and twitches itself erect.

He rolls over onto his back and pulls me on top of him. I regain enough power of speech to mumble something to the effect that I don't know anything about esoteric sexual practices. "Don't worry about it," Bud whispers. "I'll take care of all that. You just relax and do what comes naturally."

He rearranges my unresisting body so that I'm sitting astride him; I feel him slide effortlessly into me. I'm moist and soft even though I don't feel sexually aroused. I just feel as if I'm observing some predetermined course of events in which I'm an actor following a script being revealed one page at a time.

Bud places his hands on my hips and moves me back and forth; his eyes are closed, his body entirely relaxed, except for the bit that is penetrating me like a small, cylindrical probe. I understand that I am to play the active role, the shakti to his shiva. I settle obediently into a rhythmic rocking motion, which seems to please him as he sighs deeply. Maybe he isn't as disinterested as he seems?

As for myself, well, I'm not disinterested in the proceedings, but I'm not exactly excited by them either. My body is on some kind of sexual automatic pilot while my mind is wondering how long we have to keep this up before something amazing happens.

Bud's not giving me any clues as to what comes next and my mind isn't producing with any answers. Then I remember what Bud said in the casino about following your subtle bodily inclinations, the physical counterpart of intuition. What they seem to be telling me is that I have to do something more, something that Bud hasn't asked for and probably doesn't even care about. It's something I have to do for myself.

With that, there's a kind of opening in the center of my chest as if my breastbone has split down the middle. I feel a warm, vibrant energy pour out and flow over Bud's still body like a widening stream of golden light. I'm dissolving, losing my self in a flood of compassion for this being lying beneath me, whoever or whatever he is. And not just for him but for an endless expanse of mute, suffering figures I see somehow stretching behind him clear to the horizon. It's like everyone that has ever existed or ever will exist is standing there, heads bowed, and Bud is in front of them, holding their pain.

I sort of expect Bud to look at me and acknowledge whatever this is that is flowing from- or more accurately, through--me, but his face is a bland mask. I have no idea of what is going on behind it. But I don't care. I don't need an acknowledgement. I don't need anything from Bud. Not now. Not ever. I lean forward and kiss him gently—a mother's kiss—on the forehead and wish him well with all my heart.

It's not finished yet, though. I understand that I have to come, not because I feel any physical or emotional urge to, but because it's required that I reveal myself, even though, or maybe because, Bud has remained concealed. It has something to do with trust, I think. Trust in something greater than me or Bud. My body finds its way to a climax and I know the ritual is complete. I slip off Bud's motionless body and go down the ladder to find my clothes. He never opens his eyes and never utters a word.

· · · · · · ● · ● ●●●●● · · · ·

Dorie closed the journal and dropped it on the floor beside the bed. She folded her arms across her chest and stared at the ceiling. A maelstrom of charged memories was seething within her, memories of experiences that had no place in the context of her daily life. Yet they were real memories of very real experiences.

She hadn't imagined the pawn ticket that Bud handed her the day after the Winnebago episode. She hadn't imagined going to a pawn shop down the Strip to redeem it for a package containing, to her astonishment, her missing watch, traveler's check and pendant. Her possessions, which had one by one mysteriously disappeared during her stay in the Community, were now being returned, just had Bud had elliptically foretold with the undoubtedly fictional parable of his stay in a monastery. It was his way of letting her know she had gotten the answers she sought, at least in part.

Nor had she fabricated the claustrophobic timelessness that terrified her in the woods, the prescient dream of the scene in the Winnebago, or the peculiarly asexual congress with Bud and her vision of the massive suffering of humanity. The culmination of these experiences had been a state of inner peace and clarity that gave her a sense of connection to something inchoate, unknowable and eternal. Something that, while not exactly what one would call God, certainly felt like a step in that direction.

But it didn't last, did it? The inner voice that sounded so like Bud broke into her reverie. Dorie shifted uncomfortably, suddenly aware of an ache in her lower back. She got out of bed and dragged a suitcase out of her closet. Doug was picking her up at 8 a.m. and she needed to pack.

It didn't last, did it? The voice nagged her as she went into the bathroom to get her toilet kit. She tossed it in the suitcase and got a change of underwear out of her bureau. You let it all slip away, didn't you? the voice accused.

Dorie dropped a nightshirt into the suitcase on top of the underwear. Yes, she had let it slip away. It had been impossible to monitor her emotions and thoughts sufficiently to maintain the compassionate objectivity she had felt in Bud's presence. There had been too many classes to teach, too many papers to publish, too many flights to and from Toronto, and later on, too many fights with Colin.

She stood in front of her closet trying to decide what clothes she would need for the weekend but she couldn't think clearly. In her mind's eye she saw Colin, not as he was when they met in 1978, optimistic and vibrant, but as he was when she last saw him, tired and angry and hurt, standing in front of the Volvo in their driveway in Newton. Caught up in the biotech frenzy of the eighties, he too had lost his internal compass, and their marriage, which had begun with such high hopes of spiritual union, had drifted onto the shoals of imminent divorce.

Maybe if we'd remembered ourselves, maybe if we'd remembered what we learned from Bud, Dorie thought, our relationship wouldn't have gone bad. Tears stung the back of her eyes. But it had gone bad, slowly and inexorably, as a wall of mutual disappointment and resentment arose between them. Phoebe's birth had brought them together temporarily, but the wall continued to grow until it was so high and intricately constructed that only an emotional nuclear explosion would have demolished it. And then the accident ended everything.

"'Getting and spending, we lay waste our powers,'" Dorie spoke aloud. "'Little we find in nature that is ours. We have given our hearts away, a sordid boon.'" That bit of Wordsworth pretty much summed up the last two decades of her life.

She was suddenly exhausted. All she wanted to do was go to sleep. She'd finish packing in the morning. She got into bed and pulled the quilt over her head. Her last thought, before she plunged into unconsciousness, was an apology, to Bud, to Colin, and the universe in general.

"I blew it," she whispered. "Sorry everyone."

Twenty-Six

Dorie opened her eyes to a room full of sunshine. Shit, she thought, the alarm didn't go off.

She fumbled for the clock on the bedside table and realized that the alarm hadn't malfunctioned; she'd forgotten to set it. She had exactly twenty minutes to shower, wash her hair, dress and finish packing before Doug arrived. He would already be en route from his place in the mountains and she didn't have his cell number. She'd have to scramble.

She took a three-minute shower, bypassed Sharon's age-masking cosmetics for a quick slathering of sunscreen, pulled on slacks and a cotton sweater, and tossed a tank top and t-shirt into her bag.

No need for anything fancy, she thought. All I'm going to do is sit through six hours of mind-numbing discussions of literary political correctness.

"Those without expectations are open to infinite possibilities," her little inner voice, which inexplicably now sounded less like Bud's and more like a variant of her own, reminded her.

"Oh, all right," she said and added her yellow church dress and sexy sandals to the contents of her bag. Something requiring festive garb might materialize.

She bent to retrieve her patchwork quilt and pillows from the floor where they had landed during an evidently restless night.

Making the bed was her one act of compulsive housekeeping. It created the illusion that the day would proceed in an orderly fashion. She looked at the clock; it was 7: 55. She'd have to keep entropy at bay some other way this morning. She grabbed her bag and tiptoed downstairs; she'd told Phoebe she needn't get up to say goodbye.

She was in the kitchen waiting for the electric kettle to boil when she heard a car turn into her drive. She dropped an infuser full of breakfast tea into a travel mug. She wasn't leaving without a shot of caffeine to keep her alert. Doug was probably a speed freak and that silly Jeep he insisted on driving was a rag-topped death trap.

She hurried to the front door to let Doug in so he wouldn't ring the bell and wake Phoebe. When she stepped out onto the front porch she was surprised to see Doug getting out of a sporty silver sedan.

"What's with the hot wheels?" she called. "What happened to your Jeep?"

Doug bounded up her four front steps in two large strides.

"I wouldn't take that piece of junk on a road trip," he said. "It's my play toy for the back country."

Dorie squinted at the insignia on the car.

"A Lexus?" she said. "How can you afford a ritzy ride like that? You're a poet."

"Among other things," Doug replied. "One of which is an exceptionally astute investor in real estate."

Dorie looked at him inquiringly.

"I did more than ski and hang out in bars when I was in Aspen," he said. "I bought a couple of run-down Victorians, fixed them up and flipped them. I rolled the money over into condos right before Aspen boomed."

"Wow. A man of property. I'm impressed." Dorie glanced at the flaking paint on the trim around the door and hoped Doug wouldn't notice it or the splintered floorboards beneath her feet.

The kettle shrieked and she asked him to come in for a minute while she finished fixing her tea.

"It's not much," she said, as they traversed the hall to the kitchen, "but it's a real house with a big yard, which is more than I had back east."

"It's homey," Doug said. "I liked it the first time I saw it. I thought it suited you."

"You've been here before?" Dorie couldn't recall ever having Doug over.

"Yup." Doug examined the grocery list on her whiteboard. "Biked out here once. It's a good workout. And I wanted to see where you lived."

"Good grief! I was being stalked and never knew it."

Doug laughed. "Hardly. I always pick some kind of arbitrary destination on my bike rides just to make them more interesting." He pointed to an item on her grocery list. "Flax seed? You eat that or put it in the bird feeder?"

"It's full of omega somethings," Dorie replied. "Good for your joints. You should try it. Might help you kick your Advil habit." She poured a dollop of milk into her mug. "I'll just leave Phoebe a note and we can go." She drew a fat heart on the whiteboard, adorned it with wings and a smiley face and wrote "WBD, I'll call you tonight. Love, WBM."

"What's with the initials?" Doug said.

Dorie explained the pet names she and Phoebe had adopted.

"Sounds like you've got a pretty neat kid," Doug said as they made their way to the front door.

Dorie nodded. "We have our differences but we love each other."

"That's great. Don't let that Jesus thing she's into mess up your relationship." Doug picked up Dorie's suitcase and held the door open for her. She preceded him onto the front porch, tea in one hand and briefcase in the other, then stopped and turned to face him.

"You know, Doug, you were right when you told me not to meddle with Phoebe's faith. I was trying to control something that was none of my business. Everyone's got to find their own way to make sense of life."

"That's a switch. What changed your mind?"

"Something I read last night."


"I'm afraid I'm not very chatty this morning," Dorie said as they stopped at a light in the middle of Sulfer Springs, a small resort town about an hour east of West Fork. She had been responding to Doug's report on the stalemate with Dean Drescher and the Campus Christian Coalition with mute nods and monosyllabic expressions of support.

"I'm sorry," Doug said. "I've probably bored you senseless with my problems."

Dorie leaned back on the headrest and sighed deeply.

"No," she said. "It's me. I'm sort of preoccupied."

"Something's bothering you, isn't it?" Doug said. "Do you want to talk about it?"

Dorie shook her head. Doug's sympathetic inquiry triggered an avalanche of unwelcome feeling. Her throat tightened so that she couldn't speak and an unpleasant pressure constricted her chest. She closed her eyes and tried to compose herself but that recurrent image of Colin, his shoulders rigid with anger, standing by the open door of the Volvo in the gray early morning light, formed behind her lids. She tried to banish the image but her visual memory was out of control. Yet again she saw Colin look at her and shake his head, his mouth set in a tight, straight line. Yet again she watched him get into the car and slam the door. Yet again she heard the heavy thud of finely milled steel on steel, solid, precise, and final.

Hot tears welled up behind her closed lids and seeped out through her lashes. The tightness in her throat intensified into a dull ache.

She felt Doug's hand on her arm. "Something's wrong, "he said. "Do you want me to take you home? I can turn around right now."

"No, no, no." Dorie forced the words out. "I've got to go to Boulder."

"Hey, this workshop is no big deal. You don't have to go if you aren't feeling well."

"It's not the workshop." Dorie wiped her eyes. "I *need* to go to Boulder. I've got to deal with something that started there."

The light changed and Doug inched the car forward. "Must be something pretty heavy," he said. "You sure you don't want to tell me about it?"

Dorie exhaled, trying to center herself, but her breath came out in an audible moan.

"Okay, that's it," Doug said. He made an abrupt right turn onto a tree-lined residential street, stopped the car and switched off the ignition. He turned to Dorie, his brow furrowed with concern.

"Listen, I don't know what's going on with you but whatever it is, it's killing you and it's only going to get worse if you try to hold it in. I'm not about to spend the next five hours worrying that you're going to have an emotional meltdown on the interstate. So tell me what's wrong."

"It's really, really ugly," Dorie said. Her voice quavered; she was on the verge of tears. "If I tell you, you won't like me anymore." She swallowed but the lump in her throat wouldn't be dislodged. "I don't even like me anymore."

"Why? What could you possibly have done that's so awful?"

"This is really hard." She hesitated, searching for a way to begin. "You know my husband died? Phoebe's dad?"

"I knew you were widowed."

"It was in an automobile accident. Outside Boston. It was early in the morning and it was raining and the traffic on 128 is always terrible and it was Labor Day weekend so it was even worse and ..."

"Slow down," Doug said. "Breathe. We're not in a hurry. Take all the time you need." He rubbed her shoulder.

Dorie took a deep breath and let it out very slowly. Her heart, which had been pounding and threatening a fit of palpitations, reverted to a normal rhythm.

"I never knew exactly what happened," she said, "but the police report said Colin was going too fast and there was water on the road. When he hit the brakes to avoid some damn fool who pulled in front of him the car jumped the divider into oncoming traffic. That was it. He didn't have a chance. Even a Volvo can't save you in a head-on collision with an eighteen-wheeler."

Doug squeezed her shoulder. He shook his head slowly. "Dorie, that's just awful. You must have been devastated."

Dorie slumped down into her seat. She looked out the window at the street of modest ranch houses. Ordinary houses where ordinary people lived quiet, harmless lives. Unlike her own.

"That's just it," she said. "I wasn't. Not at first, anyway. When the police called me, I didn't feel anything. I just thought, this is impossible, it's a mistake. Then they described the Volvo and everything and I knew it was true. And then, just for a second..." she grimaced, "just for a tiny second, I felt... relieved."

She looked at Doug, waiting for him to recoil in horror but his hand continued to rest on her shoulder.

"And?" he said. "There's more, isn't there?"

Dorie nodded. "We'd had a huge fight right before Colin left that morning. One of many, but this one was different. I said something terrible."

The air in the car was uncomfortably close and Doug switched the ignition on so he could roll down the windows.

"I'd guess you'd be pretty good at that," he said. "What was it?"

"Colin was a microbiologist," Dorie said. "He was working on a major genome mapping project. He had this brilliant lab assistant, Nita, and she designed an experiment that was critical to the project's success. Then she went back to India and Colin published the results under his own name. No one knew but me and I only found out by accident when I borrowed his laptop and saw the paper he'd submitted to some journal. He didn't credit Nita at all."

Dorie inhaled the fresh morning air wafting in through the open window. She had a sudden urge to get out of the car and go for a very long walk. She stared at an orange cat sunning itself in the driveway in front of their car; she wanted to trade places with it, to become a simple animal, devoid of tormenting memories.

But she wasn't and now that Doug had invited a confession she might as well tell the truth and get it over with. "That morning I accused Colin of intellectual property theft and threatened to reveal him so Nita would get the credit she deserved. He was absolutely furious. He called me a cold, betraying bitch. He said I was jealous of his success. I told him he was a pretentious fraud and...." her voice dropped to a whisper "...and I wanted him to get out and never come back." She clasped her hands together in her lap, interlocking her fingers so forcefully that her knuckles cracked. She swallowed hard.

"He left," she whispered," and that was it."

"So your husband drove off in a rage because of something you said. And then he was killed on the freeway." Doug shook his head. "And you've been torturing yourself with this for all these years?"

"There's more," Dorie said. "Sometimes, when Colin worked all night at the lab I'd wake up in the early morning and wonder if he was late because he'd had an accident on the way home. And I'd think about calling him to make sure he was all right. But I never did. Because I didn't really want him to come home."

She fished a tissue out of her pocket, folded it in half and wiped her eyes. 'I didn't want him dead though." She blew her nose to clear the stuffiness. "I just wanted him to disappear."

Doug sat in silence for a few moments, gazing out over the steering wheel. When he turned towards her, Dorie was surprised to see a barely discernable smile on his face.

"Unbelievable," he said. "You're so damn smart but you can't see that you're on the mother of all guilt trips. You've convinced yourself that you killed your husband."

"By our thoughts we create our realities," Dorie said. "I thought it and it happened. So on some level, I caused it."

As soon as the words left her mouth she realized how ridiculously New Age they sounded.

"On some level you're crazy is more like it," Doug said. "You may have hated Colin and wanted him out of your life but you are not responsible for that accident. If you've got to blame someone, blame Colin. He was the one who was driving too fast."

"Yeah, uh huh, "Dorie said. "Or I could blame the driver who cut in front of him. Or the weather. I've thought this through again and again but it always comes out the same: if I hadn't said those awful things to Colin, he wouldn't have been driving like a maniac and he wouldn't have gone out of control when that car pulled in front of him. So I put the ball in play, so to speak."

Doug snapped his fingers twice. "Stop it, Dorie," he said. "You're acting like a little kid who gets mad at his mommy and says I hate you, I wish you were dead and then thinks it's his fault when she gets sick. That's childish magical thinking. It's what kids do when they feel guilty about their own anger. Can't you see that?"

Dorie drew her breath in sharply and sat up straight. Childish, magical thinking? What was Doug talking about? Did he mean she was punishing herself for hating Colin? By blaming herself for something that actually wasn't her fault?

She ran through the tantalizing contingencies that had obsessed her for eight years. If Colin had left the house one minute later he wouldn't have encountered the car that cut in front of him. If the driver of the semi had been going a little faster the truck wouldn't have been there when Colin's car crossed the divider. If any one of an infinite number of details had been different the accident wouldn't have happened. She'd pictured all this a million times, but always before her own angry actions had loomed in the foreground, dwarfing the other elements in the multiple chains of cause and effect that converged in a fiery crash.

But now, all of a sudden, she could see it differently: the hurtful words she had uttered that morning were only a tiny piece of a vast kinetic puzzle that had assembled itself in the only way possible. She felt a chill ripple down the back of her neck. She had not caused Colin's death. It was karma, the endpoint of an inexorable series of events, only some of which involved her.

I could have told you that, the quiet little not -exactly -Bud -but -not -exactly -Dorie voice in her head whispered. Once again her eyes filled with tears, but now the lump in her throat dissolved and the tension in her lower back drained away; she felt loose and floppy, as if the spaces between her joints had expanded.

Doug touched her arm gently, but didn't speak. She was grateful for his silence; she couldn't have said answered him if he'd asked her how she was. He started the motor, executed a three-point turn, and returned to the highway in silence, leaving her to process her thoughts.

She replayed the last months of her marriage, the escalating arguments and insults that led, inevitably, to the bitter scene in the driveway on the morning of Colin's death. But this time her mental movie unreeled in black and white and the actors mouthed their lines silently. She watched, as if from a distance, Dorie and Colin, unwitting actors in a preordained drama, playing out their assigned roles, neither of them innocent, neither of them guilty.

"Okay now?" Doug said as they turned onto the highway that led to the Interstate.

Dorie blinked and came back into the present. "Maybe," she said. "I'm thinking about what you told me."

Doug shook his head. " Don't think about it, Dorie. Feel it."

Twenty-Seven

Dorie didn't have much to say after they left Sulfer Springs. She was grateful that Doug didn't press her to talk. He'd simply handed her a case of CDs and invited her to play whatever she liked. She had flipped through its plastic sleeves, noting Chopin, Bach, Keith Jarrett, and the Dixie Chicks, but chose nothing. The silence in the car, rather than being uncomfortable, was reassuring and companionable, allowing her to ponder the new revised version of her role in Colin's death.

She emerged from her extended reverie as they descended La Veta Pass en route to Walsenburg.

"How come you got my number so easily?" she asked. "About the guilt trip thing, I mean."

Doug braked as they came up behind a moving van creeping down the steep grade. "Been there, done that. Got a whole drawer full of t-shirts."

"You, wracked with guilt? I can't believe it. You always seem so carefree."

"Maybe now. But not always. That example I gave you? Of the kid whose mother gets sick and he thinks it's his fault? That was me."

"How so?"

Doug downshifted to spare the brakes. There was no safe way to get around the big van.

"My mom had MS. She was in bed a lot when I was little and I used to get mad because she couldn't do anything with me. When she got worse and ended up in a wheelchair I thought it was because I'd been bad. So I turned into the best little boy in the world to make up for being so bratty."

An empty uphill passing lane came into view and Doug took advantage of it to overtake the van. When they were safely back on the right side of the road he resumed his story.

"Mom lost her eyesight when I was a freshman in high school. She liked for me to read to her at night when she couldn't sleep. Wallace Stevens, James Crowe Ransom, all the poets she loved."

Dorie looked at Doug's profile, his straight nose and strong chin, outlined against the light from the driver's side window. In her mind, the contours softened into the rounded features of a child. He must have been a sweet boy, she thought. And he really loved his mother.

"So that's why you became a poet yourself?" she said. "For your mother?"

"I guess." Doug shrugged. "Or maybe I did it to annoy my father. He's a corporate lawyer and a pretty rigid guy. He wanted me to get an MBA."

"And your mother..." Dorie hesitated. "Is she...?"

"She died when I was a senior in college. I kind of lost it afterward. Being good hadn't saved her, so I figured I might as well be bad. I headed for the mountains right after graduation." He looked sideways at Dorie and grinned. "Where, as you have so kindly pointed out, I enjoyed a protracted adolescence guzzling beer and chasing women. But now I'm officially grown up."

"Really? You who drive a red Jeep with a bumper sticker that says 'Jesus loves you, everyone else thinks you're an asshole'?"

"I also have a mortgage and an IRA. And a suit. For weddings and funerals."

They reached the bottom of the pass and entered a wide green valley backed by a range of jagged mountains.

"That suit of yours," Dorie said, "did you ever commit matrimony in it?"

"I lived with a woman for six years. That's longer than lots of marriages."

"True." Dorie nodded. "But why didn't you get married?"

"She wanted kids and I wanted to travel. We broke up, she married a doctor and had a baby a year later. I was mildly traumatized but it made me get serious about my writing. Things worked out fine for both of us."

Interesting, Dorie thought. Doug seemed to have a knack for ending relationships without rancor, which is more than she could say for herself.

The sun was low in the sky over the Front Range as they negotiated the maze of freeway interchanges on the north side of Denver. They'd run into highway construction on I-25 just past Walsenburg, where they'd stopped for lunch and the delay meant they hit the early rush hour traffic out of Colorado Springs and the late rush hour traffic out of Denver.

"Makes you appreciate West Fork, doesn't it?" Doug said as he edged the Lexus across three lanes of traffic to reach the exit to the Boulder highway. "I don't think I could ever live in a city again."

Dorie agreed; the mere thought of returning to the hectic life she'd had on the East Coast was repellant. She slipped off her shoes and maneuvered herself into a cross-legged position on the front seat. She felt good, loose and relaxed, the way she did after a long hike. The Lexus was a cushy ride, quiet and suffused with the smell of expensive leather, and Doug was a proficient and surprisingly careful driver. She couldn't remember the last time she'd been content to leave the driving to someone else. Colin had been so impatient that she was continually on guard when she rode with him, terrified that he'd try to pass on a curve or speed through a red light.

"Colin likes to take shortcuts. He outsmarts himself." Bud 's words echoed in her inner ear. He, bless his canny guru's heart, had recognized Colin's impatience and arrogance while she'd been dazzled by his good looks and intellect. That same impatience and arrogance had led to his taking credit for Nita's research and his fury at being called on it. The fault, she thought, is not in the stars but in ourselves. I didn't cause Colin's accident. He did.

She turned to look at the new industrial parks that had sprouted on either side of the Boulder-Denver highway and noticed how freely her neck moved. She wiggled her toes contentedly. Life's possibilities, while not necessarily infinite, seemed far richer than they had yesterday.

And one of those possibilities, while only an indistinct glimmer at the moment, was Doug. Dorie was acutely aware of his body less than two feet away. Despite the Lexus' exemplary climate control, she was sure she could feel a gentle warmth radiating from his skin. Out of the corner of her eye, she could see his right forearm, tanned and glinting with sun-bleached golden hairs. She had to resist the impulse to reach over and stroke it. A pleasant tingle of arousal asserted itself in her nether regions.

Hold on there, she told herself. First Viktor, now Doug? She'd really better cut back on the dong quai; it might be good for her hot flashes but the effect on her libido seemed to be dangerously cumulative.

The car crested the last hill between Denver and the Front Range and Dorie felt the thrill she always experienced at seeing the town of Boulder nestled below the monumental vertical stone slabs of the Flatirons. Her ambivalence about returning to the place where she'd first lived with Colin had vanished. She was eager to revisit her youthful hangouts.

"Well, the mountains are the same," she said, "but Boulder's about five times as big as I remember it."

"Five times as big and ten times as expensive," Doug said. "Neither of us could afford to live there even if we wanted to. Which I, for one, don't."

"Why not?" Dorie said.

"All the bike paths are paved. No fun in that."

After they checked into their rooms at a motel near the CU campus, Dorie called Phoebe to let her know they had arrived safely.

When Phoebe answered her cell phone, Dorie heard music and voices in the background. She recalled Sharon's warning about teenagers gone wild without parental supervision and wondered if her belief in the moral rectitude of Christian adolescents had been unrealistic.

"We're in Boulder," she said. "Where are you? I hope those aren't party noises I'm hearing."

"I'm at Jared's," Phoebe said. "Amber and Chris are here. We're making spaghetti and then we're going to watch a video. I called Sharon and told her where I was so she wouldn't freak out."

"Okay, but don't stay too late. And watch for deer on the way home. Remember, they travel in pairs. Call me when you get there. Or if you have any problems. Promise?" She hoped Phoebe wouldn't be driving home after dark but there wasn't much she could do about it from 300 miles away.

There was an exasperated groan on the other end of the phone. "Mom, stop obsessing. Go out to dinner with that Doug guy or something. Have fun. I promise I'll call you."

As it happened, Doug had to attend a Faculty Club dinner for workshop presenters so he suggested that Dorie drop him off, take the Lexus and explore the town.

"Do you mind if we go by my old apartment on the way to the Club?" she asked. She didn't know exactly why she wanted Doug to see where she used to live. Maybe, she thought, I need him to witness this piece of my past so I can connect the then and there to the here and now.

Doug looked at his watch. "We've got time so go for it. I'd love to see where you came of age, so to speak."

Dorie headed towards east Spruce Street via a maze of unfamiliar one-ways and miniature traffic circles. As she approached the block where she once lived, she caught sight of the conical roof of the turret that had held her bedroom. Her heart quickened; the shabby Victorian house had not been demolished to make way for condos. It was still standing. And so am I, she thought. Despite everything.

She stopped the car and stared at her former home. It gleamed with a tricolor paint job, dusty mauve with cream and teal accents. A shiny tricycle lay on its side in the front yard.

"This is it," she announced, "but it's been yuppified

"Is that good or bad?" Doug said.

Dorie looked at the house again. She had expected it to be just as it was when she lived there, a charming but deteriorating warren of student flats, home to the young, creative, and impoverished. However, the splendid dwelling in front of her, with its tidy flowerbeds and wrought iron fence, shouted upper middle-class prosperity.

"Actually," she said, "it's good. It's a family home again, which is what it was originally. It's come back into its own."

She pointed to the second story. "See that bay window? That was my sitting room. I loved it. It was my little nest. It's probably some kid's room now."

"I like Victorians," Doug said. "They're so unabashedly stolid." He stuck his head out the window. "Look at those fishtail shingles. You don't see workmanship like that anymore."

Dorie peered up at the shingled gable. "Colin hated this place. When we got married he insisted we move to this stark white contemporary thing up in the hills. It was like living in a refrigerator." She shuddered, remembering the echoing rooms and the leather, steel and glass furniture that Colin had selected. A scientist's dream house. Not hers. She should have realized then that they were ill-matched.

Doug touched her arm. "You seeing ghosts?" he asked.

"Yes." Dorie sighed. "How can things be so obvious in hindsight and so obscure when you're in the middle of them?"

Doug gave her arm a gentle pat. "We see what we want to see. Until reality bites us on the bum. Didn't anyone ever tell you that?"

"As a matter of fact," Dorie said, "a guy named Bud did. Repeatedly. But I wasn't listening."

## Twenty - Eight

After Dorie deposited Doug at the Faculty Club she left the car in a parking lot downtown and headed for the Pearl Street Mall. She was infused with energy; being back in Boulder seemed to have fooled her body into believing it was twenty -two again.

She bounced a little on her toes as she waited for the light at the Fourteenth Street intersection to change, then jogged across the street behind a girl in Lycra bike shorts and running shoes. She threaded her way through the usual throng of students and tourists crowding the pedestrian walkway before stopping to watch a dreadlocked youth spinning five plates on an elaborate contraption of poles strapped to his waist. She was happy to see the Mall still allowed street performers even though it had been invaded by a Banana Republic and a Starbucks, the vanguard of the upscale chains that would undoubtedly follow.

She turned off on a side street in search of her favorite restaurant, Sushi Banzai. Since she would be dining alone tonight she might as well enjoy the instant camaraderie of a funky sushi bar where the chefs fancied themselves standup comedians as well as samurai fish slicers.

She nearly walked past the place when she came to it. The old red and white sign over the front window had been replaced by a discreet lacquered black panel with the name inscribed in gold

Japanese characters. Only the small sans-serif lettering beneath it identified it as "Sushi Banzai" for the kanji-impaired.

The interior was as elegantly understated as the exterior. The old Air Nippon travel posters and paper lanterns were gone. The walls were panelled in split bamboo. The entry featured a stone Buddha and a granite sphere bubbling water into a small pool. Atonal music played discreetly in the background and a scattering of stylishly dressed couples occupied floor cushions at the low tables.

"How many, ma'am?" A young Asian man with a sleek ponytail that matched his black tunic glided out from behind a shoji screen.

Dorie took a step back. I can't eat here, she thought. I'll look pathetic sitting at a table by myself. "I'm just checking it out," she blurted. "For future reference."

She slunk out of the restaurant feeling conspicuously middle-aged and unattached. Who am I fooling, she thought. Maybe I'm back in Boulder, but I'm forty-eight and on my own. You can't step in the same river twice.

She retraced her path towards the car. She passed an unpretentious Mexican restaurant and a pizza parlor but the prospect of a solitary meal in any eatery full of happy couples and laughing groups of friends was depressing. She stopped in a deli at the west end of the mall and got a boxed Greek salad and a container of tapioca pudding to go. Better to hole up in the motel and watch mindless sitcoms on TV, then check in with Phoebe before bed. She'd had enough blasts from the past for one day.


By Saturday afternoon Dorie never wanted to hear another word about inter-cultural sensitivity, unconscious ethnocentrism, and the expressive power of street slang. The only thing that kept her awake during the day's final seminar, which dealt with the touchy topic of incorporating works by contemporary Islamic writers into the curriculum without appearing to condone terrorism, was the thought of dinner. Doug had told her that morning that he had something special lined up.

"It's a surprise," he had insisted. "It's a place that will give you some perspective."

"Give me a hint," Dorie pleaded.

"It's not an ethnic restaurant. After a day of refining our inter-cultural sensitivity, I thought we should eat American."

"I knew it." Dorie shook her head. "You're taking me to Denny's."

"Nope. I can promise you that the place we're going does not have menus with colored photos of the entrees."

In fact, the menus at The Flagstaff House Restaurant were substantial booklets printed on cream vellum. The location, a wooded plateau near the summit of the Flatirons, was even more awe-inspiring. The entire Boulder Valley was visible below and in the distance the plains of eastern Colorado offered a preview of the vast prairies rolling all the way to the Mississippi.

"This is amazing," Dorie said. "I think I can see my old house from here." She edged closer to the floor-to-ceiling window behind their table. "Good golly, I can practically see Iowa."

"I told you this place would give you perspective," Doug said. "Your past is spread out below you. Literally." He was standing directly behind her; he was so tall that he could easily see over her head. Dorie felt his breath stir her hair. She wobbled a bit in her strappy sandals, resisting the urge to lean back against his chest.

Fortunately, their waiter, who had been hovering nearby as they admired the view, pulled out Dorie's chair and invited her to take a seat. She did so, managing to flash a lengthy expanse of leg in the process, the result of leaving half the buttons on her yellow dress undone. She intended for Doug to notice and he did.

"I like that dress," he said, "especially the way you didn't finish putting it on."

"Thank you," Dorie replied. "I bought it for church."

Doug looked at her incredulously.

"It's a long story," she said. "I'll tell you sometime."

Dorie turned her attention to their damask-swathed table. "How are we supposed to use all this equipment?" An array of crystal wine glasses and silver flatware flanked the silver chargers at their places. "No wonder I never came here when I lived in Boulder. It was way out of my league."

"Well, tonight's on me," Doug said. "A token of appreciation for your company during six hours on the road."

"Fine company I was. Lost in the past for most of the trip."

She cupped her chin in her hands and propped her elbows on the table. Maybe it wasn't good manners, but she didn't think Doug would mind.

Doug copied her position so that they were eye to eye across the formidable table setting. "Road trips encourage reflection," he said. "And like it or not, the past is always with us. Kind of like those Russian nesting dolls. Each former self is contained within the ones that come after. You can't get rid of any of them so you'd better help them get comfortable with each other."

"That's not so easy," Dorie said, "when you see the stupid mistakes some of them made."

"Hey, from up here," Doug swept his hand in an arc towards the window, "there are no mistakes. There's just what is."

Dorie smiled. "That sounds like a guru I used to know."

Doug shrugged his shoulders and tucked his chin in a show of mock modesty. "I'm a poet, ma'am," he said. "Our job is to wake people up with words."

After they settled on entrees, wild catch salmon for Dorie and seared ahi tuna for Doug, the sommelier presented Doug with a leather-bound wine list as thick as a dictionary.

Doug feigned alarm and handed it back to him unopened. "I can't cope with this. You pick something for us."

Smart move, Dorie thought approvingly. Viktor would have staged an embarrassingly public display of vinology but Doug was willing to admit the limits of his expertise.

Dorie studied him surreptitiously over the edge of her menu while he and the sommelier discussed the merits of various Pinot Blancs. She noted the crows' feet at the edges of his eyes and the fine horizontal lines banding his forehead. He wasn't really that boyish when you looked closely. No one who saw them together would think she was seven years older. She certainly wasn't old enough to be his mother. So, if by any remote chance, they did develop a relationship--her stomach flipped over at the thought-- it wouldn't have weird Oedipal overtones. On the other hand, when she was seventy Doug would only be sixty -three, which meant he'd still be attractive to the literary groupies who swarmed around good-looking poets.

Doug concluded his conversation with the sommelier and looked at her questioningly.

"You're unusually quiet," he said. "What are you thinking about?"

"Oh, nothing," Dorie lied.

"I don't believe you. I've never known you not to be thinking about something."

"Well," Dorie hedged, "I was thinking about what a bad judge of men I am. My first serious boyfriend cheated on me, my husband was an intellectual property thief, and this guy I went out with last week tried to grope me in a parking lot."

Doug nodded. "You *are* a bad judge of men. I've done everything I can to show you that I find you physically attractive, intellectually fascinating—and amusingly neurotic--and you've brushed me off as some kind of playboy jock. I hope all this..." he gestured at the lavishly appointed dining room, "...will convince you I'm for real." He paused and looked at her intently, then grinned. "If not, we're leaving right now. There's a Denny's on 28th Street and you can have the soup and salad senior's special."

Dorie rearranged the multiple forks to the left of her silver charger so that the handles were all evenly aligned. Her stomach was so jittery she didn't think she would be able to eat. She could no longer pretend that Doug wasn't serious. His flirtatious overtures had always been sufficiently light-hearted that she could dismiss them without either of them losing face, but now, after the incident in Sulfer Springs, she couldn't deny his sincerity.

Nor could she deny that it terrified her. Unlike Viktor, who was so beyond the pale that there had been no possibility of a real relationship, Doug presented a risk. She could fall for him in a big way. In fact, if her sudden loss of appetite was any indication, she was already dangerously off balance.

"Well?" Doug prompted. "Say something. I can't keep asking you to take a chance on me. Either say you'll give it a go or tell me once and for all that you aren't interested. I won't be ticked off. You'll still get dessert."

Dorie burst out laughing. Doug's sense of humor was irresistible. Men like this came along once in a lifetime. She'd be crazy to pass him up. She reached over the table and took his hand. His fingers were surprisingly long and delicate as they closed around hers. An artist's hands, she thought, as her heart began to race.

"I am interested," she said. "And even though I'm scared to death, I want to take a chance on you." She hesitated, then added, her cheeks burning with a five-alarm blush, "On us." Yecch, she thought, that sounds so soppy.

Doug exhaled with exaggerated relief and smiled broadly. "Thank God," he said, enclosing her hand firmly in both of his. "I'm getting that wine guy back over here. We need champagne."

Two hours later, after a liberal infusion of strong coffee to counteract the effects of the champagne and Pinot Blanc, they emerged from the restaurant into the cool night air. Doug kept his arm around Dorie's waist to steady her as she traversed the cobbled pathway in her heels. She pressed against his side, enjoying the solidity of his lean well-muscled torso. He's like a big tree, she thought. The kind you're supposed to hug when you're lost in the woods.

Doug drove the twisting road down the mountain slowly, steering with his left hand so he could massage the back of Dorie's neck.

"That's nice," she said, sinking back into the leather cushions. "I can feel all the little knots dissolving." Her limbs were pervaded with a sweet, heavy lassitude and she felt the familiar itch of lust stirring deep behind her pubic bone. If she let her body have its way, it would proceed directly from the car to Doug's bed, shedding items of clothing along the way. But she was getting ahead of herself. They hadn't even kissed yet. This is ridiculous, she thought. I'm as giddy as a teenager.

Uh oh. Dorie jerked upright and fumbled for her purse, looking for her phone. She'd been so besotted with alcohol and Doug that she'd completely forgotten her very own teenager, home alone back in West Fork.

"You okay?" Doug asked, removing his hand. "Did I hit a sore spot?"

"No, no," Dorie said. "I just remembered that Phoebe was going to call me at nine. I've had my phone off since we went in to eat."

Dorie located her phone in the depths of her bag and turned it on. It chimed into life but there was no service in the canyon they were winding down on their way back to town. How could she have been so thoughtless? Phoebe had probably been trying to get through to her for hours.

The moment they emerged into the electronic airspace of the flatlands Dorie checked for missed calls and voicemails but there were none. She called her landline in case Phoebe's cell had been malfunctioning, and, if truth be told, to make sure her daughter was in the right bed in the right house at this late hour.

Her home phone rang eight times before the answering machine picked up. No surprise there. Phoebe was probably in her room plugged into her iPod. Dorie tried her daughter's cell. The call went straight to Phoebe's greeting: "Hi. It's Phoeb. Tell me the good news." Perhaps she'd fallen asleep? Dorie hit redial but before the call went through her own cell beeped, signaling the delayed arrival of a voicemail.

"Finally," she told Doug as she pulled up the voicemail screen, "Phoebe's left me a message. I was getting worried."

But the message she received made her heart plummet to the pit of her stomach.

"Dorie, it's Sharon. Now don't panic, but it's way after dark and Phoebe's not home and she's not answering her cell. What do you want me to do?"

# Twenty-Nine

"Everything okay?" Doug asked. "You look discombobulated."

"I'm not sure," Dorie said. "I can't reach Phoebe and my next-door neighbor left me a message saying she's not at the house. I'm calling her right now."

Sharon answered on the first ring.

"Dorie, thank heavens it's you. Listen, I saw Phoebe come home from work about four and then we took the boys out to MacDonald's and the park. When we came back your car was gone and the lights were off. She still hasn't shown up. Have you heard from her?"

Dorie's stomach did a flip-flop. What if Phoebe had been in an accident and was lying unconscious by the side of the road? Was their tragic family history about to repeat itself?

Dorie bit her index finger, hard. Stop that, she told herself, you're over-reacting. There's bound to be a reasonable explanation.

"It's okay, Sharon," she said, with more assurance than she felt. "I bet she's out with Jared. I'll call his dad; he probably knows where they are." Unless they're both lying unconscious by the side of the road, she thought and no one knows where they are. A wave of nausea hit her and she wished she hadn't drunk so much at dinner.

"You want me to pull over into the light up there?" Doug said, indicating a service station on Broadway. "I've got a pad and pen in the console if you need to write something down."

Dorie shook her head as she searched her phone for Viktor's number, which she hoped she hadn't deleted in a fit of pique.

"No," she said. "I'll get this sorted out in a minute. I hope."

She found the number, pressed "call" and steeled herself to speak to Viktor in a dignified, concerned parent-to-parent manner. But no one answered. Viktor's recorded greeting invited her to leave a message and to remember that it was a great day to be alive in Christ.

It's Saturday night, she thought. Viktor's out on the town. She left a terse message explaining the situation and asking him to contact her immediately, no matter how late.

"Try calling Phoebe again," Doug suggested.

Dorie did. This time she got a recorded message that the wireless party she was trying to reach was unavailable at this time.

"Where is she?" she wailed. "It's not like Phoebe to stay out late when I specifically asked her to not to drive at night. Something's wrong."

She snapped her phone shut and nibbled her thumbnail in frustration. She shouldn't be here, 300 miles away. She should be back in West Fork, pounding on Viktor's door in case Phoebe and Jared had foregone their vows of chastity and were safe and sound in Jared's bed. Which would be a lot better than lying unconscious by the side of the road.

Doug squeezed her arm. "Don't panic, Dorie. We'll go back to the motel and contact the highway patrol and the sheriff and the hospital just to set your mind at rest. Then we'll wait for Jared's father to call you back."

"I need to go home," Dorie said miserably. "I should never have left Phoebe alone. She's only sixteen."

"Rubbish," Doug said, "Sixteen is the new twenty. Kids these days are so sophisticated they scare me. Phoebe and Jared are probably downtown hitting the bars with fake i.d.s."

"Not these two," Dorie said. "Jared's idea of the high life is playing in a Christian garage band and Phoebe practically calls AlAnon every time I have a beer."

"Whoops," Doug replied. "In that case, we might have a problem."

By midnight it was clear that they did have a problem. Dorie had phoned all the relevant West Fork authorities twice and spoken to Sharon three times while Doug brewed coffee in the courtesy pot in her room, collected their luggage and loaded it in the car. When her cell rang she was so hyper-caffeinated that the sound went through her like an electric shock.

It was Viktor, who reported that he had just gotten in, from where he did not say and Dorie did not ask, and that Dorie's Subaru was in his driveway but Jared's truck was gone.

"So they're together," he said. "But where? I'm calling the police. An accident maybe happened." The reversion to his ancestral eastern European sentence structure betrayed his stress.

"I already did," Dorie said. "Nothing. But they're on the lookout for my Subaru. Call them and tell them to look for Jared's truck instead." She managed to speak calmly although her mouth was so dry her tongue felt as if it might stick to her palate.

"Yes, yes, of course," he said. "And I'll call Jared's buddy, Chris French. And Kimberly. Maybe they'll know something."

"The Medderlys are out of town," Dorie said, "But try Chris. Amber and Nicole too. And anyone else you can think of." She wanted to sound decisive but she couldn't control the tremor in her voice.

"Pastor Charlie," Viktor said. "I'll call Pastor Charlie. He'll start a prayer chain."

A prayer chain? Dorie stifled a groan. What a bunch of superstitious crap. Then, picturing mangled vehicles and distorted limbs, she thought, why not? Hadn't some experiment indicated that hospital patients got better when they were prayed for even though they didn't know about it? If Jared and Phoebe were bleeding to death in a ditch somewhere maybe a collective outpouring of positive energy could keep them alive until the EMTs arrived.

"Yes," she said, her voice quavering. "Do it, Viktor. Call Pastor Charlie."

She sat down on the bed, clutching her phone like a talisman. Her jaw ached and she realized that she'd been grinding her teeth. Doug sat down beside her and put his arm around her, pulling her close.

"Whatever you're thinking," he said, "it's probably wrong. Chances are the kids are fine. They might just be stuck out in the boonies where their phones don't work."

"But Jared's good with cars. He wouldn't get stuck." Dorie said. She buried her nose in Doug's oxford cloth shirt. His skin exuded a faint scent of vetiver and masculinity that was deeply comforting.

"No," Doug agreed. "But sitting here trying to figure things out isn't going to help. Let's go."

"Okay," Dorie said. "If I keep moving I'll be all right." She managed a wry smile as she stood up and ran her fingers through her hair, which felt sticky and matted even though she had just washed it that afternoon. "How does that saying go? 'When in trouble and in doubt, run in circles, scream and shout?'"

"Whatever works for you," Doug said. "Just don't do it while I'm driving."

Since it was early Sunday morning I-25 was deserted and Doug was able to make good time to Walsenburg, where they bought gas and yet more coffee at a truck stop. Dorie tried calling Phoebe again but heard the same recorded announcement of unavailability she'd gotten on her previous attempts.

"This tells me exactly nothing," she said. "Her phone could be turned off or it could be in an arroyo with the truck on top of it. I'm calling the sheriff's department. They aren't looking hard enough."

Doug sighed. "You've already called them three times. They have your number. They'll contact you if they find anything. Try to relax just a little. You're exhausting yourself."

Dorie crushed her cardboard coffee cup in her fist and threw it at a trashcan. It fell two feet short but she didn't bother to retrieve it from the floor. Her shoulders ached and her jaw muscles were knotted. What the hell did Doug know? He'd never had children. He'd never even grown up enough to get married. How could she relax when it was Phoebe, her baby, her only family, who was lost?

"We're wasting time," she said. She glanced at her watch. "It's 3:30 now. We'll be in West Fork by dawn if we hustle. I'll drive if you're too tired."

Doug started back to the car. "No, I'm not too tired," he said, without looking at her. His voice was tight. "I'll hustle; you pay for the traffic ticket I'm probably going to get."

Doug slowed to something resembling the legal speed limit as they entered Sulfer Springs. Dorie took advantage of the resumption of cell service to check in with Sharon and Viktor. Sharon still had no news, but Viktor did and it was disturbing.

"I finally tracked down Chris French," he reported. "He says he was on the phone with Jared late yesterday afternoon. Jared put him on hold to take a call from Phoebe and then got back to him and said he had to go because Phoebe was hysterical about something."

Hysteria wasn't Phoebe's style, Dorie thought. Either Jared was exaggerating or something awful had happened to Phoebe at work. Could she have scalded a customer with espresso? Or had the trashy barista with the skunk-striped hair made trouble for her? Maybe some pervert had followed her home and committed atrocities too horrible to contemplate. Dorie blinked to dispel the sickening images that flitted across her mind. Focus, she told herself. Stay in the moment. Be positive.

"Did Chris say anything else?" she asked. "Anything at all?"

"Just that Jared hung up right away and never called back to tell him if they had band practice Monday night."

Dorie stared at the red light that had halted their progress through town, willing it to change. Her stomach was cramping and the skin on her forehead felt taut and dry. She should never have taken this silly trip to Boulder. And she should have called Phoebe before she went out to dinner and let Doug ply her with wine. Then she could have helped Phoebe with whatever had happened to her.

"I'll be home in an hour," she told Viktor. "Call me if you hear anything from the police. That red truck isn't invisible. Someone has to have seen it somewhere." She twitched her foot impatiently. Why didn't the light change, dammit?

The light turned green and Doug accelerated with a satisfying burst of speed. Dorie's shoulders dropped a few millimeters. At least they were moving again, getting closer to Phoebe, wherever she was.

"How are you holding up?" Doug asked, glancing over at her. "You want me to pick up some fast food? Might be a good idea to eat something."

"No," Dorie snapped, "How can you think about stopping? This could be a life or death situation."

"You don't have to bite my head off," Doug said. "I'm going as fast as I can."

Dorie swallowed hard to dispel the lump in her throat, She shouldn't take out her frustration on Doug. He was making this ghastly all night drive for her sake. He barely knew Phoebe, so why should he too be overwrought?

"I'm sorry," she said. "You must be starved. It's okay to grab a muffin or something."

"No problem," Doug said. "I can hold out until we get to your place. I'll fix us breakfast while you hit the phones." He reached over and tousled her hair. "We'll find Phoebe. And Jared. Anyway, if Jared is as resourceful as you say he is, he'll be looking out for her if they're in trouble."

Dorie nodded. Jared, competent, caring, Christian Jared, was with Phoebe. She wasn't alone. No one should be in trouble and alone. Dorie looked at Doug as he guided the Lexus around a curve, monitoring his speed to counteract the centrifugal force.

"Doug?" she said. "Thank you for putting up with me. I'd probably be falling apart if you weren't here."

Doug glanced at her. "No, you wouldn't," he said. "But it's nice to know you appreciate my efforts."


When Dorie opened her front door she automatically called Phoebe's name, hoping against all reason, for a reply. A pervasive silence, broken only by the distant hum of the refrigerator, confirmed that the house was empty. Nevertheless, she checked the dining room, the kitchen and even her study, as if Phoebe might be hiding somewhere anticipating the thrill of discovery, a game she had played as a toddler.

Doug went to the kitchen to scramble eggs and make toast, insisting that they both needed to eat. Dorie, whose stomach writhed at the prospect of receiving food, went upstairs. Maybe something in Phoebe's room would provide a clue to where she'd gone. But the room was uncharacteristically tidy; the bed was neatly made and the floor cleared of the usual piles of discarded clothing and shoes. Dorie shook her head, bewildered. It made no sense. Why would Phoebe have suddenly cleaned her room? Had she wanted to leave a good impression before running away to elope with Jared?

Dorie crossed the hall to her room and, suddenly felled by exhaustion, flopped down on her own neatly made bed. She reached for the bedside phone, hoping that Phoebe, or the police, might have left a message since she'd last checked her landline. As she listened to an automated voice reminding her of an upcoming appointment to get her teeth cleaned, she noticed her journal on the nightstand. She recalled her rushed departure Friday morning. Evidently she had neglected to put the journal in the drawer where she usually hid it. She also recalled that she hadn't made the bed. Which meant that Phoebe, or some newly acquired invisible housekeeper, had. And if Phoebe had tidied her room, she must have seen the journal, with the slip of paper still marking the final chapter that Dorie had been reading Thursday night. The chapter that contained the blow by blow, so to speak, description of her night in the mobile bordello.

Dorie groaned, recalling her words *"...his cock comes to life and twitches itself erect..."* This was why Phoebe was so upset when she called Jared. She'd just found out that her mother had fucked her guru.

Of course she's run away, Dorie thought. She must really hate me now. I don't care. I just want her home in one piece.

She heard a vehicle turn into her driveway and ran to the window hoping to see Jared's truck. But a much larger truck, white with the Ace Auto Repair logo on the side, was there, closely followed by her Subaru. Her heart thudded with relief and excitement. Phoebe was back! Viktor found the kids!

She cranked open the casement window, ready to call out a greeting, but the words stuck in her throat. Viktor got out of the truck but only his brother Frank exited the Subaru. No Phoebe. No Jared.

Dorie squeezed her eyelids shut to stop the tears that threatened to turn into uncontrollable weeping. Get it together, she told herself. This is no time to fall apart. She went to the bathroom, splashed her face with cold water and quickly brushed her teeth to remove the gritty aftertaste left by truck stop coffee.

When she got downstairs Viktor and Frank were in the living room. Doug was standing in the hall with a spatula in one hand and a potholder in the other.

"Listen," Viktor said. "I think I've figured out what's happened." His words tumbled out in a rush. "Look in the garage for Phoebe's bike. Jared's is missing and if Phoebe's is too that means they went mountain biking. We need to check the bike trails."

"West Fork is surrounded by trails," Dorie wailed. "We can't check them all."

"No need to do that," Doug said. "Just check the more remote trailheads with parking areas that you can't see from a regularly traveled road. The sheriff's department would have spotted Jared's truck if he left it anywhere along the main highways and county roads."

Viktor looked at Doug, then at Dorie. "Who's this guy?" he asked.

"This is Doug Brenner, a ..." she started to say "colleague of mine" but realized that was both misleading and insulting to Doug. "A good friend of mine," she finished. She didn't wait to see Viktor's reaction but sprinted through the kitchen to the door into the garage. There was one bike leaning against the wall. Hers. She ran back to the living room.

"Phoebe's bike's not there," she said. "Does anybody have a trail map? We need a trail map."

"No, we don't," Doug said. "I've ridden all the trails. I can tell you which ones have obscured parking areas."

"We should get a map, though," Dorie insisted. "To be sure. You can't know them all."

"Dorie, that will just waste time," Doug said. "Let's split up and each check a couple of likely areas. I can tell you exactly where to go."

"But we might miss one without a map," Dorie protested. "How can you be sure you know all of them? That's presumptuous."

Doug stared at her, incredulous. "For once, can you trust that someone other than yourself is competent?"

"No chance of that," Viktor muttered.

Dorie glared at him, then at Doug, who shook his head and sighed.

"Okay, okay, let's all calm down," Frank said. "We'll make a list and divvy up the areas and get on it."

"We could use more people," Doug said. "We should search in pairs. Just in case the kids are hurt and someone needs to stay with them while the other one goes for help."

"That's easy," Viktor said. "Where's your phone?"

"Are you calling Search and Rescue?" Doug asked.

"No, "Viktor replied. "They can't do anything until we have a specific area to search. I'm calling Pastor Charlie. He'll send some of the congregation over."

"Trust in the Lord, Dorie," Frank said, giving her arm a reassuring squeeze. "With His help we'll find them."

Doug looked at Dorie questioningly. She shrugged.

"Whatever," she said and went upstairs to get her hiking boots.

Thirty

"**P**raise be! We've got a PLS!" Rick Tibbets jumped up from Dorie's kitchen table, where he'd been poring over a topo map of Mesa County.

Rick held his phone up in the air. It emitted a high-pitched scramble of words. Dorie recognized the voice: Paul Greenberg.

"What? What do you mean?" Dorie stuttered. "Did someone find the kids?"

"Paul found the truck. Up in Hawk Canyon behind some aspens. That gives us a Point Last Seen," Rick exclaimed. He put the phone back to his ear. "Good job, Paul. I'll tell the State Police to dispatch Search and Rescue. It'll take them a while to get their act together so we'll go ahead and deploy. See you at ten hundred hours."

He pocketed his phone and bowed his head briefly. "Thank you, Lord, for guiding Paul to the truck. Please look after Phoebe and Jared until we can get them out of that frigging canyon."

Dorie pressed her hands to her eyelids to quell the flurry of palpitations in her chest. Maybe the kids were just lost. Tired and hungry but none the worse for a night in the rough. Night? Her stomach lurched into her chest. Mountain lions hunted at night. And bears roamed the forest at that elevation. Irascible mother bears with cubs. Anything could have happened.

Rick broke into her dark thoughts.

"Call your friend Doug. We need him and that riding buddy he mentioned—-Tony something—up there with their bikes ASAP."

Dorie did as she was told. Rick, in full-bore Marine mode, was a force to be reckoned with. He'd arrived at her house an hour ago, attired head to toe in camo gear and bristling with survival equipment, binoculars, GPS, radio and a hunting knife big enough to gut an elephant.

"Pastor Charlie's put me in charge," he said, and proceeded to turn her kitchen into a command center as he converted the prayer chain into a search team. He had dispatched Viktor and Frank to check two trailheads west of town, called Paul Greenberg to cover the northern "sector", and instructed Dorie to make sandwiches and load a cooler with iced tea and bottled water. "Got to keep the troops hydrated," he muttered, while laying out a topo map, a compass, and colored pencils on the table.

Doug had gone to meet Tony Begay and pick up their bikes. They were heading towards the eastern mountains when Dorie reached him on his cell.

"We found the truck," she announced happily. "Hawk Canyon trailhead. Meet us there."

She heard Doug draw in his breath sharply. "Hawk Canyon? Man, those trails are technical bastards. Narrow switchbacks and monster drop offs."

"Thanks for sharing, "Dorie said sharply. "You've just made my day immeasurably brighter."

"Spare the sarcasm," Doug shot back. We're doing the best we can here."

"You don't have children," Dorie said. "You don't even have a dog. You have no idea how I feel."

"You're not giving me much of a chance," Doug snapped. "So let's drop it, okay? We'll see you in about twenty minutes."

Dorie's phone went silent. Prick, she thought. Macho mountain biking prick. What did he mean, the trails were "technical bastards?" Phoebe was used to riding on gravel roads but she wasn't experienced with the rugged trails used by West Fork's serious bikers. Maybe Jared took her into terrain she couldn't handle so he could show off. Little Christian macho mountain biking prick.

She turned to Rick, who was chugging water from a metal canteen.

"What do you know about Hawk Canyon?" she asked.

"Nada," Rick said cheerfully. "Those trails are too narrow for my ATV and if I can't get somewhere on it I don't go. Got a gutful of hiking in Nam."

Dorie swallowed hard and wiped her sweaty palms on her shorts. Finding the truck had seemed like such a lucky break but it was just the beginning of the search. And she had no idea of when or how it might end.


The drive to up Hawk Canyon was an acrophobe's nightmare. A gravel road with skid-inducing washboard corrugations had been carved into the side of a cliff, leaving a precipitous drop to the Rio del Norte far below. Dorie put the Subaru in low gear and followed Rick's truck as it swerved to avoid the larger potholes. Every time she glanced over the edge her stomach dropped six inches. If this was the road, what was the trail like?

Rick's truck rumbled across a cattle guard, made a sharp turn to the right, and came to a stop beside an old white Honda Civic. Paul Greenberg hopped out and frantically waved them to a stop, hardly necessary since the road ended in a deeply rutted parking area. Dorie glimpsed a flash of red through the aspen leaves. Jared must have pulled his truck out of the way to leave space for other vehicles to turn around. It wouldn't have been easy to see even if the sheriff's deputies had ventured this far off the main roads.

Paul bounded up to Dorie, hesitated, then embraced her awkwardly and patted her shoulder. The Circle of Friends greeting hug didn't come easily to him.

"Don't you worry, Dorie," he said. "The Lord's looking after those young 'uns. We'll find them."

Dorie forced a smile. Paul seemed to have taken the Circle of Friends bait of instant community and swallowed the party line in the process. What an anodyne we have in Jesus, she thought. He's got the whole world in His hands so don't worry, be happy.

She took a second look at Paul. He was wearing elastic-waisted red poplin shorts, white tennis shoes with navy blue socks and one of those inverted bucket hats favored by golfers; he was as out of place in this rugged canyon as his little car. Yet he'd been brave enough to make it all the way up this road that had given her more than one white-knuckle moment. She felt a wave of affection for the little guy. He'd stepped up. She shouldn't have judged him so harshly.

Rick unrolled his map on the truck's tailgate and weighted the corners with stones. He was walking in circles while holding his GPS aloft—"locking in satellites" he explained--when Doug's Jeep careened into the clearing and jolted to a stop, rattling the two bikes strapped to a carrier on the rear. Tony Begay got out and gave Dorie a considerably more energetic hug than Paul had managed, but Doug just nodded and began unloading the bikes.

"Okay, guys," Rick said. "You got a GPS, right? If you find the kids, send me your coordinates. If we can't evacuate them ourselves Search and Rescue will go in with a litter. No way we're going to get a chopper into those box canyons." He handed Doug one of his radios. "Check all the side trails for fresh bike tracks.

Stay together and..." he raised a warning finger "... be careful out there. We don't want any more casualties."

Dorie's heart lurched in her chest. Any more casualties? Did Rick really think Phoebe and Jared were injured? Or was he having some sort of PTSD combat flashback?

When Doug radioed in a second negative report, the only thing that kept Dorie from bursting into tears was her determination not to break down in front of Rick and Paul. They'd be even more embarrassed than she would. And by no means did she feel like having them comfort her with uplifting snippets of Scripture.

She wriggled into her backpack. "I'm going up the trail," she said. "I can't just sit and wait like this."

"No point," Rick said. "Doug and Tony are miles ahead of you already. You can't catch up to them."

Dorie squared her shoulders and turned towards the trail. "I'm going. Phoebe's out there somewhere. I've got to find her."

"But you don't have a radio," Paul said. "You can't communicate with anyone even if you find her."

"I don't care," Dorie said. Her throat was so constricted she could barely squeeze the words out. She turned away so Rick and Paul wouldn't see her quivering lips and reddened eyes. What she really wanted was to get away from them so she could fall apart in private.

Rick's radio blasted static. Dorie jumped. She turned back towards him, all her senses on high alert.

"Doug to Rick." Doug's voice came through, scratchy but clearly excited. Dorie held her breath as Rick replied, "Copy that. Go ahead."

"We've spotted them. They're down in the canyon by the river. Jared's waving at us and shouting but I can't make out what he's saying. "

"What about Phoebe?" Dorie interrupted. "Is Phoebe all right?"

She chewed the cuticle on her thumb as Rick relayed her question. Her heart was beating so hard that her pulse reverberated in her ears.

Doug's response was interspersed with the sound of heavy breathing. "Can't tell. We're going down. It's all scree and practically vertical."

The next ten minutes seemed endless. Dorie paced back and forth between Rick, the cars, and the trailhead, kicking up small clouds of dust with the toes of her boots. Why was Doug taking so long? A chilling thought brought her to a standstill. What if Doug wasn't calling in because Phoebe was dead and he didn't know what to say?

The radio crackled into life. "Doug to Rick." There was another burst of static, then a broken transmission with only a few clear phrases: "They're...a mess...out of here...concussed."

Dorie clutched Paul's arm. "What did he say? I couldn't understand what he said."

Paul put a finger to his lips and Rick held his hand up to silence her as he spoke into the radio's microphone.

"You're breaking up. Say again."

"They're both okay. Phoebe's ankle is a mess and her bike's totaled but I think we can carry her out. She's got a nasty bump on the head but she says she didn't black out so she's probably not concussed."

The tension drained from Dorie so suddenly that her legs almost buckled. Phoebe was all right! She staggered to the nearest boulder and collapsed, laughing and crying simultaneously.

Rick was still on the radio. "Roger that, Doug. Give me your coordinates. Dorie and I will meet you on the trail. We'll leave Paul here in case Jared's dad or Search and Rescue shows up."

Dorie set off at a quick jog despite Rick's admonitions to slow down and conserve her energy.

"Can't," Dorie panted, "I want to see Phoebe." But after a quarter of a mile she had to admit Rick was right; she couldn't sustain her pace at this altitude. She slowed to a brisk walk, which kept her several yards ahead of Rick, whose dogged plodding confirmed his preference for traveling by ATV.

About forty -five minutes later, Dorie rounded a rock outcropping and spotted Jared riding slowly towards her on Tony's bike. His face was smudged and his hair matted with dirt but he raised a hand in greeting. Then Phoebe appeared, perched on the seat of Doug's bike and supported by Doug on one side and Tony on the other. Her left leg was propped up, tied to the bike's crossbar by a bandanna around her ankle. Dorie's joy at seeing her upright and relatively unharmed was tempered by alarm; Phoebe was shockingly pale and drooping with exhaustion.

Dorie rushed past Jared to wrap her arms around Phoebe's shoulders and kiss her dusty hair. She held her close, taking care not to dislodge her immobilized leg..

"Baby, I am so glad to see you," she said, her voice hoarse with unshed tears. "I was worried sick."

"Sorry," Phoebe mumbled. "I didn't mean to cause so much trouble."

Dorie fumbled with the tube to her Camelback. "Do you want a drink?" she said. "Or something to eat? I've got bananas and chocolate."

"I'm okay," Phoebe murmured. "Doug gave me water and some crackers but I don't really feel like eating."

"What about you, Jared?" Dorie said.

"No thank you ma'am," he replied. He leaned forward, resting his forearms on the handlebars of the bike. His head drooped and he spoke without looking up. "I'm really sorry we screwed up like this. I tried to carry Phoebe back up to the trail but it was too steep and I was afraid if something was broken I'd just make it worse. I tried to call 911 but I couldn't get a signal."

"I just wish you'd thought to leave a note saying where you were going," Dorie said. "We could have found you lots sooner. What happened anyway?" She realized that she sounded accusing but she couldn't help herself. Jared was responsible for bringing Phoebe out here.

"Phoebe hit a rock and flipped out over the side of the trail. I think her foot got caught in the frame on the way down. It was, like, a major wreck. And her helmet came off, too."

"That was my fault," Phoebe whispered. "It made my head itch so I unbuckled it."

Dorie touched the lump visible on the side of Phoebe's head. "Wow," she said, "this is some goose egg. Next time you'll keep your helmet fastened. And tell people where you're going when you head out into the boonies."

"Yeah," Jared said, "I know we should of, but we were in a hurry to get on the trail before it got too dark. Phoebe, uh, needed to burn off some energy." He glanced at Phoebe, who frowned and shook her head.

I'll bet I know why, Dorie thought, remembering the journal entry Phoebe must have read.

"It doesn't matter, "she said, "We're just glad you're both okay." She massaged Phoebe's shoulders gently. She'd deal with the touchy subject of her night of Tantric revels later.

# Thirty-One

Paul was waiting for them at the edge of the parking area. He pumped his fist in the air in a victory salute. His face was nearly split in two by a jubilant grin that made Dorie smile despite her nagging concern over Phoebe's pallor. He's a real sweetheart, she thought. I'm glad he's found a community. Everyone needs friends. Including me. She made a mental note to call Pastor Charlie when she got home and thank him for rallying the troops on Phoebe's behalf.

Doug and Tony helped Phoebe into the back seat of the Subaru while Dorie filled a plastic bag with ice from the cooler. Phoebe winced when she placed it on her ankle, which was so red and puffy that Dorie couldn't tell if it was broken or just badly sprained.

"If you ladies are okay," Doug said, "I'd like to head down the mountain. But I can wait and follow you if you want. Just to make sure you make it."

"No, we're fine," Dorie said. Doug was so stiff and distant that she wasn't about to impose on him any more than she already had. She tried to dispel the tension that charged the air between them. "You've already done too much and all I've done is grouch at you. I'm really sorry."

Doug took a step towards her and Dorie half-expected him to hug her, but instead he patted her shoulder. "No problem. I'm glad you had a happy ending."

Just what does he mean by that, Dorie wondered, as he opened the door to his Jeep, then turned to look at her. His expression was unreadable; not exactly frowning but solemn and unsmiling.

"Be careful," he cautioned. "The washboarding on that big curve can throw you into a skid so take it in low gear and don't brake." He got in the Jeep but glanced at her through the open window as he started the engine.

"Give me a call when things calm down. I'd like to know how Phoebe's doing."

"Will do, "Dorie said. A lump was forming in her throat but she waved jauntily as Doug turned the Jeep downhill and vanished around a curve.

Well, Dorie thought, that's the end of that. I blew it, as usual. What the hell, he was too young for me anyway. She took a deep breath and looked around for Tony, who had volunteered to drive Jared's truck home and come back the next day to extract the kids' bikes from the canyon. She thanked him profusely for pitching in on short notice.

"Hey," he said, "it was an excellent adventure. Happy to help. Any friend of Doug's is a friend of mine."

Make that ex-friend, Dorie thought. I've burned that bridge beyond repair.

Paul Greenberg gave Dorie a parting hug, this time with a spontaneity that surprised her, and got into his little car to follow Tony down the canyon.

"Take care, Dorie," he called out the window, seemingly emboldened by his foray into the wilderness. "Maybe we'll see you at church next Sunday?"

Dorie smiled and shrugged, a combination she hoped would be pleasantly noncommittal. Paul was so obviously sincere that she didn't want to hurt his feelings, but despite her gratitude to the Circle of Friends she had no intention of attending another performance of their evangelical circus.

"We better get back to the highway," Rick said, "I need to call off Search and Rescue and deliver Jared to his dad before Frank and him come charging up the canyon. And I'm going to follow you down, make sure you make it okay, whether you like it or not. So don't give me a hard time."

Dorie saw that Jared was already in the passenger seat of Rick's truck, leaning back against the headrest with his eyes closed. Poor kid, she thought, he must be utterly exhausted.

She hugged Rick, told him he deserved a medal for service above and beyond the call of duty, and did a quick check on Phoebe, who was stretched out on the back seat with her foot propped up on Dorie's daypack.

"We're going straight to the ER," she told her. "We need to get that ankle x-rayed to make sure nothing's broken."

"Nothing's broken," Phoebe protested. "I can wiggle all my toes. Let's just get home. I've got an awful headache."

"No way," Dorie said. "This is one of those times that mother knows best. I want a doctor to look at your ankle."

"You don't know best," Phoebe retorted. "You always think you do, but you don't."

"What are you talking about?" Dorie was pretty sure she knew but she wanted Phoebe to come out with it herself.

"Nothing," Phoebe said and lapsed into silence.

Best to let her tell me in her own time, Dorie decided. She got into the driver's seat, did a careful three-point turn to exit the parking area without backing over the edge of the cliff, put the car in low gear and inched down the road, with Rick following a safe distance behind.

When she reached the highway she tooted the horn, waved him past, and paused the car to peer around her headrest at the backseat.

"You doing okay, babe?"

"Yeah." Phoebe didn't meet her eyes.

Dorie ventured another invitation to share. "Phoebe, I understand you were really upset about something yesterday before you and Jared came up here. Did it have anything to do with me?"

Phoebe didn't respond for several seconds. Then, slowly and deliberately, she spoke.

"I looked at that notebook in your room. I was going to surprise you by making the beds and everything so the house would be nice when you came back. So it was, like, lying open under the quilt and I couldn't help seeing the part where you were in that orgy. What you did with that guru? How could you?" she wailed. "It was disgusting."

"It was the quickest way to find out something I needed to know," Dorie said. "It's kind of hard to explain. You had to be there."

"But it was just plain fornication," Phoebe declared. "You weren't even in love with him or anything. It was fornication and the Bible says that's a sin."

Dorie shifted in her seat, flipped on the turn signal, and turned towards town. Her relief at Phoebe's recovery was giving way to annoyance.

"The Bible also says judge not that ye be not judged," she stated firmly. "Phoebe, you have no idea what I was thinking or feeling at that point in my life. You're condemning me for something you can't even begin to understand."

She checked herself. Phoebe was recovering from a terrifying experience. She shouldn't be arguing with her. Nevertheless, her daughter's self-righteous tone and accusation of "fornication" were insufferable.

"I have a big problem with your brand of Christianity," she continued. "It preaches love and forgiveness while it judges and damns everything and everybody that diverges from its own biased reading of the scriptures. It's a basically hypocritical religion."

"It is not!" Phoebe protested vehemently. "It's based on God's commandments. And I know He says to honor your parents but I can't honor you."

Suddenly she gasped and moaned. "Something's wrong," she whimpered. "I …."

Dorie braked, pulled onto the shoulder, and jammed the shift lever into park. She swiveled around and looked into the backseat. Phoebe's eyes were closed and her head lolled to one side.

"Phoebe? Phoebe?" Dorie's heart thumped erratically. "Are you okay?" There was no answer, only an empty silence. She jumped out of the car, opened the back door and shook Phoebe's shoulder. There was no response. Her daughter was as limp as a rag doll.

Check for a pulse, she admonished herself. Check to see if she's breathing. She fumbled with Phoebe's wrist but couldn't locate a pulse with her trembling fingers. But she could see Phoebe's chest rise and fall. She's breathing, she thought. So she must have a pulse.

She closed the back door and got behind the wheel, accelerating so fast that the wheels spun with a horrible screeching sound and she smelt burning rubber. With a dry mouth and pounding heart, she overtook several cars, honking the horn so furiously that they swerved onto the shoulder to let her pass. When she reached a clear stretch of highway she extracted her phone from her shirt pocket and called 911.

Her voice, brittle and cracked, seemed like a disembodied stranger's when she spoke to the dispatcher.

"My daughter's unconscious. She has a head injury. I'm on the way to St. Joseph's ER. Call ahead for me."

Mechanically, Dorie answered the dispatcher's calm questions concerning Phoebe's name and age, the circumstances of her injury, and the present location and description of the Subaru. The dispatcher promised to dispatch a patrol car to escort her to the hospital.

When she reached the city limits, Dorie was forced to slow down. The road was jammed with impossibly slow-moving cars full of tourists and families on their way home from Sunday outings. Stuck behind a mammoth SUV with Texas plates, she adjusted the rearview mirror to reflect the back seat. Phoebe's chest rose and fell with her shallow breaths. However, her face was ashen and her jaw slack. Frantic, Dorie scanned the oncoming traffic for a sign of the promised police cruiser while silently repeating an improvised mantra: "Please God, let Phoebe be all right. Please God, let Phoebe be all right."

Thirty - Two

The cruiser that had escorted Dorie to St. Joseph's halted abruptly at the ambulance entrance to the emergency wing. Dorie stopped the Subaru within inches of his rear bumper, jumped out of the car and flung open the door to the back seat. Phoebe was flat on her back, eyes shut and mouth agape. Her face was paper white. Her left arm dangled limply into the off the seat. Dorie placed it across her chest with some vague notion of making her more comfortable.

"Don't try to move her, ma'am. We'll take over from here."

A voice spoke from somewhere behind her and she turned to see two men in green scrubs trotting towards the car with a gurney. She stepped aside and they slid a board-like contraption under Phoebe, secured her head and neck with foam blocks and transferred her to the gurney. One of the men put a finger to her neck while leaning close to her mouth. He nodded to his companion.

"Pulse and respiration are steady. Let's go."

Brushing Dorie aside, they rushed the gurney towards the double doors to the emergency wing. Dorie started to follow them, then stopped. She should move her car. It was blocking the ambulance entrance. But she didn't want to leave Phoebe for even a moment. She spied the patrolman, who was standing outside his cruiser, speaking into a handheld microphone. She waved at him and pointed to her car and then the parking area. He nodded and made an o. k. sign with his fingers. She mouthed "thank you" at him, then turned and sprinted to the double doors just as they were closing.

She found herself in a tiled corridor so brightly lit that she had to blink repeatedly to regain her focus. The two men and the rolling gurney were just ahead of her and she could hear them questioning Phoebe: "Can you hear me? Can you tell us your name?" She followed them though another set of double doors into a large room with even brighter lights. Curtained cubicles lined the walls on either side of her.

A white-coated man, shockingly young and well-muscled, burst through a door at the rear of the room, intercepted the gurney, and bent over Phoebe with a stethoscope.

He fired a series of questions at Dorie as he examined Phoebe: her daughter's name, and age, the circumstances preceding her collapse, any pre-existing medical conditions.

"Does she have a history of drug use?" he inquired, as he pulled back Phoebe's eyelids and peered closely at her eyes.

"None," Dorie replied, adding needlessly, "She's a Christian." And if it weren't for her Christian boyfriend, she added silently, this would never have happened.

A wave of guilt hollowed her stomach. She was lying to herself. If she hadn't left her journal on the bed and rushed off to that idiotic conference Phoebe wouldn't have seen it and run to Jared for comfort. She herself was the cause of this disaster.

She edged around the nurses who were attaching a tube to a plastic bag of clear liquid dangling from metal pole. Phoebe didn't even twitch as they slid an IV needle into a vein in the back of her hand. She was so still and colorless that she looked like a wax effigy of herself.

Dorie turned to the young doctor, who was talking to a woman with a clipboard. "What's the matter with my daughter?" she demanded, tugging at his sleeve. "Why is she unconscious?" She remembered something about fixed and dilated pupils being a bad sign and wondered what he had seen when he pulled back Phoebe's lids and aimed a light at her eyes.

"Too soon to say," the doctor replied. He turned to the nurses. "She's stable for the moment but I want a CAT scan STAT. Let's get her into imaging." He walked towards a door at the rear of the room and held it open for the gurney to pass through.

Dorie started to follow it but the woman with the clipboard stopped her.

"It's better if you wait outside," she said gently. "We've got a bunch of high-tech devices back there and not a lot of standing room." She took Dorie by the arm and turned her around.

"But she's my daughter," Dorie protested, pressing her hand to her chest. The door closed with a hydraulic sigh and she felt as if an invisible cord stretching from her heart to Phoebe's inert form had been severed.

"I know." The woman smiled. "I can see the resemblance. And we'll get her back to you as soon as possible. But right now I need you to fill out some forms so we can take care of her." She placed her hand on Dorie's back and guided her through a side door and into a public corridor.

"I'm Dr. Lenninger, chief ER resident. And that good-looking kid who whisked your daughter away is Dr. Sanberg, our attending. Don't worry; he's older than he looks and he's highly experienced." She guided Dorie through an intersecting corridor. "And you are…?"

Dorie squeaked her name. Her voice sounded tinny and thin, like an old radio recording. She cleared her throat and managed to slide into a lower octave.

"I understand that you don't know anything definitive," she said, trying to sound reasonable and intelligent, "but what's your best guess about what's going on?" Maybe Dr. Lenninger, being a woman, would be more open than taciturn Dr. Sanberg.

They had arrived at an office marked "Admitting." Dorie had no idea how they had gotten there or how to find here way back to the emergency wing. Dr. Lenninger ushered her inside, pulled out a chair in front of a desk, and dinged a little circular bell to summon the office's occupant. Dorie, suddenly weak with exhaustion, lowered herself into the chair.

Dr. Lenninger perched on the edge of the desk and cleared her throat. "Your daughter has what appears to be an injury to the temporal area of her skull," she said softly, almost whispering. "The CAT scan will tell us exactly what kind of damage she's incurred. And then," she smiled reassuringly, "we'll do everything we can to fix it."

"Everything we can to fix it." The phrase replayed itself in Dorie's mind as she sat in the emergency wing waiting area, where she had been sent after filling out innumerable forms in Admissions. "Everything we can" was far too tentative to be reassuring.

She stared at a lithograph of a desert sunset on the far wall. Its colors were painstakingly coordinated with the room's carpet and upholstery. Everything was muted sage and apricot and peach, a soothing palette undoubtedly chosen to ward off hysteria on the part of those who waited for their ill and injured loved ones. But the color therapy wasn't working for her. She dropped the inane Hollywood gossip magazine she'd picked up to distract herself and got to her feet. Walking around and feeling helpless was better than sitting still and feeling helpless.

"Can I get you something, ma'am? Some water? A cup of coffee?"

The sweet-faced blonde at the receptionist's desk, a girl who looked only a few years older than Phoebe, stood up as Dorie paced by her. Dorie shook her head.

"No thank you," she said. "But could you try again to find out what's happening to my daughter?"

The girl sighed. "Ma'am, Dr. Sanberg said he'd get back to you just as soon as they finish the CAT scan. There's nothing I can do to hurry that up."

Dorie nodded and wandered to the entry doors of the waiting area and pressed her forehead against the cool glass. She looked out at the puffy white clouds floating in the midday sky. How could the day be so beautiful when her world was disintegrating? She rubbed her hands together. They were as cold as the glass but her cheeks felt hot and prickly. I've got to calm down, she thought. I'm no use to anyone like this.

For an instant, she imagined her parents' old black Chrysler pulling into the parking lot outside, her mother and her father getting out, walking towards the door where she was standing, coming to her aid. If they were here, I could get through this, she thought. But they'd been dead for decades; the only comfort they could offer was her memory of their love.

She needed help. She needed to call someone. But whom? She couldn't call Doug, not after their frosty farewell. Sharon had already been up most of last night on the phone and besides she had the twins to look after.

Viktor. She'd call Viktor. He'd been as worried as she was about Phoebe and Jared. And Jared had a right to know what was going on. It was obvious that he cared about Phoebe and felt terrible about getting her into trouble.

She located Viktor's number in the recent calls list on her phone, thankful that she hadn't deleted it in a fit of pique. He didn't answer until the sixth ring and he sounded groggy and irritated.

"I guess you're going to chew Jared out for taking Phoebe to Hawk Canyon and getting her banged up."

"No, no, no. That's not it. Listen, Viktor, Phoebe's really hurt. She passed out on the way down the mountain and she's still unconscious. We're at the hospital."

Viktor's intake of breath was clearly audible. "But Jared said she was okay except for her ankle and a headache."

"She's not. They're doing a CAT scan right now. One of the doctors told me there was trauma to her skull." Dorie choked up and the last four words came out in a croak.

"Dorie, is anyone with you?" Viktor asked.

"No, but I'm okay." What had she been thinking? She couldn't ask Viktor to come sit with her. There was too much ill feeling between them.

"Bullshit," Viktor said. "You can't be okay. I wouldn't be if it was Jared getting a CAT scan. Don't go anywhere. Jared and I will be there in two shakes."

Dorie sank down in one of the waiting room chairs and rested her forehead in one hand. Relief washed over her like a soothing balm.

"Thank you," she said. "Thank you so much."

"Mrs. MacKenzie?" Dr. Sanberg had materialized beside her. Dorie sprang to her feet as if galvanized. She didn't bother to correct his attribution of Colin and Phoebe's surname to her.

"How's my daughter?" she asked, hoping that he would smile and say that Phoebe was awake and asking for her mother.

"Please come with me," he said." I want you to see something." He led her down the hall and through the doors to the emergency room.

"Where's Phoebe?" Dorie asked, scanning the curtained cubicles, which were empty save for one in which an elderly man in overalls sat on the edge of a bed talking softly to an old woman who was propped up with pillows and tethered to an IV and an oxygen feed. Her face was a wrinkled mask of fear. The man leaned forward and caressed her disheveled white hair.

It's not so bad if *she* dies, Dorie thought, she's had a life. Phoebe hasn't. She scanned the room again, her attention registering vivid but irrelevant details: pale blue thermal blankets that looked as if they belonged in a nursery, resuscitation equipment in oddly decorative wall-hung steel baskets, a nurse with a cellphone to her ear, ordering Chinese takeout.

"Where's Phoebe?" she repeated.

"She's being prepped for the O.R.," the doctor said.

Dorie gasped and clapped her hand to her mouth.

"What?" She swayed backwards, off balance, then righted herself. "Why are you operating? What's wrong?"

"I'm going to show you," the doctor said. He took her elbow and guided her to a computer monitor on a desk in an alcove. A gray oval was superimposed on a black background. "This is Phoebe's CAT scan. "

Dorie searched her pockets for her reading glasses. When she put them on the convoluted folds of what she guessed were the cerebral hemispheres came into focus within the gray oval. She realized that she looking at the inside of Phoebe's head; it was as if her skull had been sliced in half from front to back exposing the soft vulnerable brain within. Dorie recoiled from the monitor. Even though the image was a digital reconstruction, it seemed violent and intrusive.

"See this?" The doctor pointed to a white ellipse on the left side of the oval. "That's an epidural hematoma." Dorie looked at him mutely. What did he mean? Why didn't he speak plain English?

"Your daughter incurred a skull fracture that tore the middle meningeal artery," the doctor continued. "The clot you see here is compressing the brain. That's why she's in a coma."

Dorie closed her eyes as the room started to spin around her. A coma. Phoebe was in a coma. People in comas could die. Or wake up as someone else, someone spastic and non-verbal. Or worst of all, lapse into--what was that awful phrase--a "persistent vegetative state."

She gripped the edge of the desk to steady herself.

"How do you fix this?" she whispered. "And what's the prognosis?"

Dr. Sanberg clicked his ballpoint pen repeatedly as he spoke. Dorie stifled the impulse to rip it out of his hand.

"We've got a neurosurgeon on his way. Don't worry, he's the best guy in town. He'll remove a small section of skull over the hematoma and extract it. That will relieve the intercranial pressure and let the brain expand."

"And then?"

"Then we'll be monitoring Phoebe in intensive care so we can keep everything in working order until her brain has a chance to recover."

He's waffling, Dorie thought. She forced herself to take a deep breath. "What are the chances that her brain won't recover?"

Dr. Sanberg clicked the pen more rapidly and stared at the monitor, as if the gray and white image held an answer.

"To be frank," he said, "I have to tell you that these cases are a little unpredictable. There is always the possibility of brain damage or...." He hesitated. "Or death." He gave the pen a final definitive click and dropped it on the desk. "We'll just have to wait and see."

# Thirty-Three

Phoebe was rushed into surgery so quickly that Dorie only saw her for a minute as she was being rolled into the operating room. She was barely recognizable in a pale blue hospital gown, her hair hidden under a puffy cloth cap. IV's were attached to both arms, and wires emerged from beneath the sheets and terminated in a monitoring device perched on the end of the wheeled hospital bed.

Dorie was hesitant to touch her for fear of detaching some vital cord or tube but one of the two nurses guiding the bed reassured her.

"Go ahead, Mom. Give her a kiss and talk to her. Sometimes they can hear you even when you think they can't."

Dorie leaned over and touched her lips to Phoebe's cheek. It was cool and dry. Like Snow White, like Sleeping Beauty, Dorie thought. But this kiss can't wake you up, can it, my love?

"Hang in there, Phoebe. You're going to be fine," she whispered. "I love you. I'll be there when you wake up."

The nurse pushed a round button on the wall and the doors to the operating room swung inwards. Dorie caught a glimpse of white tile, glaring lights, and complex monitors swathed in protective plastic. Androgynous masked figures swathed in green scrubs were moving about purposefully, fiddling with dials on the monitors and arranging shiny instruments on trays. A white-sheeted operating table mounted on a stainless steel pedestal sat in the center or the room. Dorie shuddered. It looked like the setting of an alien abduction movie.

The nurses rolled Phoebe's bed through the doors and they closed silently behind it. Once again Dorie was overwhelmed with a sense of separation that left her hollow and desolate. She wanted to curl up on the floor outside the operating room until the doors opened and Phoebe reappeared.

Get a grip, she admonished herself. Do not fall apart. It's self-indulgent and useless. She took a deep breath and stumbled towards an alcove down the hall where a sofa and chairs were provided for families to hold vigil.

"Dorie, thank God! We've been looking everywhere for you."

Viktor, with Jared close behind, emerged from the elevator across from the alcove. He stepped forward as if to embrace Dorie but checked himself and simply patted her arm instead.

Jared peered over Viktor's shoulder. His hair had been washed and combed and he was wearing clean clothes but his face was drawn.

"Where's Phoebe?" he said. His voice cracked as it regressed to a preadolescent countertenor. "Can I see her?"

Dorie shook her head and pointed at the doors to the operating room. Jared's mouth dropped open and his prominent Adam's apple traced a gulp.

"What are they doing to her?" he said. "Will she be all right?"

Dorie explained the planned procedure as briefly as possible, omitting the graphic details the neurosurgeon had included. There was no point in upsetting Jared; he looked as if he might burst into tears any moment.

As Dorie was searching for a euphemism for "craniotomy", the elevator chime sounded and the doors slid back to reveal Pastor Charlie, Janelle and Ev Medderly.

Dorie recoiled as Pastor Charlie strode towards her, his arms opened wide. Before she knew it, she was surrounded. Charlie enfolded her upper body in an embrace while Janelle grasped one of her wrists and Ev squeezed her shoulder.

She extricated herself and glared at Viktor.

"What are they doing here?"

"I called them." Viktor was unapologetic. "I know you don't think much of us but Phoebe needs all the help she can get right now."

"That's right, Dorie," Pastor Charlie added. "We don't mean to intrude but we love Phoebe and we want to be here for her. And you, too."

"There's nothing worse for a mother than when her child's in trouble," Ev said. "We're here to support you."

Dorie softened momentarily, but then Janelle spoke.

"As a mom myself, I've been praying for the Lord to give you strength from the very minute Viktor called us."

Dorie gritted her teeth.

"We all have, "Charlie added. "We know the Lord loves you just like he loves our Phoebe." He paused and glanced up and down the hall. "And where is she?"

What the fuck does he mean, "our Phoebe"? Dorie's lips curled in an incipient snarl. She pointed at the doors to the operating suite. "She's in there," she spat. "They're sawing a piece of her skull out and then they're going to suck a big blood clot off her brain and then we'll see whether she ends up a vegetable or not."

Ev gasped and Janelle clasped her hand to her mouth. Jared's lower lip trembled and Dorie immediately regretted her outburst.

Charlie, however, didn't flinch.

"I see," he murmured. "She is indeed in mortal peril." He looked directly at Dorie. "We all know the Lord's will must be done but I don't think it would be amiss to encourage Him to steady that surgeon's hand and sustain Phoebe through her ordeal."

Janelle nodded vigorously. "Jesus looks after his lambs and Phoebe is truly one of his." She sighed deeply. "In fact, I can just feel His presence right there with her in that operating room."

Dorie closed her eyes. If these people didn't shut up her head was going to explode.

Charlie took her hand. "Dorie, I can see how upset you are and I wish I could do something to ease your pain. But all I can do is to ask for God's help. Would you be willing to join us in a prayer for Phoebe?"

Dorie jerked her hand away.

"No!" she yelled. "I'm sick of this crap. I never got any help from your God when I needed it. Not when my parents died and not when my husband was killed. I don't expect to get it now."

She brushed pass Viktor and stalked to the elevator. She jabbed at both the up and down buttons, not caring which way she went as long as it was out of here. How dare these people presume to understand her grief? How dare they offer her their sanctimonious platitudes?

"Dorie! Don't go, dear." Ev was at her elbow. "It doesn't matter whether you believe what we do. We just want to help. You shouldn't be alone at a time like this."

Dorie jigged in place. The elevator was making no progress. She had to escape before she hit someone. She bolted towards a door marked "Stairs" and jerked it open. As it swung shut behind her, she spoke into the silence of the stairwell.

"Yes, I should be alone. I'm always alone."

She stopped on the top step. Her declaration reverberated off the concrete walls. It wasn't true. She wasn't alone. She had Phoebe. But if Phoebe died she would be alone. Horribly, irrevocably, forever alone.

"No," she whispered. "Not again." She remembered the angry words Phoebe had hurled at her in the car: "...but I can't honor you." If Phoebe were to die, those words would hang in the void between them for all eternity, along with her own hateful last words to Colin before he drove away: "...and I hope you never come back."

She descended the stairs haltingly, grasping the cold metal railing to keep from tripping as tears flooded her eyes.

"I can't lose her. I just can't." Her voice rose from somewhere deep in her chest, hoarse and guttural and barely recognizable.

Two flights down she came upon a door she thought might lead to an outside exit. She needed space. Fresh air and sunshine. The sounds and smell of the hospital, the bells and beeps and acrid medicinal odors, were driving her mad. But when she opened the door she found herself in a wide hall connected to the main lobby, a glassy atrium full of people and offering no privacy.

She looked around, desperate for a refuge, somewhere she could sit down and pull herself together. Across the lobby a discreet sign read "Chapel." Why not? It should be dark and quiet inside, as good a place to hide as any. And it would be the last place Pastor Charlie and company would think of looking for her.

## Thirty - Four

Dorie hurried across the lobby, slipped through the chapel door, and stopped, startled by the glare of light from a wall of windows and, in front of it, a massive metal sculpture, the figure of a man, suspended in mid-air, arms outstretched and legs crossed at the ankles. An abstract, Christ, flayed and crucified.

Dorie eased herself into one of the chairs arrayed in front of the figure. She couldn't look take her eyes off it. The suggestion of exposed muscle, bone and sinew wrought in varying shades of bronze, conveyed unbearable suffering; the bowed featureless head, depicted resignation and acceptance.

Dorie swallowed to ease the ache in her throat and wiped away the tears blurring her vision. That's the way it is, she thought. The Buddha was right. Life is suffering. The vision that Bud had mysteriously transmitted to her that night in the Winnebago, the panoramic view of an infinite multitude of anonymous souls, heads bowed in silent, inescapable misery, appeared in her mind's eye and a shiver passed down her spine.

She looked up at the sculpture. Reflected sunlight radiated from its variegated contours, imbuing the figure with a mysterious vitality that defied its posture of death. Dorie smiled sadly as she remembered Bud's elliptical aphorism, "the only way out is up it and through it." Wasn't that the real lesson of the crucifixion? By taking on the suffering of others we transcend our own inevitable personal tragedies. We learn compassion. We learn to love.

She took a tremulous breath as tears spilled from her eyes and wet her cheeks. A sweet liquid heat grew behind her breastbone and spread like melting honey throughout her body. She remembered Phoebe standing in the living room clutching a Bible to her chest. "I know it's true, because I feel it. Here."

Phoebe, dear Phoebe, had been blessed with the gift of faith. Maybe her faith came wrapped in a cloak of dogma, but there was something live and burning at its core.

I had that once, Dorie thought. I had that same sense of union with something infinite and eternal. Her scalp and the back of her arms tingled and the boundary between her envelope of skin and its surroundings dissolved. Suddenly she was no longer Dorie; she was only a point of awareness in a field of ecstatically dancing particles of energy, an energy that annihilated her with a sense of an incomprehensibly boundless, timeless love so powerful, so self-evidently true that there was no question of its existence.

Yes, she thought. That's it. That's what lies beneath everything. That's what's real. How could I have forgotten?

The instant this thought formed her sense of self returned. Her body solidified and time resumed. Dazed, she pressed her hand to her forehead, then blinked as the vertical lines of the wood paneled chapel walls came into focus. I must remember this, she thought. It's a gift.

"Thank you," she said aloud. "Thank you, thank you, thank you."

Then, she remembered where she was and why. How long had she been sitting here? She looked at her watch. It was 4:06 pm. Phoebe's surgery must have started. The neurosurgeon had said the procedure would take at least three hours, more if there were complications. The operation should be over before sunset.

And then maybe Phoebe would wake up, groggy and disoriented, but still herself. Or maybe not. But there was no point in being negative. What would be would be, but just in case her thoughts mattered she would picture Phoebe alert and talkative, her cheeks rosy, her eyes bright.

She summoned a memory of Phoebe at her birthday party, happy and laughing, but the image morphed into an ugly scene of Phoebe unconscious, surrounded by green clad alien doctors wielding bone-piercing drills and suction tubes. The knot of anxiety that lived under her ribcage re-formed, writhing like a clutch of nervous snakes. Dorie groaned.

"This sucks," she muttered. "This just sucks." She looked out the vertical expanse of windows at the foothills dotted with pinons and junipers, their dark green silhouettes dramatic against the rocky ochre soil.

"I will lift up my eyes unto the hills from whence cometh my help." The words floated to the surface of her mind from some storehouse of childhood memories. She realized that it was the one hundred and twenty first Psalm, the one Pastor Charlie had urged her to read.

"My help cometh from the Lord," she whispered, "who made heaven and earth." The phrase seemed to calm the snakes so she repeated it aloud as she gazed at the uncaring and implacable hills.

Night and day did not exist in the Intensive Care Unit. The glass walled cubicles surrounding the central nursing station were illuminated at all hours, the better to monitor the precarious condition of their occupants.

Dorie pushed herself upright in the uncomfortable reclining chair besides Phoebe's bed and looked at the big clock on the opposite wall. Seven fifteen, which meant it was Monday morning. She must have dozed off around three a.m., right after an anonymous doctor had come in, checked the monitor displaying Phoebe's vital signs, tried to rouse her and failed, then scribbled something on a chart. He had reassured Dorie that, while Phoebe was still unconscious, all her systems seemed to be functioning normally.

Dorie removed the hospital blanket that someone had placed over her legs and extricated herself from the chair. She studied her daughter as she worked the kinks out of her back and neck. Phoebe's appearance was far less frightening than it had been in the recovery room, where a plastic tube had tethered her to a wheezing respirator. She was still receiving supplementary oxygen through a nasal cannula as well as intravenous fluids, but her pallor was gone. She looked almost like a normal, sleeping girl with black mascara smudges beneath her eyes and a bulky white turban covering a head full of hair rollers. Except the smudges were black eyes, the aftermath of her surgery, and the turban was a thick gauze bandage hiding a partially denuded scalp and an irregular oval of sutured skull.

And who knew what was happening under that Frankenstein patch of bone? Were the traumatized brain cells healing themselves, reconstructing the neural networks that made Phoebe herself? Or had some vital circuits been damaged beyond repair, damage that would manifest itself in palsy, aphasia, an altered personality?

Dorie listened to Phoebe's even breathing for a moment to reassure herself that it was safe to leave her alone, then hurried to the restroom near the nursing station. She splashed cold water on her face, plastered some wayward tufts of hair into place, and scrubbed her sticky teeth with a brush from a packet of courtesy toiletries supplied by a sympathetic nurse. She looked in the mirror. She had bags beneath her eyes and lines from her nostrils to the corners of her lips. Yesterday had been unspeakably bad day followed by an unimagineably worse night.

Phoebe's surgery had taken four and a half hours. When the neurosurgeon, still clad in his scrubs, found Dorie at the coffee machine by the family waiting room he had delivered a guardedly positive prognosis.

"Overall it went well," he said, rubbing his eyes wearily. "We had one dicey moment when her blood pressure dropped through the floor. But we got her stabilized right away so I think everything will be okay."

Dorie had mentally edited his words at the time, allowing only "went well" and "everything will be okay" to register, but now, staring at her haggard reflection in the restroom mirror, she couldn't stop obsessing about how that moment of diminished cerebral blood flow might have worsened the preexisting trauma. What if Phoebe's bright intelligence were permanently dimmed? Would Phoebe know what she had lost and be devastated? What if her motor functions were impaired and she couldn't walk? And what would their life together be like if Phoebe no longer was no longer an active, independent teenager but a young woman with what was so awkwardly termed "special needs"?

Dorie patted her face dry with rough paper towels and hurried back to Phoebe's room. The monitor was still beeping evenly, the green and amber lines tracing their roller coaster patterns across the screen. Phoebe lay immobile beneath a smooth expanse of thermal blanket, her hands atop it in exactly the same position they had been since she was wheeled out of the recovery room. Dorie laid her palm on her daughter's cheek. It was reassuringly warm, plump and resilient, but Phoebe gave no sign she was aware of being touched.

"Phoebe? It's me, Mom," Dorie said. "Can you open your eyes?"

There was no response. Phoebe's face remained a placid, expressionless mask. Dorie felt the twinge of incipient tears but willed them way. She'd done enough weeping. It was time to move on, time to play whatever cards she and Phoebe had been dealt. She pulled her chair close the bed, settled into it, and clasped Phoebe's hand.

"Time to wake up, baby," she said. "I'm right here waiting for you and I'm not going anywhere. So you wake up and talk to me, okay?"

For the next two hours Dorie alternated pacing the cubicle with sitting by the bed to massage Phoebe's hands and promise her anything she thought might ring a bell in some auditory center deep in her brain: pizza with anchovies, a new puppy, a trip to San Francisco, even a homecoming party involving the entire membership of Teens for Christ. She was exhausting her list of enticements to consciousness when a nurse appeared in the open doorway.

"Someone called from reception asking if he could come up. He said he was Phoebe's pastor."

"It's all right," Dorie said. "Phoebe would want him here."

A few minutes later there was a rap on the door and Charlie entered hesitantly. He was carrying two paper cups from the coffee bar in the lobby.

"Good morning," he said. "I don't mean to barge in on you but..." he took another step into the room "but I wanted to come by just in case you needed anything. I hope you don't mind."

"It's all right." Dorie said. "I acted like a jerk last night. You all were trying to help and I blew you off. I'm really sorry."

"I understand," Charlie said. "You were stressed." He held up the cups. "I brought coffee. Didn't know how you took it so I got one black and one with cream." He nodded at the bed. "How's our girl? She been awake yet?"

"Not yet. The surgeon said it would take a while for the swelling in her brain to go down." Dorie accepted the light coffee and closed her eyes for a moment. The coffee smelled like mornings at home, like normality and hope. "Thanks," she said. "I needed this."

Charlie approached the bed, walking softly as if Phoebe were a sleeping baby who might startle at the slightest sound.

"Is it okay to touch her?" he asked.

Dorie nodded. "The nurse says it helps. I've been rubbing her arms and hands all morning but so far she hasn't responded."

Charlie placed his palm on Phoebe's forehead, closed his eyes, and took a deep breath. Dorie wondered if he was doing some kind of faith healing but if so, she didn't mind. It might actually help. She leaned forward, hoping Phoebe might suddenly open her eyes and sit up like a latter-day Lazarus but Charlie's touch had no more effect than her own.

Charlie stepped back from the bed. He retrieved his coffee from the bedside tray table where he'd set it down and took a sip. He shifted from foot to foot as he glanced at the screen monitoring Phoebe's vital signs. Dorie thought he seemed uncharacteristically ill at ease. Perhaps he was embarrassed that his laying on of hands hadn't elicited a response.

"Got to tell you something," he said. "Hospitals kind of give me the creeps."

"How so?" Dorie asked. "I thought pastors were supposed to be good with sick people."

"It's not the sick part," Charlie said. "It's the technology. I sat with my Daddy after he had a stroke and I was scared to death to look at that thing…" he pointed at the monitor…"because I was afraid I'd see the lines go flat like they do on those hospital soap operas." He took another sip of his coffee and shook his head slowly. "Besides," he continued," I didn't care about what was going on with Daddy's blood pressure. I wanted to know that his soul was at peace. A machine couldn't tell me that. All this hightech stuff they've got, it keeps the body going but that's no use if the spirit isn't healed."

"I'm with you on that," Dorie said. She looked at Phoebe's motionless form. The surgical intervention and the anti-inflammatory drugs could only deal with the physical damage. Ultimately, it would be Phoebe's vital young spirit, her will to live, and possibly her innocent faith, that would sustain her through the healing process.

And what sustains me, Dorie wondered, thinking of her regimen of vitamins and health foods and exercise and fancy skin creams. She had a well-nourished body but it was inhabited by a semi-starved soul. Like one of the Buddhist hungry ghosts, whose tiny mouths and constricted necks won't allow them to partake of the abundance surrounding them.

"Yes, indeed," Charlie went on, following his own train of thought. "When I sat there with my Daddy praying for him live so he could carry on his ministry, the Lord took him away." He looked down at his shoes. "Kind of shook me up for a while." He smiled ruefully. "But Janelle got me back on track. Janelle and the good Lord. Together they lit a fire under me and I went through with the purchase of our new sanctuary."

"I'd guess Janelle can be quite a powerful motivating force," Dorie said.

Charlie shot her an assessing glance followed by a hint of a smile. Dorie realized he was considerably sharper than the "oh shucks" and "yes ma'ams" his countrified diction suggested.

A sound like the mewling of a tiny kitten broke the silence.

Dorie's heart thudded. She scrambled from her chair and leaned over Phoebe, studying her face for signs of consciousness.

Phoebe's lips parted. She moaned again, louder this time, and her eyelids fluttered.

"Phoebe, it's me. Wake up, baby," Dorie patted Phoebe's hand. "Charlie, call the nurse." She prodded Phoebe's shoulder. "I'm right here, sweetie. Talk to me."

Phoebe opened her eyes slowly.

"Mo.. om?" Her voice was halting and weak but the word was clearly audible. Her eyeballs rolled upwards and her lids shuttered them again.

Dorie shook her shoulder. "Stay with me," she commanded. "You've got to stay with me."

She felt a hand on her own shoulder. "It's all right, Ms. Winslow," the nurse said. "She's likely to slip in and out of consciousness for a while. But this is a good sign."

"Praise the Lord," Charlie exclaimed. "He's heard our prayers and he's brought Phoebe back to us."

Dorie was too elated to suggest that the dexamethasone administered to reduce the cerebral edema was finally kicking in. There was no need to challenge Charlie's faith in the collective prayers of his congregation. Besides, it was entirely possible that all that focused emotion might have, in some mysterious non-linear way, enhanced the effect of the steroids.

"Phoebe's doctor will be making his rounds this afternoon," the nurse told Dorie. "In the meantime, you keep on talking to her. That will help her wake up."

After Pastor Charlie had recited the Lord's Prayer at the foot of Phoebe's bed, given his cell phone number to Dorie, and excused himself to attend a Rotary Club luncheon, Dorie started talking. She talked all afternoon. She recounted the story of Phoebe's life, from her midnight emergence at Brigham and Women's Hospital in Boston up to her "best ever" birthday party just two weeks ago. She told Phoebe how much she loved her. She told her how much her father had loved her, and how, when she was six weeks old, he had bought a giant Steiff teddy bear bigger than she was.

"You were always loved and wanted, Phoebe." Dorie wove a lifeline of words close to her daughter's ear. "And you always will be. You are the heart of my heart."

Phoebe's right arm twitched and her fingers plucked at the thermal blanket.

"Phoebe, if you hear me, raise your hand," Dorie whispered. "Just raise your hand. Please."

Slowly, almost imperceptibly, Phoebe uncurled the fingers of her right hand and lifted them two inches above the bedclothes. Then, even more slowly, she opened her eyes. Dorie held her breath, afraid to anticipate what might come next. Phoebe's gaze was unfocussed and random, like that of a blind person. Dizzy with rising panic, Dorie imagined a damaged visual cortex, Phoebe in dark glasses with a white cane. Phoebe's eyes moved erratically to the right and left. Dorie forced herself to breathe slowly so she wouldn't pass out. Phoebe rolled her head to the side and frowned. She blinked rapidly and her eyes began to track normally. She looked directly at Dorie.

"Mom? What's happening?" Phoebe's voice was hoarse and scratchy but stronger. "My head hurts."

Dorie didn't bother to wipe away the tears that spilled freely down her cheeks. "You had a little accident," she replied. "But you're going to be all right. You're going to be just fine."

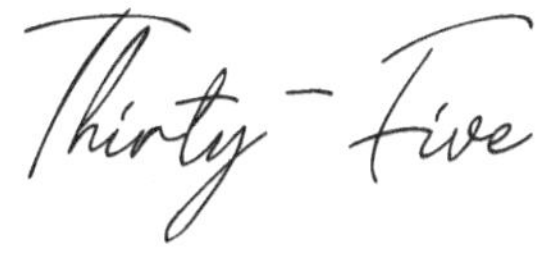

"**P**hoebe, I need to talk to you."

Dorie stood in the doorway of Phoebe's bedroom holding a silver foil gift bag. Phoebe, nestled in bed among multiple pillows and stuffed animals, was paging through a *People* magazine while listening to her iPod. She looked up blankly.

"What did you say?"

Three weeks ago, when Phoebe came home from the hospital, this query would have sent Dorie into a tailspin of worry about hearing loss but now, with Phoebe's recovery proceeding smoothly, aside from late afternoon headaches, Dorie reacted normally. She pantomimed removing the iPod's earbuds and shouted, "Take those things out so you can hear me."

Phoebe extracted the earbuds. "That is the most awesome music," she sighed. "It gives me goose bumps."

"What is it?" Dorie asked. "A new JC Rox production?"

"No," Phoebe smiled. "Something way more righteous. Bach's Prelude and Fugue in D Minor."

Dorie did a double take.

"Since when did you develop a taste for Baroque music?"

"This guy I met at physical therapy. He turned me on to it."

Dorie imagined a Humbert Humbert type lurking in the halls of the rehab facility where Phoebe had been going to strengthen her injured ankle.

"What kind of guy?" she asked.

"A musician. He plays the cello. He's got some kind of carpal tunnel problem. That's why he's getting therapy."

"An old guy or a young guy?"

"Really, Mother. He's eighteen. His name, since I'm sure you're going to ask, is Aaron Waldbaum. He goes to Andover but he's here for the summer because his parents have a vacation house in the mountains."

She glanced at her laptop, close at hand on her bedside table. "He's sending me links to the whole Art of the Fugue. It is so cool. Did you know that Wanda Landowski was the greatest harpsichordist that ever lived?"

Dorie moved a plush buffalo wearing a CU letter sweater, a get well present from Kimberly and Amber, and sat down on the bed.

"I was more or less aware of that. But about this Aaron Waldbaum? Should Jared be worried?"

Phoebe wrinkled her nose. "I guess not," she said. "I mean, I still like Jared. It's just that Aaron's, like, really interesting, you know? He's into all kinds of stuff. Not just music. Books, too. And physics. That's his other passion. Besides the cello, I mean."

"Oh, a scientist," Dorie said. "Like your dad. Cool."

Phoebe looked at her warily. "I thought you didn't like scientists," she said.

"Why? Because Colin and I couldn't get along?"

"I guess. You sure didn't like him."

It's time, Dorie thought, to lay this issue to rest.

"I did at first, Phoebs. I was crazy about your father. But people change, and not always in the same way. We became so different from each other that the only thing we had in common was you. You were the light of our lives but we didn't have anything else to keep us together."

Phoebe looped the cords of her earbuds around her hand. She bit her lower lip.

"I've been really mad at you ever since Dad died, you know?"

"I know, baby. You thought it was my fault. Well, guess what. So did I."

"No," Phoebe said. "I knew the car crash was an accident. But I thought you didn't care that he died. You got rid of all his things and went back to work like nothing happened. It was like you didn't miss him at all and you didn't want me to miss him either."

Dorie nodded. "I didn't miss the tension and the fights, which is about all we had left, but I felt just awful about his death. So awful I had to clear out everything that reminded me of him and our marriage."

Phoebe considered this for a moment. "That wasn't very fair on me," she said.

"No," Dorie agreed. "It wasn't. And I'm sorry. You needed to grieve for your father and I didn't let you."

Phoebe leaned back against her pillows. She stared at the ceiling for a long moment.

"Are you all right?" Dorie asked, concerned that she might have triggered emotions that Phoebe wasn't yet strong enough to handle.

Phoebe turned a level gaze on Dorie. A smile tweaked the corners of her lips.

"Don't look so worried, Mom. I'm not freaking out. I just can't believe you finally said you were sorry."

Dorie shook her head and sighed. "I've been apologizing a lot lately," she said. "I have a lot of fences to mend. Which reminds me, I came up here to give you something." She put the foil bag on the bed.

Phoebe grabbed at it. "Goody. Another present. I should get brain surgery every day."

Dorie put her hand Phoebe's wrist. "Wait," she said. "It is a present, in a way, but if you don't want it I won't be offended."

Phoebe looked at her questioningly.

"It's my journal. You read a piece of it but it was out of context. I wish you'd read the whole thing. You'll like the part about how your father and I met. And what I did might not seem so shocking if you knew more about who I was back then."

Phoebe looked at the gift bag dubiously. "I don't know," she said slowly.

Dorie stood up. "It's your choice. But that journal's an important part of my past and I'd like to share it with you."

Phoebe gazed at her, head cocked to the side, lips pursed. "Okay," she said. "I'll consider it. But right now I need to take a nap."

Dorie went downstairs to fix macaroni and cheese for dinner. During the quiet weeks of Phoebe's convalescence she had prepared the simple foods of childhood: meat loaf and mashed potatoes, cream of tomato soup, chocolate pudding. As she grated curls of bright orange cheddar cheese into a bowl she realized how much this interlude reprised their early years together. Lots of nurturance, lots of naps, just the two of them close and cozy in their little house, the confusion and complexity of the world beyond their front door reduced to a dim background noise.

She set the grated cheese aside and mixed a paste of flour and milk to thicken the cream sauce she would make while the pasta cooked. This peaceful seclusion would end when Phoebe returned to school in a few months and Dorie's fall term courses began. Once again their lives would diverge, Dorie's into the increasingly dull routine of teaching, research, and mountain hikes; Phoebe's into a flurry of friends, dates, and college applications. Then, in two years, Phoebe would be gone, probably to a distant east coast school, and her room would be neat, quiet, and empty.

And what will I do then? Dorie asked herself as she folded the cheese into the thickened sauce. Get that big dog I keep talking about? Hang out at the Senior Center line dancing with a bunch of geriatric singles?

She transferred the cooked pasta to a casserole and poured the steaming sauce over it. Too bad she'd ruined her chances with Doug. She sighed as she slid the casserole into the oven. She could understand why he didn't want anything to do with her. He'd called when he heard about Phoebe's surgery and was sympathetic but impersonal. She had apologized again for being such a bitch but all he said was "You were under a lot of pressure." That was it. No suggestion that they get together, no inquiries about her future plans and nothing revealed about his own.

If it hadn't been for Phoebe's accident, she mused, recalling the powerful attraction that had been so obvious during their dinner at The Flagstaff House, there was no question that they would have gone to bed. And that she, high on post-coital oxytocin, would have been swept away in a tidal wave of romantic fantasies.

Dorie removed her apron, picturing, Doug waving a spatula as he emerged from her kitchen to greet Viktor and Frank. Even under the strained circumstances, his presence in her house had seemed natural and comfortable. It was so easy to imagine him sprawled on the sofa beside her as they shared a beer and watched the BBC news, or in her bathroom, shaving while she brushed her hair.

Stop torturing yourself, she admonished. You'd have screwed things up sooner or later. Maybe, baby, her inner Tina Turner voice observed. But it would have been a helluva lot of fun while it lasted.

The following Tuesday, Dorie stopped at her college mailbox after her morning class in Southwestern Literature. Class had gone particularly well. She'd brought enlargements of black and white archival photographs of a Hopi village to accompany her lecture on Frank Waters and her students had responded with genuinely interested questions about Hopi beliefs and daily life.

As she wrestled the latest MLA journal out of her box, her class notes and the folder of photographs slipped from under her arm and cascaded to the floor. She was on her knees reassembling them when a large pair of hiking boots came into view.

"Hey, Dr. Winslow, let me give you a hand." Tony Begay knelt and retrieved some of the outlying papers.

"Nice pix," he said, examining a photo. "How's Phoebe doing?"

"Great. Still got a bald spot but she's growing hair like a chia pet," Dorie said. She reinserted the photos into their folder and Tony extended his hand to help her up.

"Thanks, Tony," she said. Then, with studied casualness, she asked, "What's up with your boss? His name's still on his mailbox so I guess he hasn't been sacked."

"No way," Tony said, "he's been reinstated."

Dorie felt her cheeks redden. She hoped Tony wouldn't notice.

"What happened? she asked.

Tony grinned wickedly. "I fought fire with fire."

"What do you mean?"

"You know how Drescher caved when the Christian students complained? Well, out here Native Americans trump Christians. I drew up a petition that said Doug helped Native kids express their identities and get in touch with their culture, blah, blah, blah. Got about sixty signatures in a couple of days. We sent it over the dean's head to the prez and Drescher went down like Custer."

"Good for you. So Doug's not leaving."

"Nope. And he still gets to hold the high school poetry slams on campus. The prez thinks they'll help recruit minority students."

"Tony, you're a genius," Dorie said. "Forget poetry. You should go into politics."

Dorie took her bundle of mail to her office and dumped it on the desk. She sat down and stared at the MLA journal, then pushed it aside. She rummaged in a drawer for a pad of Post-it notes. If she didn't do this now, she never would. She tried to think of something clever to write, something equal to Doug's goofy rhymed dinner invitations, but her mind was blank. She settled for the simple and direct: "Doug, I'm glad you're back. Can I buy you a drink to celebrate? Dorie."

She tore the note off the pad and quickly, before she lost her nerve, scurried out and stuck it on Doug's office door. He could take it whatever way he wanted, as collegial congratulations or as an invitation to reconnect. She'd made her move. The next one was up to him.


The following day Dorie was sitting in her home office correcting a quiz when Phoebe came in. She had her hands behind her back and a knowing grin on her face.

"What are you smiling about?" Dorie asked. "Is there something I should know?"

Phoebe sat down on a still unpacked carton of books.

"I read your journal," she said. "You were really, like, mixed up, weren't you?" She didn't give Dorie a chance to answer. "I know you were trying to find God. But those Community people and all that New Age stuff? They were weirdos."

"No more so than the fanatics who think J.K. Rowling is a mouthpiece for Satan," Dorie responded, knowing that Phoebe, a stalwart Hogwarts fan, took issue with the position of some of the more literal-minded members of her church.

"Okay," Phoebe conceded. "Anyway, I just wanted to tell you that I get where you were coming from. At least sort of. So I'm cool with what you did."

"Praise Jesus," Dorie said, then, hastily, "Excuse me. That just slipped out."

Phoebe smiled. "It's okay. You can't help it." She took her hands out from behind her back and waved a piece of paper at Dorie. "It's my turn to give you something to read."

Dorie took the paper. It was a printout of an email exchange. She read the first line and looked up in disbelief. "How did you find him?"

"Google."

Dorie wiped her glasses on the bottom of her tee shirt, leaned back in her chair, and read:

> "From: PhoebeMac@aol.com
> To: Bud@IMBudd.org
>
> Dear Mr. Bud,
>
> My name is Phoebe MacKenzie. My parents met on your ashram in 1978. (My mom is Dorie Winslow and my dad, who died when I was eight, was Colin MacKenzie.)
>
> My mom let me read a journal she kept while she was with you. Some of the things you did were totally gross but you made a big impression on her and she's usually not impressed by anybody so you must have something going for you.

So, what I want to know is, what do you think about Jesus and Christianity? This is a serious question because I consider myself a Christian but I don't agree with everything my church teaches. Like, the world is only 4000 years old. So, duh, all that fossil evidence of evolution is some kind of cosmic joke? And if God loves us, why do people who aren't Saved because they never even heard of Jesus go to Hell? It's not their fault the missionaries didn't get to them before they died.

I hope you'll answer this. You kind of owe me, because if it weren't for you my mom and dad wouldn't have met and I wouldn't exist. So this is like your karma, okay?

Yours truly,
Phoebe"

"To: PhoebeMac@aol.com
From Bud@IMBudd.org

Dear Phoebe,

Your note brightened an otherwise dreary day spent dealing with people who hang on my every word and worship the ground I walk on. You clearly don't and in that you remind me of your mother. (That's a compliment.)

Now, what I think about Christianity and Jesus doesn't matter. What you think does. And I mean think. Don't leave your head at the door when you enter a church or a mosque or a synagogue or a temple or a sweat lodge. Those places are full of religion and religion is a product of the rational mind, which is inevitably self-interested and highly fallible. Not to mention finite and therefore incapable of experiencing the Infinite or God or the Absolute or whatever you want to call the unknowable substrate of our existence. Religious doctrines contain shredded and distorted bits of truth that can be interpreted in whatever way suits the psychological, social and political needs of the so-called authorities who promulgate them.

So you must use your head to question the doctrines, Phoebe. But to find the highly elusive Divine, for that, my dear, you must use your heart. And no one, not even me, can tell you how to do that.

Yours truly,
Bud

P.S. Give my regards to Cookie."

As Dorie read Bud's reply, time collapsed and the Community dining hall at Marmot Rock superimposed itself upon the present. The words came to life in Bud's distinctive gravelly voice. He might as well have been present, slouched against the bookcase in his jeans and cowboy boots, addressing Phoebe in person. The effect was temporally dislocating. For a moment Dorie didn't know *when* she was.

She handed the emails back to Phoebe.

"So what do you think of Bud's advice?" she asked.

Phoebe carefully folded the paper in thirds and put it in her pocket.

"I'm not sure. I'm still thinking."

"Good," Dorie said. "That's exactly what you're supposed to do."

*Thirty - Six*

Dorie was in the shower Wednesday afternoon, washing away the residue of some aggressive weeding in her vegetable garden, when the phone rang. She fumbled for a towel and dripped her way into the bedroom. Phoebe's physical therapist was supposed to call back to confirm an appointment and she knew Phoebe would be keen to keep it, given the possibility of encountering the musically prodigious Aaron Waldbaum.

Much to her surprise, the caller was Doug.

"I got your note," he said, "I'm up for a drink if you are."

Dorie's tummy butterflies fluttered happily.

"That's great I was afraid you were so disgusted with me that you wouldn't even respond."

"I've never been disgusted with you, Dorie. But I think you have some issues to deal with and I'm not sure there's room for anyone in your life but your daughter."

Dorie traced a spiral of water on the floor with her big toe.

"You're right. That crisis with Phoebe pushed all my hot buttons. But I'm happy to report the big ones have been disabled."

"Interesting," Doug said. "That's sort of what Tony told me. He said he ran into you on campus and you were different. Softer. Quieter." Doug chuckled. "Actually what he said was, and I quote, 'Her spirit has returned.'"

"About time, too," Dorie said. "It went AWOL years ago. I'll tell you all about it over that drink. You want to come to my place or meet at the Cantina?"

"Neither one," Doug said firmly. "If we're going to give this thing another shot I want the home team advantage."

"What do you mean?"

"We have drinks and dinner at my house."

"That's very generous of you."

"No, it's not. It's a test. I want to see if you can give up control when you're on someone else's turf."

Dorie wasn't sure what to say. Doug's willingness to consider the possibility of a relationship was encouraging but it was clear that he had some well-considered reservations about her.

"That's understandable," she replied. "I accept the challenge."

Their dinner date was set for Friday night. Dorie called Sharon and asked her to look in on Phoebe at hourly intervals during her absence.

"I know that's excessive," she confessed, "but last time I had dinner with this person Phoebe nearly got herself killed."

"This person?" Sharon echoed. "Is this a male type person, by any chance?"

"Yes. Someone I know from work. He teaches poetry."

"Ooooo, Dorie. A poet. I hear they're very passionate. I'll expect you back late."

Dorie started to say, "don't count on it," but stopped herself. Why jinx the evening? Better to go with the flow. And if by chance she got swept away, well, so be it.

Doug's house was in the mountains about thirty minutes north of town. His meticulous directions included visual landmarks, the last of which was a white barn where she turned right on a gravel road that wound through the pines to his house, a sprawling log cabin nestled in a small meadow.

"This place is incredible," she exclaimed when Doug opened the rustic front door. "How did you find it?"

"I shopped 'til my real estate agent nearly dropped. Took me a year but I knew what I wanted and I held out until I got it. Come in."

Dorie stepped into a large room with a beamed ceiling, pine floors and a huge stone fireplace. A leather sofa layered with sheepskins faced the fireplace and a plank dining table sat in a deep bay of windows. Shelves filled with books, Puebloan pottery, and photos flanked the fireplaces.

Moving closer, Dorie examined a framed black and white photo of a tall, unsmiling man in a blazer and tie standing beside a dark-haired woman in a wheelchair. Her expression was gentle and serene, a dramatic contrast to the man's severity.

"Are these your parents?" Dorie asked, remembering Doug's description of his mother's MS.

"Yes. That was taken about a year after my mother started using a wheelchair. I was seven."

"And who's this handsome fellow?" Dorie said, pointing to a snapshot of Doug in a ski jacket looking eye to eye with a Bernese Mountain Dog who was standing up with its paws on his chest. "I mean the one with the fluffy tail."

"That's Plato. Great dog. I got him as a puppy and trained him for avalanche rescue." He picked up the photo and studied it. "I had to put him down when he was nine. His hips were so bad he couldn't walk. It nearly killed me."

He likes dogs, Dorie thought. Big dogs. That's a good sign.

She turned from the bookcase to an arrangement of small paintings on an adjacent wall. They were meticulously detailed but the content was even more striking than the technical expertise.

They were portraits: a seated judge with a gavel, a little girl with a kitten and ball of yarn, a formally posed multigenerational family. The subjects wore contemporary clothing but their faces were rendered in the flat style of Byzantine icons. The overall effect was both witty and disconcerting.

"These are good, "Dorie said, "in an eerie sort of way. Are they your work?"

"Yup," Doug said

"Wow," Dorie said. "You're always so upbeat that I never suspected you had a dark side."

"I have a highly developed dark side," Doug said. I let it come out and play with paint. That way it doesn't get frustrated and try to run my life."

He looked at his watch. "I need to put a chicken in the oven. And pour you a glass of wine."

"What else are we having? Can I help?" Dorie followed him into a tidy kitchen with pine cabinets and Mexican tile countertops.

"Baked potatoes and salad. That's the extent of my culinary repertoire." Doug uncorked a bottle of Semillon and poured two glasses of wine.

"I can do something creative with the potatoes if you want," Dorie said. "Or would that be exerting too much control on your turf?"

"Feel free to doctor the spuds. But I'll choose the music to cook by. Providing that won't threaten you."

He fiddled with an iPod sitting in a dock on the counter and a track from Bob Dylan's new album flooded the room with guitar chords.

"I knew you were too young for me," Dorie said. "You know how to use an iPod."

"Hardly. My students gave me a tutorial."

Doug stripped the plastic wrap off a chicken and rubbed it with seasoning from a jar labeled "Poultry Magic." "Speaking of kids, how's Phoebe getting along?"

Dorie told him about Phoebe's dual infatuation with Bach and Aaron Waldbaum and her questions about Christianity.

"Sounds like she's ready to broaden her horizons," Doug said. "I've got a chapbook for her. It's a collection of pieces from last year's poetry slam finals. It might give her a new perspective. Show her how minority kids experience the world."

With the chicken and potatoes in the oven, Dorie and Doug adjourned to the living room with the bottle of wine and a bowl of pistachios that Doug placed on the split log coffee table in front of the sofa.

"Sit," he said, patting the sheepskin next to him as he slipped off his moccasins. "Unless, of course, you want to avoid intimacy by taking a chair across the room. Where you won't be able to reach the pistachios."

Dorie sank down into the sheepskin, kicked off her sandals and put her feet up on the coffee table. The two glasses of wine she'd drunk on an empty stomach were taking effect, or maybe it was the proximity to Doug. She caught a whiff of his distinctive scent, that mix of new cut hay and leather with an indefinable bottom note of something very male. She had a nearly irresistible urge to bury her nose in his neck.

"Now," Doug said, "it's time for you to tell me what you mentioned on the phone. How your soul went AWOL."

Dorie snuggled deeper into the sheepskin as Doug refilled their wine glasses.

"It started a long time ago, "she began, "when I went looking for God and got lost on the way home." She told Doug about Bud and the Community and the priceless moments she had experienced there, about the bad years with Colin, and the worse ones after his death.

"I just shut down inside," she said. "Pulled the blinds and didn't answer the door. Not the best survival strategy but it worked. Until now, when I thought I was going to lose Phoebe. Then it failed utterly and I sort of went over the edge." She made a face. "Ugh. That is one painfully mixed metaphor."

Doug reached over and brushed a wisp of hair off her forehead. "You've had a lot of losses, Dorie, and you survived them. But you deserve more." He traced the ridge of her cheekbone with his fingertip. Dorie's skin tingled in its wake. He slid his finger down her neck and along her collarbone to the u-shaped depression in its center.

"I can feel your heart beat," he whispered. "I can feel …your life."

Dorie closed her eyes. A liquid fire radiated from his fingertip throughout her body, weakening her limbs. I shouldn't have had that second glass of wine, she thought. This is all going too fast.

She stood up abruptly. "How about giving me a tour of your property before dinner?" she asked. "It's so beautiful outside, I'd like to see it before dark."

Doug looked up at her, frowning, then shrugged.

"Okay," he said, "if that's what you want."

Dorie winced. She could see she'd hurt him by pulling away. She looked at him apologetically.

"I'm sorry," she said. "I just need some air. Or some time. Or maybe just some courage." She shook her head ruefully.

Doug smiled. "Cold feet, huh?" he said. "I get it." He pulled on his shoes and stood up. "Best cure for cold feet is action. Let's go for a walk."

The air was noticeably cooler when they stepped outside and the wisps of clouds over the mountains were rose-tinged from the alpenglow of the setting sun. An evening breeze carried the clean, cutting scent of evergreens as it wafted down the hillside towards the cabin.

"I'm going to show you my pride and joy," Doug said. He took Dorie by the elbow and steered her around the corner of the house.

"Look," he said, pointing at a shed filed with split logs.

"I'm looking," Dorie said. "What's the big deal?"

"My woodpile. Split entirely by me. Me man. Me make fire. Keep woman warm. You're supposed to be impressed."

Dorie laughed. "Okay. But I did see a propane tank on my way in."

"That's only back up," Doug said. "For those days when I can't haul my ass out of bed. Furthermore, I have a freezer full of elk steaks. From a buck I shot myself. Now are you impressed?"

Dorie turned to face him. The setting sun backlit his unkempt graying curls. He looks, Dorie thought, rather like an aging cherub. Behind him, the irregular tips of pines and firs were silhouetted against the deepening blue of the sky. The breeze died down, and silence descended on the high valley. Dorie was transfixed by the perfection of the moment.

She stepped towards Doug and put her hands on his shoulders.

"I am impressed," she said. "More than you can possibly know."

Doug cupped her face in his hands, pulling her close. His breath tickled her forehead as he slowly bent forward and his lips brushed hers, a delicate invitation to a kiss. Then, as her own lips parted, he kissed her wholeheartedly, and she responded in kind, welcoming the new, yet unaccountably familiar, taste of his mouth.

After a long dizzying moment, they drew back, slowly and reluctantly and gazed at each other, giddy with the possibilities that had suddenly come into being.

Suddenly Dorie sniffed the air. "The chicken! It's burning."

"Damn and blast," Doug said. "I should have set a timer. See, I really can't cook worth shit."

"That's okay," Dorie replied. "I can. Just wait 'til you see what I'm going to do with your elk steaks."

Together, they raced to the house to save their dinner.

**THE END**